ELECTIONS IN
METROPOLITAN LONDON
1700 -1850

VOLUME 2

METROPOLITAN POLLS

ELECTIONS IN METROPOLITAN LONDON 1700 -1850

Edmund M Green

Penelope J Corfield

Charles Harvey

Bristol Academic Press

Published by
Bristol Academic Press
7 Grange Park
Westbury-on-Trym
Bristol
BS9 4BU

ISBN: 978-0-9544138-0-4

Typeset by Bristol Academic Press and
Printed in Great Britain by
The Print Room, Newcastle upon Tyne

CHAPTER 8
METROPOLITAN POLLS

8.1 PARLIAMENTARY POLLS

Note: In all tables, the names of elected candidates are in SMALL CAPITALS and those of unsuccessful candidates in lower case.

8.1.1 Middlesex, 1701-1852: 24 polls

For details of the Middlesex freeholder franchise, see Section 3.2.

Table 8.1.1.1
Poll for Members of Parliament for Middlesex, 3 December 1701

Candidate	Votes received
WARWICK LAKE	902
JOHN AUSTEN	869
Nicholas Wolstenholme	862
Hugh Smithson	848
Scorie Barker	214
John Bucknall	212

Source: *Hist. Parl., 1690-1715.*

Table 8.1.1.2
Poll for Members of Parliament for Middlesex, 30 July 1702

Candidate	Votes received
WARWICK LAKE	1,175
HUGH SMITHSON	1,159
Nicholas Wolstenholme	1,127
John Austen	1,114

Source: *Hist. Parl., 1690-1715.*

Table 8.1.1.3
Poll for Members of Parliament for Middlesex, 28 May 1705

Candidate	Votes received
SCORIE BARKER	1,657
JOHN WOLSTENHOLME	1,630
Warwick Lake	1,349
Hugh Smithson	1,336

Source: *Hist. Parl., 1690-1715.*

Table 8.1.1.4
Poll for Members of Parliament for Middlesex, 12 October 1710

Candidate	Votes received	
	Post Boy	BL Add. Ms.
JAMES BERTIE	1,916	1,920
HUGH SMITHSON	1,876	1,886
Scorie Barker	1,313	1,316
John Austen	1,239	1,234

Source: *Hist. Parl., 1690-1715.*

Table 8.1.1.5
Poll for Members of Parliament for Middlesex, 27 January 1715

Candidate	Votes received
JAMES BERTIE	1,604
HUGH SMITHSON	1,553
John Austen	1,330
Henry Barker	1,325

Source: *Hist. Parl., 1715-54.*

Table 8.1.1.6
Poll for Members of Parliament for Middlesex, 30 March 1722

Candidate	Votes received
JAMES BERTIE	1,800
JOHN AUSTEN	967
Henry Barker	908
George Cooke	662
William Withers	228

Source: *Hist. Parl., 1715-54.*

Table 8.1.1.7
Poll for Members of Parliament for Middlesex, 6 September 1727

Candidate	Votes received
JAMES BERTIE	1,410
FRANCIS CHILD	1,305
Thomas Catesby Paget	1,039
Henry Barker	1,074

Source: *Hist. Parl., 1715-54.*

Table 8.1.1.8
Poll for Member of Parliament for Middlesex, 15 May 1740

Candidate	Votes received
HUGH SMITHSON	382
Henry Barker	147

Source: *Hist. Parl., 1715-54.*

Table 8.1.1.9
Poll for Members of Parliament for Middlesex, 2 July 1747

Candidate	Votes received
HUGH SMITHSON	1,797
WILLIAM BEAUCHAMP PROCTOR	1,457
George Cooke	899
Roger Newdigate	794

Source: *Hist. Parl., 1715-54.*

Table 8.1.1.10
Poll for Member of Parliament for Middlesex, 8 March 1750

Candidate	Votes received
GEORGE COOKE	1,617
Frazer Honywood	1,201

Source: *Hist. Parl., 1715-54.*

Table 8.1.1.11
Poll for Members of Parliament for Middlesex, 28 March 1768

Candidate	Votes received
JOHN WILKES	1,297
GEORGE COOKE	827
William Beauchamp Proctor	802

Source: *Hist. Parl., 1754-90.*

Table 8.1.1.12
Poll for Member of Parliament for Middlesex, 14 December 1768

Candidate	Votes received
JOHN GLYNN	1,548
William Beauchamp Proctor	1,272

Source: *Hist. Parl., 1754-90.*

Table 8.1.1.13
Poll for Member of Parliament for Middlesex, 13 April 1769

Candidate	Votes received
JOHN WILKES	1,143
HENRY LAWES LUTTRELL	296
William Whitaker	5

Source: *Hist. Parl., 1754-90.*

Table 8.1.1.14
Poll for Members of Parliament for Middlesex, 22 April 1784

Candidate	Votes received
WILLIAM MAINWARING	2,118
JOHN WILKES	1,858
George Byng	1,792

Source: *Hist. Parl., 1754-90.*

Table 8.1.1.15
Poll for Members of Parliament for Middlesex, 13 July 1802

Candidate	Votes received
GEORGE BYNG	3,848
FRANCIS BURDETT	3,207
William Mainwaring	2,936

Source: *Hist. Parl., 1790-1820.*

Table 8.1.1.16
Poll for Member of Parliament for Middlesex, 23 July 1804

Candidate	Votes received
GEORGE BOULTON MAINWARING	2,828
Francis Burdett	2,823

Source: *Hist. Parl., 1790-1820.*

Table 8.1.1.17
Poll for Members of Parliament for Middlesex, 10 November 1806

Candidate	Votes received
WILLIAM MELLISH	3,213
GEORGE BYNG	2,804
Francis Burdett	1,197

Source: *Hist. Parl., 1790-1820.*

Table 8.1.1.18
Poll for Members of Parliament for Middlesex, 18 May 1807

Candidate	Votes received
WILLIAM MELLISH	2,706
GEORGE BYNG	2,368
Christopher Baynes	1,252

Source: *Hist. Parl., 1790-1820.*

Table 8.1.1.19
Poll for Members of Parliament for Middlesex, 17 March 1820

Candidate	Votes received
GEORGE BYNG	4,004
SAMUEL CHARLES WHITBREAD	3,585
William Mellish	3,093

Source: *Hist. Parl., 1820-32.*

Table 8.1.1.20
Poll for Members of Parliament for Middlesex, 17 December 1832

Candidate	Plumpers	Votes received
JOSEPH HUME	498	3,238
GEORGE BYNG	414	3,033
Charles Forbes	492	1,494
J.S. Lillie	16	1,004

Source: Craig.

Table 8.1.1.21
Poll for Members of Parliament for Middlesex, 15 January 1835

Candidate	Votes received
GEORGE BYNG	3,505
JOSEPH HUME	3,096
Thomas Wood	2,707

Source: Craig.

Table 8.1.1.22
Poll for Members of Parliament for Middlesex, 31 July 1837

Candidate	Plumpers	Votes received
GEORGE BYNG	157	4,796
THOMAS WOOD	72	4,582
Joseph Hume	80	4,380
Henry Pownall	18	4,273

Source: Craig.

Table 8.1.1.23
Poll for Members of Parliament for Middlesex, 4 August 1847

Candidate	Votes received
ROBERT GROSVENOR	4,944
RALPH B. OSBORNE	4,175
Thomas Wood	3,458

Source: Craig.

Table 8.1.1.24
Poll for Members of Parliament for Middlesex, 17 July 1852

Candidate	Votes received
ROBERT GROSVENOR	5,241
RALPH B. OSBORNE	4,390
Marquess of Blandford	4,258

Source: Craig.

8.1.2 London, 1701-1852: 45 polls

Poll for Members of Parliament for London, 17 May 1705

Following LEH website conventions, 'London' refers to the parliamentary constitutency of London. For details of the London liverymen franchise, see Sections 3.3.1, 3.3.3 and 3.3.4.

Table 8.1.2.1
Poll for Members of Parliament for London, 1 February 1701

Candidate	Votes received	
	Poll	Scrutiny
ROBERT CLAYTON	3,124	3,088
WILLIAM ASHURST	3,291	3,245
GILBERT HEATHCOTE	3,182	3,135
WILLIAM WITHERS	2,798	2,758
Charles Duncombe	2,714	2,631
John Fleet	2,544	2,480
Francis Child	2,255	2,189
William Prichard	2,126	2,068

Source: *Hist. Parl., 1690-1715.*

Table 8.1.2.2
Poll for Member of Parliament for London, 20 March 1701

Candidate	Votes received
JOHN FLEET	2,356
Thomas Stamp	2,089

Source: *Hist. Parl., 1690-1715.*

Table 8.1.2.3
Poll for Members of Parliament for London, 24 November 1701

Candidate	Votes received
GILBERT HEATHCOTE	2,769
WILLIAM ASHURST	2,759
THOMAS ABNEY	2,647
ROBERT CLAYTON	2,602
Charles Duncombe	1,494
John Fleet	1,428
John Houblon	995
Richard Levitt	945
John Parsons	137

Source: *Hist. Parl., 1690-1715.*

Table 8.1.2.4
Poll for Members of Parliament for London, 18 August 1702

Candidate	Votes received
JOHN FLEET	3,177
GILBERT HEATHCOTE	3,038
WILLIAM PRICHARD	2,993
FRANCIS CHILD	2,849
Robert Clayton	2,791
Charles Duncombe	2,777
William Ashurst	2,738
Thomas Abney	2,713

Source: *Hist. Parl., 1690-1715.*

Table 8.1.2.5
Poll for Members of Parliament for London, 17 May 1705

Candidate	Votes received
GILBERT HEATHCOTE	3,346
SAMUEL SHEPHEARD	3,015
WILLIAM ASHURST	2,961
ROBERT CLAYTON	2,919
Richard Hoare	2,195
John Fleet	2,187
William Withers	1,964
John Parsons	1,700

Source: *Hist. Parl., 1690-1715.*

Table 8.1.2.6
Poll for Member of Parliament for London, 16 December 1707

Candidate	Votes received	
	Poll	Scrutiny
WILLIAM WITHERS	3,146	3,109
John Buckworth	2,893	2,842

Source: *Hist. Parl., 1690-1715.*

Table 8.1.2.7
Poll for Members of Parliament for London, 14 May 1708

Candidate	Votes received
JOHN WARD	3,353
GILBERT HEATHCOTE	3,216
WILLIAM ASHURST	3,209
WILLIAM WITHERS	3,189
Samuel Stanier	3,012
John Buckworth	2,284
Richard Hoare	2,245
Francis Child	2,026

Source: *Hist. Parl., 1690-1715.*

Table 8.1.2.8
Poll for Members of Parliament for London, 16 November 1710

Candidate	Votes received
WILLIAM WITHERS	3,629
RICHARD HOARE	3,572
GEORGE NEWLAND	3,385
JOHN CASS	3,240
John Ward	3,224
Gilbert Heathcote	3,185
James Bateman	3,104
William Ashurst	3,048

Source: *Hist. Parl., 1690-1715.*

Table 8.1.2.9
Poll for Members of Parliament for London, 12 November 1713

Candidate	Votes received
RICHARD HOARE	3,842
GEORGE NEWLAND	3,826
JOHN CASS	3,802
WILLIAM WITHERS	3,763
John Ward	3,730
Robert Heysham	3,688
Peter Godfrey	3,657
Thomas Scawen	3,625

Source: *Hist. Parl., 1690-1715.*

Table 8.1.2.10
Poll for Members of Parliament for London, 29 January 1715

Candidate	Votes received
ROBERT HEYSHAM	3,499
JOHN WARD	3,475
PETER GODFREY	3,471
THOMAS SCAWEN	3,439
John Cass	2,884
William Withers	2,879
William Stewart	2,828
George Mertinns	2,774

Source: *Hist. Parl., 1715-54.*

Table 8.1.2.11
Poll for Members of Parliament for London, 9 May 1722

Candidate	Votes received	
	Poll	Scrutiny
RICHARD LOCKWOOD	4,235	4,025
JOHN BARNARD	3,980	3,840
PETER GODFREY	3,852	3,723
FRANCIS CHILD	3,784	3,575
Humphry Parsons	3,593	3,393
Robert Heysham	3,573	3,441

Source: *Hist. Parl., 1715-54.*

Table 8.1.2.12
Poll for Member of Parliament for London, 11 December 1724

Candidate	Votes received
RICHARD HOPKINS	3,332
Charles Goodfellow	2,911

Source: *Hist. Parl., 1715-54.*

Table 8.1.2.13
Poll for Members of Parliament for London, 24 November 1727

Candidate	Votes received	
	Poll	Scrutiny
JOHN EYLES	3,643	3,539
JOHN BARNARD	3,620	3,514
MICAJAH PERRY	3,494	3,396
HUMPHRY PARSONS	3,370	3,255
John Thompson	3,340	3,244
Richard Lockwood	3,086	2,977
John Williams	3,017	2,914
Richard Hopkins	3,010	2,921

Source: *Hist. Parl., 1715-54.*

Table 8.1.2.14
Poll for Members of Parliament for London, 10 May 1734

Candidate	Votes received
HUMPHRY PARSONS	3,932
JOHN BARNARD	3,841
MICAJAH PERRY	3,725
ROBERT WILLIMOT	2,984
John Barber	2,381
Robert Godschall	1,078

Source: *Hist. Parl., 1715-54.*

Table 8.1.2.15
Poll for Members of Parliament for London, 13 May 1741

Candidate	Votes received
JOHN BARNARD	3,769
GEORGE HEATHCOTE	3,322
DANIEL LAMBERT	3,217
ROBERT GODSCHALL	3,143
Micajah Perry	1,713
Edward Bellamy	1,312
Edward Vernon	1,175

Note: Vernon was proposed without his knowledge, and withdrew.
Source: *Hist. Parl., 1715-54.*

Table 8.1.2.16
Poll for Members of Parliament for London, 10 July 1747

Candidate	Votes received
WILLIAM CALVERT	3,806
JOHN BARNARD	3,781
SLINGSBY BETHELL	3,146
STEPHEN THEODORE JANSSEN	3,008
Daniel Lambert	2,530
Robert Ladbroke	1,986
Henry Marshall	73

Note: Marshall was proposed without his knowledge, and withdrew.
Source: *Hist. Parl., 1715-54*; *Whitehall Evening Post*, 30 June 1747.

Table 8.1.2.17
Poll for Members of Parliament for London, 7 May 1754

Candidate	Votes received
JOHN BARNARD	3,553
SLINGSBY BETHELL	3,547
ROBERT LADBROKE	3,390
WILLIAM BECKFORD	2,941
Richard Glyn	2,655
William Calvert	2,650

Source: *Hist. Parl., 1754-90.*

Table 8.1.2.18
Poll for Members of Parliament for London, 4 April 1761

Candidate	Votes received
ROBERT LADBROKE	4,306
THOMAS HARLEY	3,983
WILLIAM BECKFORD	3,663
RICHARD GLYN	3,285
Samuel Fludyer	3,193

Source: *Hist. Parl., 1754-90.*

Table 8.1.2.19
Poll for Members of Parliament for London, 25 March 1768

Candidate	Votes received
THOMAS HARLEY	3,729
ROBERT LADBROKE	3,678
WILLIAM BECKFORD	3,402
BARLOW TRECOTHICK	2,957
Richard Glyn	2,823
John Paterson	1,769
John Wilkes	1,247

Source: *Hist. Parl., 1754-90.*

Table 8.1.2.20
Poll for Member of Parliament for London, 23 December 1773

Candidate	Votes received
FREDERICK BULL	2,695
John Roberts	2,481

Source: *Hist. Parl., 1754-90.*

Table 8.1.2.21
Poll for Members of Parliament for London, 18 October 1774

Candidate	Votes received
JOHN SAWBRIDGE	3,456
GEORGE HAYLEY	3,390
RICHARD OLIVER	3,354
FREDERICK BULL	3,096
William Baker	2,802
Brass Crosby	1,913
John Roberts	1,398

Source: *Hist. Parl., 1754-90.*

Table 8.1.2.22
Poll for Members of Parliament for London, 19 September 1780

Candidate	Votes received
GEORGE HAYLEY	4,062
JOHN KIRKMAN	3,804
FREDERICK BULL	3,150
NATHANIEL NEWNHAM	3,036
John Sawbridge	2,957
Richard Clarke	1,771

Source: *Hist. Parl., 1754-90.*

Table 8.1.2.23
Poll for Member of Parliament for London, 2 October 1781

Candidate	Votes received
WATKIN LEWES	2,685
Richard Clarke	2,387

Source: *Hist. Parl., 1754-90.*

Table 8.1.2.24
Poll for Member of Parliament for London, 26 January 1784

Candidate	Votes received
BROOK WATSON	2,097
Brass Crosby	1,043

Source: *Hist. Parl., 1754-90.*

Table 8.1.2.25
Poll for Members of Parliament for London, 7 May 1784

Candidate	Votes received	
	Poll	Scrutiny
BROOK WATSON	4,789	4,776
WATKIN LEWES	4,554	4,541
NATHANIEL NEWNHAM	4,479	4,467
JOHN SAWBRIDGE	2,823	2,812
Richard Atkinson	2,816	2,803
Samuel Smith	277	286
William Pitt	52	56

Note: Pitt was proposed without his knowledge, and withdrew.
Source: *Hist. Parl., 1754-90*; *Morning Herald and Daily Advertiser,* 7 April 1784.

Table 8.1.2.26
Poll for Members of Parliament for London, 26 June 1790

Candidate	Votes received
WILLIAM CURTIS	4,346
BROOK WATSON	4,101
WATKIN LEWES	3,747
JOHN SAWBRIDGE	3,586
Nathaniel Newnham	2,670
William Pickett	1,064

Source: *Hist. Parl., 1790-1820.*

Table 8.1.2.27
Poll for Member of Parliament for London, 12 March 1795

Candidate	Votes received
WILLIAM LUSHINGTON	2,334
Harvey Christian Combe	1,560

Source: *Hist. Parl., 1790-1820.*

Table 8.1.2.28
Poll for Members of Parliament for London, 2 June 1796

Candidate	Votes received
WILLIAM LUSHINGTON	4,379
WILLIAM CURTIS	4,313
HARVEY CHRISTIAN COMBE	3,865
JOHN WILLIAM ANDERSON	3,170
William Pickett	2,795
Watkin Lewes	2,357

Source: *Hist. Parl., 1790-1820.*

Table 8.1.2.29
Poll for Members of Parliament for London, 6 July 1802

Candidate	Votes received
HARVEY CHRISTIAN COMBE	3,377
CHARLES PRICE	3,236
WILLIAM CURTIS	2,989
JOHN WILLIAM ANDERSON	2,387
Benjamin Travers	1,371
Watkin Lewes	652
William Lushington	113

Source: *Hist. Parl., 1790-1820.*

Table 8.1.2.30
Poll for Members of Parliament for London, 31 October 1806

Candidate	Votes received
HARVEY CHRISTIAN COMBE	2,294
JAMES SHAW	2,275
CHARLES PRICE	2,254
WILLIAM CURTIS	2,213
John Atkins	314
John Peter Hankey	164

Source: *Hist. Parl., 1790-1820.*

Table 8.1.2.31
Poll for Members of Parliament for London, 6 May 1807

Candidate	Votes received
CHARLES PRICE	3,117
WILLIAM CURTIS	3,059
JAMES SHAW	2,863
HARVEY CHRISTIAN COMBE	2,583
John Peter Hankey	226

Note: Hankey died on the first day of polling.
Source: *Hist. Parl., 1790-1820.*

Table 8.1.2.32
Poll for Members of Parliament for London, 5 October 1812

Candidate	Votes received
HARVEY CHRISTIAN COMBE	5,125
WILLIAM CURTIS	4,577
JAMES SHAW	4,082
JOHN ATKINS	3,645
Robert Waithman	2,622
Matthew Wood	2,373
Claudius Stephen Hunter	8

Source: *Hist. Parl., 1790-1820.*

Table 8.1.2.33
Poll for Members of Parliament for London, 6 June 1818

Candidate	Votes received
MATTHEW WOOD	5,715
THOMAS WILSON	4,846
ROBERT WAITHMAN	4,617
JOHN THOMAS THORP	4,349
William Curtis	4,236
John Atkins	1,693

Source: *Hist. Parl., 1790-1820.*

Table 8.1.2.34
Poll for Members of Parliament for London, 7 March 1820

Candidate	Votes received
MATTHEW WOOD	5,370
THOMAS WILSON	5,358
WILLIAM CURTIS	4,908
GEORGE BRIDGES	4,259
Robert Waithman	4,119
John Thomas Thorpe	3,921

Source: *Hist. Parl., 1820-32.*

Table 8.1.2.35
Poll for Members of Parliament for London, 9 June 1826

Candidate	Votes received
WILLIAM THOMPSON	6,845
ROBERT WAITHMAN	5,045
WILLIAM WARD	4,992
MATTHEW WOOD	4,891
William Venables	4,514
John Garratt	330

Source: *Hist. Parl., 1820-32.*

Table 8.1.2.36
Poll for Members of Parliament for London, 12 December 1832

Candidate	Votes received
GEORGE GROTE	8,412
MATTHEW WOOD	7,488
ROBERT WAITHMAN	7,452
JOHN KEY	6,136
George Lyall	5,112
Michael Scales	569

Source: Craig.

Table 8.1.2.37
Poll for Member of Parliament for London, 27 February 1833

Candidate	Votes received
GEORGE LYALL	5,569
William Venables	4,527

Source: Craig.

Table 8.1.2.38
Poll for Member of Parliament for London, 12 August 1833

Candidate	Votes received
WILLIAM CRAWFORD	4,041
Francis Kemble	2,004

Source: Craig.

Table 8.1.2.39
Poll for Members of Parliament for London, 5 January 1835

Candidate	Votes received
MATTHEW WOOD	6,418
JAMES PATTISON	6,050
WILLIAM CRAWFORD	5,961
GEORGE GROTE	5,955
George Lyall	4,599
William Ward	4,559
T. Wilson	4,514

Source: Craig.

Table 8.1.2.40
Poll for Members of Parliament for London, 22 July 1837

Candidate	Votes received
MATTHEW WOOD	6,517
WILLIAM CRAWFORD	6,071
JAMES PATTISON	6,070
GEORGE GROTE	5,879
John Horsley Palmer	5,873

Source: Craig.

Table 8.1.2.41
Poll for Members of Parliament for London, 28 June 1841

Candidate	Votes received
JOHN MASTERMAN	6,339
MATTHEW WOOD	6,315
GEORGE LYALL	6,290
JOHN RUSSELL	6,221
Matthew Wolverley Attwood	6,212
James Pattison	6,070
William Crawford	6,065
John Pirie	6,017

Source: Craig.

Table 8.1.2.42
Poll for Member of Parliament for London, 20 October 1843

Candidate	Votes received
JAMES PATTISON	6,532
Thomas Baring	6,367

Source: Craig.

Table 8.1.2.43
Poll for Members of Parliament for London, 28 July 1847

Candidate	Votes received
JOHN RUSSELL	7,137
JAMES PATTISON	7,030
LIONEL NATHAN DE ROTHSCHILD	6,792
JOHN MASTERMAN	6,722
George Gerard de Hochpied Larpent	6,719
Robert Cooper Lee Bevan	5,268
John Johnson	5,069
James William Freshfield	4,704
William Payne	513

Source: Craig.

Table 8.1.2.44
Poll for Member of Parliament for London, 4 July 1849

Candidate	Votes received
LIONEL NATHAN DE ROTHSCHILD	6,017
John Manners	2,814

Source: Craig.

Table 8.1.2.45
Poll for Members of Parliament for London, 6 July 1852

Candidate	Votes received
JOHN MASTERMAN	6,195
JOHN RUSSELL	5,537
JAMES DUKE	5,270
LIONEL NATHAN DE ROTHSCHILD	4,748
R. Wigram Crawford	3,765

Source: Craig.

8.1.3 Westminster, 1701-1852: 33 polls

For details of the Westminster rate-payer franchise, see Section 3.4.

Table 8.1.3.1
Poll for Members of Parliament for Westminster, 21 January 1701

Candidate	Votes received
JAMES VERNON	2,646
THOMAS CROSSE	2,485
Henry Dutton Colt	2,057
Walter Clarges	1,177
Charles Bonython	1,040

Source: *Hist. Parl., 1690-1715.*

Table 8.1.3.2
Poll for Members of Parliament for Westminster, 9 December 1701

Candidate	Votes received
HENRY DUTTON COLT	3,013
JAMES VERNON	2,997
Thomas Crosse	1,649
John Leveson Gower	1,623

Source: *Hist. Parl., 1690-1715.*

Table 8.1.3.3
Poll for Members of Parliament for Westminster, 6 August 1702

Candidate	Votes received	
	Daily Courant	*Post Man*
THOMAS CROSSE	3,195	2,992
WALTER CLARGES	2,932	2,909
Henry Dutton Colt	2,605	2,829
James Cavendish	2,298	2,371

Source: *Hist. Parl., 1690-1715.*

Table 8.1.3.4
Poll for Members of Parliament for Westminster, 30 May 1705

Candidate	Votes received
HENRY BOYLE	3,746
HENRY DUTTON COLT	3,356
Thomas Crosse	2,424

Source: *Hist. Parl., 1690-1715.*

Table 8.1.3.5
Poll for Members of Parliament for Westminster, 7 July 1708

Candidate	Votes received		
	Poll	Scrutiny	Recount
HENRY BOYLE	4,410	4,428	4,430
THOMAS MEDLYCOTT	3,695	3,815	3,815
Henry Dutton Colt	3,724	3,791	3,856

Note: A recount held after the scrutiny revealed a discrepancy in voting figures. The return was based on the result of the scrutiny
Source: *Hist. Parl., 1690-1715.*

Table 8.1.3.6
Poll for Members of Parliament for Westminster, 9 October 1710

Candidate	Votes received
THOMAS MEDLYCOTT	4,153
THOMAS CROSSE	3,542
James Stanhope	1,870
Henry Dutton Colt	1,509

Source: *Hist. Parl., 1690-1715.*

Table 8.1.3.7
Poll for Members of Parliament for Westminster, 27 March 1722

Candidate	Votes received
ARCHIBALD HUTCHINSON	4,024
JOHN COTTON	3,853
William Lowndes	2,215
Thomas Crosse	2,197

Source: *Hist. Parl., 1715-54.*

Table 8.1.3.8
Poll for Members of Parliament for Westminster, 3 December 1722

Candidate	Votes received
CHARLES MONTAGUE	4,835
GEORGE CARPENTER	4,515
John Cotton	3,485
Thomas Clarges	2,827

Source: *Hist. Parl.,1715-54.*

Table 8.1.3.9
Poll for Members of Parliament for Westminster, 7 May 1741

Candidate	Votes received
CHARLES WAGER	3,686
WILLIAM CLAYTON	3,533
Edward Vernon	3,290
Charles Edwin	3,161

Source: *Hist. Parl., 1715-54.*

Table 8.1.3.10
Poll for Members of Parliament for Westminster, 1 July 1747

Candidate	Votes received
GRANVILLE LEVESON GOWER	2,873
PETER WARREN	2,858
Thomas Clarges	544
Thomas Dyke	514

Source: *Hist. Parl., 1715-54.*

Table 8.1.3.11
Poll for Member of Parliament for Westminster, 15 May 1750

Candidate	Votes received	
	Poll	Scrutiny
GRANVILLE LEVESON GOWER	4,811	4,103
George Vandeput	4,654	3,933

Source: *Hist. Parl., 1715-54.*

Table 8.1.3.12
Poll for Members of Parliament for Westminster, 20 April 1754

Candidate	Votes received
EDWARD CORNWALLIS	3,385
JOHN CROSSE	3,184
James Edward Oglethorpe	261
Charles Sackville	209

Source: *Hist. Parl., 1754-90.*

Table 8.1.3.13
Poll for Members of Parliament for Westminster, 26 October 1774

Candidate	Votes received
HUGH PERCY	4,994
THOMAS PELHAM CLINTON	4,774
Hervey Redmond Morres	2,531
Charles Stanhope	2,342
Humphrey Cotes	130

Source: *Hist. Parl., 1754-90.*

Table 8.1.3.14
Poll for Members of Parliament for Westminster, 10 October 1780

Candidate	Votes received
GEORGE BRYDGES RODNEY	5,298
CHARLES JAMES FOX	4,878
Thomas Pelham Clinton	4,157

Source: *Hist. Parl., 1754-90.*

Table 8.1.3.15
Poll for Members of Parliament for Westminster, 17 May 1784

Candidate	Votes received	
	Poll	Scrutiny
SAMUEL HOOD	6,694	6,588
CHARLES JAMES FOX	6,234	6,126
Cecil Wray	5,998	5,895

Source: *Hist. Parl., 1754-90.*

Table 8.1.3.16
Poll for Member of Parliament for Westminster, 4 August 1788

Candidate	Votes received
JOHN TOWNSHEND	6,392
Samuel Hood	5,569

Source: *Hist. Parl., 1754-90.*

Table 8.1.3.17
Poll for Members of Parliament for Westminster, 2 July 1790

Candidate	Votes received
CHARLES JAMES FOX	3,516
SAMUEL HOOD	3,217
John Horne Tooke	1,697

Source: *Hist. Parl., 1790-1820.*

Table 8.1.3.18
Poll for Members of Parliament for Westminster, 13 June 1796

Candidate	Votes received
CHARLES JAMES FOX	5,160
ALAN GARDNER	4,814
John Horne Tooke	2,819

Source: *Hist. Parl., 1790-1820.*

Table 8.1.3.19
Poll for Members of Parliament for Westminster, 15 July 1802

Candidate	Votes received
CHARLES JAMES FOX	2,671
ALAN GARDNER	2,431
John Graham	1,693

Source: *Hist. Parl., 1790-1820.*

Table 8.1.3.20
Poll for Members of Parliament for Westminster, 19 November 1806

Candidate	Votes received
SAMUEL HOOD	5,478
RICHARD BRINSLEY SHERIDAN	4,758
James Paull	4,481

Source: *Hist. Parl., 1790-1820.*

Table 8.1.3.21
Poll for Members of Parliament for Westminster, 23 May 1807

Candidate	Votes received
FRANCIS BURDETT	5,134
THOMAS COCHRANE	3,708
Richard Brinsley Sheridan	2,645
John Elliott	2,137
James Paull	269

Source: *Hist. Parl., 1790-1820.*

Table 8.1.3.22
Poll for Members of Parliament for Westminster, 4 July 1818

Candidate	Votes received
SAMUEL ROMILLY	5,339
FRANCIS BURDETT	5,238
Murray Maxwell	4,808
Henry Hunt	84
Douglas James William Kinnaird	65
John Cartwright	23

Source: *Hist. Parl., 1790-1820.*

Table 8.1.3.23
Poll for Member of Parliament for Westminster, 3 March 1819

Candidate	Votes received
GEORGE LAMB	4,465
John Cam Hobhouse	3,861
John Cartwright	38

Source: *Hist. Parl., 1790-1820.*

Table 8.1.3.24
Poll for Members of Parliament for Westminster, 25 March 1820

Candidate	Votes received
FRANCIS BURDETT	5,327
JOHN CAM HOBHOUSE	4,882
George Lamb	4,436

Source: *Hist. Parl., 1820-32.*

Table 8.1.3.25
Poll for Members of Parliament for Westminster, 12 December 1832

Candidate	Votes received
FRANCIS BURDETT	3,248
JOHN CAM HOBHOUSE	3,214
George DeLacy Evans	1,096

Source: Craig.

Table 8.1.3.26
Poll for Member of Parliament for Westminster, 11 May 1833

Candidate	Votes received
GEORGE DELACY EVANS	2,027
John Cam Hobhouse	1,835
Bickham Escott	738

Source: Craig.

Table 8.1.3.27
Poll for Members of Parliament for Westminster, 10 January 1835

Candidate	Votes received
FRANCIS BURDETT	2,747
GEORGE DELACY EVANS	2,588
Thomas J. Cochrane	1,528

Source: Craig.

Table 8.1.3.28
Poll for Member of Parliament for Westminster, 12 May 1837

Candidate	Votes received
FRANCIS BURDETT	3,567
John Temple Leader	3,052

Source: Craig.

Table 8.1.3.29
Poll for Members of Parliament for Westminster, 27 July 1837

Candidate	Votes received
JOHN TEMPLE LEADER	3,793
GEORGE DELACY EVANS	3,715
George Murray	2,620

Source: Craig.

Table 8.1.3.30
Poll for Members of Parliament for Westminster, 1 July 1841

Candidate	Votes received
HENRY JOHN ROUS	3,338
JOHN TEMPLE LEADER	3,281
George DeLacy Evans	3,258

Source: Craig.

Table 8.1.3.31
Poll for Member of Parliament for Westminster, 19 February 1846

Candidate	Votes received
GEORGE DELACY EVANS	3,843
Henry John Rous	2,906

Source: Craig.

Table 8.1.3.32
Poll for Members of Parliament for Westminster, 30 July 1847

Candidate	Votes received
GEORGE DELACY EVANS	3,139
CHARLES LUSHINGTON	2,831
Charles Cochrane	2,819
Viscount Mandeville	1,985

Source: Craig.

Table 8.1.3.33
Poll for Members of Parliament for Westminster, 9 July 1852

Candidate	Votes received
JOHN VILLIERS SHELLEY	4,199
GEORGE DELACY EVANS	3,756
George Finch-Hatton	3,373
William Coningham	1,716

Source: Craig.

8.1.4 Southwark, 1701-1852: 40 polls

For Southwark's rate-payer franchise, see comments in Section 1.9.2.

Table 8.1.4.1
Poll for Members of Parliament for Southwark, 9 January 1701

Candidate	Votes received
CHARLES COX	2,605
JOHN CHOLMLEY	2,374
Arthur Moore	1,626

Source: *Hist. Parl., 1690-1715.*

Table 8.1.4.2
Poll for Members of Parliament for Southwark, 24 November 1701

Candidate	Votes received
CHARLES COX	322
JOHN CHOLMLEY	295
Edmund Bowyer	47

Source: *Hist. Parl., 1690-1715.*

Table 8.1.4.3
Poll for Members of Parliament for Southwark, 17 July 1702

Candidate	Votes received
CHARLES COX	1,877
JOHN CHOLMLEY	1,772
John Lade	1,194

Source: *Hist. Parl., 1690-1715.*

Table 8.1.4.4
Poll for Members of Parliament for Southwark, 25 November 1702

Candidate	Votes received
JOHN CHOLMLEY	816
CHARLES COX	745
John Lade	664

Source: *Hist. Parl., 1690-1715.*

Table 8.1.4.5
Poll for Members of Parliament for Southwark, 7 October 1710

Candidate	Votes received
JOHN CHOLMLEY	784
CHARLES COX	765
John Lade	641
Isaac Chard	576

Source: *Hist. Parl., 1690-1715.*

Table 8.1.4.6
Poll for Member of Parliament for Southwark, 12 January 1712

Candidate	Votes received
GEORGE MATHEWS	831
EDMUND HALSEY	815
Stiles	8
Cormel	5

Source: *Hist. Parl., 1690-1715.*

Table 8.1.4.7
Poll for Members of Parliament for Southwark, 27 August 1713

Candidate	Votes received
JOHN LADE	792
FISHER TENCH	770
George Mathews	721
Samuel Rush	710

Source: *Hist. Parl., 1690-1715.*

Table 8.1.4.8
Poll for Members of Parliament for Southwark, 3 May 1714

Candidate	Votes received
JOHN LADE	807
FISHER TENCH	805
Samuel Rush	708
Thomas Lant	704

Source: *Hist. Parl., 1690-1715.*

Table 8.1.4.9
Poll for Members of Parliament for Southwark, 31 March 1722

Candidate	Votes received
GEORGE MEGGOTT	1,136
EDMUND HALSEY	921
Samuel Rush	719
Fisher Tench	521

Source: *Hist. Parl., 1715-54.*

Table 8.1.4.10
Poll for Member of Parliament for Southwark, 17 January 1724

Candidate	Votes received
JOHN LADE	790
Fisher Tench	533
Walter Bagnall	199

Source: *Hist. Parl., 1715-54.*

Table 8.1.4.11
Poll for Member of Parliament for Southwark, 23 January 1730

Candidate	Votes received
THOMAS INWEN	826
Richard Lewin	540

Source: *Hist. Parl., 1715-54.*

Table 8.1.4.12
Poll for Members of Parliament for Southwark, 6 June 1734

Candidate	Votes received	
	Poll	Scrutiny
THOMAS INWEN	1,239	1,210
GEORGE HEATHCOTE	874	852
Richard Sheppard	850	824

Source: *Hist. Parl., 1715-54.*

Table 8.1.4.13
Poll for Members of Parliament for Southwark, 6 May 1741

Candidate	Votes received
THOMAS INWEN	929
RALPH THRALE	904
Joseph Chitty	323

Source: *Hist. Parl., 1715-54.*

Table 8.1.4.14
Poll for Member of Parliament for Southwark, 30 June 1743

Candidate	Votes received	
	Poll	Scrutiny
ALEXANDER HUME	792	732
William Hammond	863	691

Source: *Hist. Parl., 1715-54.*

Table 8.1.4.15
Poll for Members of Parliament for Southwark, 4 August 1747

Candidate	Votes received	
	Poll	Scrutiny
ALEXANDER HUME	1,158	
WILLIAM BELCHIER	831	801
James Creed	778	740

Source: *Hist. Parl., 1715-54.*

Table 8.1.4.16
Poll for Members of Parliament for Southwark, 16 April 1754

Candidate	Votes received
WILLIAM BELCHIER	797
WILLIAM HAMMOND	597
Crisp Gascoyne	523

Source: *Hist. Parl., 1754-90.*

Table 8.1.4.17
Poll for Members of Parliament for Southwark, 1 April 1761

Candidate	Votes received
JOSEPH MAWBEY	981
ALEXANDER HUME	950
William Hammond	608

Source: *Hist. Parl., 1754-90.*

Table 8.1.4.18
Poll for Members of Parliament for Southwark, 23 March 1768

Candidate	Votes received
HENRY THRALE	1,248
JOSEPH MAWBEY	1,159
William Belchier	994

Source: *Hist. Parl., 1754-90.*

Table 8.1.4.19
Poll for Members of Parliament for Southwark, 18 October 1774

Candidate	Votes received
NATHANIEL POLHILL	1,195
HENRY THRALE	1,026
William Lee	741
Abraham Hume	457

Source: *Hist. Parl., 1754-90.*

Table 8.1.4.20
Poll for Members of Parliament for Southwark, 13 September 1780

Candidate	Votes received
RICHARD HOTHAM	1,300
NATHANIEL POLHILL	1,138
Henry Thrale	855

Source: *Hist. Parl., 1754-90.*

Table 8.1.4.21
Poll for Member of Parliament for Southwark, 24 September 1782

Candidate	Votes received
HENRY THORNTON	978
James Adair	588

Source: *Hist. Parl., 1754-90.*

Table 8.1.4.22
Poll for Member of Parliament for Southwark, 25 June 1784

Candidate	Votes received
PAUL LE MESURIER	995
Richard Hotham	924

Source: *Hist. Parl., 1754-90.*

Table 8.1.4.23
Poll for Members of Parliament for Southwark, 28 May 1796

Candidate	Votes received
HENRY THORNTON	1,584
GEORGE WOODFORD THELLUSSON	1,373
George Tierney	976

Source: *Hist. Parl., 1790-1820.*

Table 8.1.4.24
Poll for Member of Parliament for Southwark, 22 November 1796

Candidate	Votes received
GEORGE WOODFORD THELLUSSON	1,282
George Tierney	1,119

Source: *Hist. Parl., 1790-1820.*

Table 8.1.4.25
Poll for Members of Parliament for Southwark, 8 July 1802

Candidate	Votes received
HENRY THORNTON	1,644
GEORGE TIERNEY	1,395
Thomas Turton	1,226

Source: *Hist. Parl., 1790-1820.*

Table 8.1.4.26
Poll for Member of Parliament for Southwark, 29 June 1803

Candidate	Votes received	
	Poll	Scrutiny
GEORGE TIERNEY	1,573	1,542
Thomas Turton	1,492	1,446

Source: *Hist. Parl., 1790-1820.*

Table 8.1.4.27
Poll for Members of Parliament for Southwark, 4 November 1806

Candidate	Votes received
THOMAS TURTON	1,753
HENRY THORNTON	1,592
George Tierney	1,349

Source: *Hist. Parl., 1790-1820.*

Table 8.1.4.28
Poll for Members of Parliament for Southwark, 8 May 1807

Candidate	Votes received
THOMAS TURTON	2,152
HENRY THORNTON	1,824
Charles Calvert	1,634

Source: *Hist. Parl., 1790-1820.*

Table 8.1.4.29
Poll for Members of Parliament for Southwark, 13 October 1812

Candidate	Votes received
CHARLES CALVERT	2,180
HENRY THORNTON	1,804
William James Burdett	542

Source: *Hist. Parl., 1790-1820.*

Table 8.1.4.30
Poll for Member of Parliament for Southwark, 17 February 1815

Candidate	Votes received
CHARLES BARCLAY	1,661
William Jones Burdett	424

Source: *Hist. Parl., 1790-1820.*

Table 8.1.4.31
Poll for Members of Parliament for Southwark, 22 June 1818

Candidate	Votes received
CHARLES CALVERT	1,932
ROBERT THOMAS WILSON	1,377
Charles Barclay	1,090

Source: *Hist. Parl., 1790-1820.*

Table 8.1.4.32
Poll for Members of Parliament for Southwark, 10 March 1820

Candidate	Votes received
CHARLES CALVERT	1,264
ROBERT THOMAS WILSON	1,155
Thomas Turton	458

Source: *Hist. Parl., 1820-32.*

Table 8.1.4.33
Poll for Members of Parliament for Southwark, 14 June 1826

Candidate	Votes received
CHARLES CALVERT	1,807
ROBERT THOMAS WILSON	1,712
Edward Polhill	1,342

Source: *Hist. Parl., 1820-32.*

Table 8.1.4.34
Poll for Members of Parliament for Southwark, 5 August 1830

Candidate	Votes received
JOHN RAWLINSON HARRIS	1,664
ROBERT THOMAS WILSON	1,434
Charles Calvert	995

Source: *The Times*, 5 August 1830; Stooks Smith.

Table 8.1.4.35
Poll for Member of Parliament for Southwark, 25 November 1830

Candidate	Votes received
CHARLES CALVERT	1,066
Thomas Farncomb	663

Source: *Hist. Parl., 1820-32.*

Table 8.1.4.36
Poll for Members of Parliament for Southwark, 12 December 1832

Candidate	Votes received
WILLIAM BROUGHAM	2,264
JOHN HUMPHERY	1,708
L. Baugh Allen	1,040
T. Lamie Murray	0

Source: Craig.

Table 8.1.4.37
Poll for Members of Parliament for Southwark, 25 July 1837

Candidate	Votes received
JOHN HUMPHERY	1,941
DANIEL WHITTLE HARVEY	1,927
John Richards	847
Benjamin Harrison	2

Source: Craig.

Table 8.1.4.38
Poll for Member of Parliament for Southwark, 24 January 1840

Candidate	Votes received
BENJAMIN WOOD	2,059
John Walter	1,535

Source: Craig.

Table 8.1.4.39
Poll for Member of Parliament for Southwark, 12 September 1845

Candidate	Votes received
WILLIAM MOLESWORTH	1,943
Jeremiah Pilcher	1,182
E. Miall	352

Source: Craig.

Table 8.1.4.40
Poll for Members of Parliament for Southwark, 9 July 1852

Candidate	Votes received
WILLIAM MOLESWORTH	3,941
APSLEY PELLATT	3,887
George Scovell	2,909

Source: Craig.

8.1.5 Finsbury, 1832-52: five polls

Post 1832, the Finsbury franchise consisted of adult male householders occupying property worth £10 pa or more, who were registered on the electoral register.

Table 8.1.5.1
Poll for Members of Parliament for Finsbury, 12 December 1832

Candidate	Votes received
ROBERT GRANT	4,278
ROBERT SPANKIE	2,842
Charles Babbage	2,311
Thomas Wakley	2,151
Christopher Temple	787

Source: Craig.

Table 8.1.5.2
Poll for Member of Parliament for Finsbury, 2 July 1834

Candidate	Votes received
THOMAS SLINGSBY DUNCOMBE	2,514
HENRY POWNALL	1,915
Thomas Wakley	695
Charles Babbage	379

Source: Craig.

Table 8.1.5.3
Poll for Members of Parliament for Finsbury, 10 January 1835

Candidate	Votes received
THOMAS SLINGSBY DUNCOMBE	4,497
THOMAS WAKLEY	3,359
Robert Spankie	2,332
Henry W. Hobhouse	1,817

Source: Craig.

Table 8.1.5.4
Poll for Members of Parliament for Finsbury, 26 July 1837

Candidate	Votes received
THOMAS WAKLEY	4,957
THOMAS SLINGSBY DUNCOMBE	4,895
Dudley M. Perceval	2,470

Source: Craig.

Table 8.1.5.5
Poll for Members of Parliament for Finsbury, 9 July 1852

Candidate	Votes received
THOMAS CHALLIS	7,504
THOMAS SLINGSBY DUNCOMBE	6,678
James Wyld	2,010

Source: Craig.

8.1.6 Greenwich, 1832-52: eight polls

Post 1832, the Greenwich franchise consisted of all adult male householders occupying property worth £10 pa or more, who were registered on the electoral register.

Table 8.1.6.1
Poll for Members of Parliament for Greenwich, 14 December 1832

Candidate	Votes received
JAMES WHITLEY DEANS DUNDAS	1,633
EDWARD GEORGE BARNARD	1,442
John Angerstein	1,033
F. George Hammond	15

Source: Craig.

Table 8.1.6.2
Poll for Members of Parliament for Greenwich, 10 January 1835

Candidate	Votes received
JOHN ANGERSTEIN	1,826
EDWARD GEORGE BARNARD	1,102
Matthew Wolverley Attwood	1,063

Source: Craig.

Table 8.1.6.3
Poll for Members of Parliament for Greenwich, 27 July 1837

Candidate	Votes received
MATTHEW WOLVERLEY ATTWOOD	1,368
EDWARD GEORGE BARNARD	1,194
C. Napier	1,158

Source: Craig.

Table 8.1.6.4
Poll for Members of Parliament for Greenwich, 1 July 1841

Candidate	Votes received
JAMES WHITLEY DEANS DUNDAS	1,747
EDWARD GEORGE BARNARD	1,592
George Cockburn	1,274

Source: Craig.

Table 8.1.6.5
Poll for Members of Parliament for Greenwich, 31 July 1847

Candidate	Votes received
JAMES WHITLEY DEANS DUNDAS	2,409
EDWARD GEORGE BARNARD	1,511
David Salomons	1,236

Source: Craig.

Table 8.1.6.6
Poll for Member of Parliament for Greenwich, 28 June 1851

Candidate	Votes received
DAVID SALOMONS	2,165
David Williams Wire	1,278

Source: Craig.

Table 8.1.6.7
Poll for Member of Parliament for Greenwich, 11 February 1852

Candidate	Votes received
HOUSTON STEWART	2,956
Montagu Chambers	1,211

Source: Craig.

Table 8.1.6.8
Poll for Members of Parliament for Greenwich, 8 July 1852

Candidate	Votes received
PETER ROLT	2,415
MONTAGU CHAMBERS	2,360
Houston Stewart	2,026
David Salomons	1,102

Source: Craig

8.1.7 Lambeth, 1832-52: seven polls

Post 1832, the Lambeth franchise consisted of all adult male household-ers occupying property worth £10 pa or more, who were registered on the electoral register.

Table 8.1.7.1
Poll for Members of Parliament for Lambeth, 12 December 1832

Candidate	Votes received
CHARLES TENNYSON	2,716
BENJAMIN HAWES	2,166
Daniel Wakefield	819
John Moore	155

Source: Craig.

Table 8.1.7.2
Poll for Members of Parliament for Lambeth, 12 January 1835

Candidate	Votes received
BENJAMIN HAWES	2,008
CHARLES TENNYSON	1,995
Charles Farebrother	931

Source: Craig.

Table 8.1.7.3
Poll for Members of Parliament for Lambeth, 26 July 1837

Candidate	Votes received
BENJAMIN HAWES	2,934
CHARLES TENNYSON D'EYNCOURT	2,811
Charles Baldwin	1,624

Source: Craig.

Table 8.1.7.4
Poll for Members of Parliament for Lambeth, 1 July 1841

Candidate	Votes received
BENJAMIN HAWES	2,601
CHARLES TENNYSON D'EYNCOURT	2,568
Charles Baldwin	1,999
Thomas Cabbell	1,753

Source: Craig.

Table 8.1.7.5
Poll for Members of Parliament for Lambeth, 31 July 1847

Candidate	Votes received
CHARLES PEARSON	4,614
CHARLES TENNYSON D'EYNCOURT	3,708
Benjamin Hawes	3,344

Source: Craig.

Table 8.1.7.6
Poll for Member of Parliament for Lambeth, 7 August 1850

Candidate	Votes received
WILLIAM WILLIAMS	3,834
CHARLES NAPIER	1,182
John Hinde Palmer	585

Source: Craig.

Table 8.1.7.7
Poll for Members of Parliament for Lambeth, 8 July 1852

Candidate	Votes received
WILLIAM ARTHUR WILKINSON	4,752
WILLIAM WILLIAMS	4,022
Charles Tennyson D'Eyncourt	3,829

Source: Craig.

8.1.8 Marylebone, 1832-52: seven polls

For details of the Marylebone franchise of all adult male householders in properties worth £10 pa or more, who were registered on the electoral register, see Section 3.5.

Table 8.1.8.1
Poll for Members of Parliament for Marylebone, 12 December 1832

Candidate	Votes received
EDWARD BERKELEY PORTMAN	4,317
WILLIAM HORNE	3,320
Samuel Swithin St Burden Whalley	2,185
Thomas Murphy	913
Leslie Grove Jones	316

Source: Craig.

Table 8.1.8.2
Poll for Member of Parliament for Marylebone, 20 March 1833

Candidate	Votes received
SAMUEL SWITHIN ST BURDEN WHALLEY	2,869
Henry Thomas Hope	2,055
Charles A. Murray	791
Thomas Murphy	172

Source: Craig.

Table 8.1.8.3
Poll for Members of Parliament for Marylebone, 9 January 1835

Candidate	Votes received
SAMUEL SWITHIN ST BURDEN WHALLEY	2,956
HENRY LYTTON BULWER	2,781
William Horne	1,862
Gilbert Ainslie Young	738

Source: Craig.

Table 8.1.8.4
Poll for Members of Parliament for Marylebone, 26 July 1837

Candidate	Votes received
BENJAMIN HALL	3,512
SAMUEL SWITHIN ST BURDEN WHALLEY	3,350
Charles John Shore	2,952
Gilbert Ainslie Young	764
William Horne	662

Source: Craig.

Table 8.1.8.5
Poll for Member of Parliament for Marylebone, 3 March 1838

Candidate	Votes received
CHARLES JOHN SHORE	4,166
William Ewart	3,762
Thomas Perronet Thompson	186

Source: Craig.

Table 8.1.8.6
Poll for Members of Parliament for Marylebone, 2 July 1841

Candidate	Votes received
BENJAMIN HALL	4,661
CHARLES NAPIER	4,587
Benjamin Bond Cabbell	3,410
James Hamilton	3,383
W. Villiers Sankey	61

Source: Craig.

Table 8.1.8.7
Poll for Members of Parliament of Marylebone, 31 July 1847

Candidate	Votes received
DUDLEY STUART	5,367
BENJAMIN HALL	5,343
James John Hamilton	3,677
W. Shee	662
R. Owen	1

Source: Craig.

8.1.9 Tower Hamlets, 1832-52: five polls

Post 1832, the Tower Hamlets franchise consisted of all adult male householders occupying property worth £10 pa or more, who were registered on the electoral register.

Table 8.1.9.1
Poll for Members of Parliament for Tower Hamlets, 12 December 1832

Candidate	Votes received
STEPHEN LUSHINGTON	3,978
WILLIAM CLAY	3,751
Leicester Stanhope	2,952
F. Marryat	1,934

Source: Craig.

Table 8.1.9.2
Poll for Members of Parliament for Tower Hamlets, 9 January 1835

Candidate	Votes received
WILLIAM CLAY	2,779
STEPHEN LUSHINGTON	2,580
J.R. Burton	465

Source: Craig.

Table 8.1.9.3
Poll for Members of Parliament for Tower Hamlets, 30 June 1841

Candidate	Votes received
WILLIAM CLAY	4,706
CHARLES RICHARD FOX	4,096
G.R. Robinson	2,183
A.K. Hutchinson	1,775
Thomas Perronet Thompson	831

Source: Craig.

Table 8.1.9.4
Poll for Members of Parliament for Tower Hamlets, 31 July 1847

Candidate	Votes received
GEORGE THOMPSON	6,268
WILLIAM CLAY	3,839
Charles Richard Fox	2,622

Source: Craig.

Table 8.1.9.5
Poll for Members of Parliament for Tower Hamlets, 8 July 1852

Candidate	Votes received
WILLIAM CLAY	7,728
CHARLES SALISBURY BURTON	7,718
George Thompson	4,568
A.S. Ayrton	2,792
W. Newton	1,095

Source: Craig.

8.2 POLLS IN COMMON HALL

8.2.1 Candidates for Lord Mayor of London, 1700-1832: 21 polls

Note (1): See section 3.3.5 for details of mayoral elections.

Note (2): Two candidates for the mayoralty were elected by the London liverymen in Common Hall: one candidate from the two elected then being chosen by the Aldermen.

Note (3): The names of successful candidates are in SMALL CAPITALS and those of unsuccessful candidate in lower case.

Table 8.2.1.1
Poll for candidates for Lord Mayor of London, 1 October 1700

Candidate	Votes received
CHARLES DUNCOMBE	2,752
THOMAS ABNEY	1,919
William Hedges	1,907

Source: LMA COL/CC/01/01/050, fo 341.

Table 8.2.1.2
Poll for candidates for Lord Mayor of London, 1 October 1701

Candidate	Votes received
WILLIAM GORE	2,073
CHARLES DUNCOMBE	1,650
Owen Buckingham	1,380
Samuel Dashwood	1,345

Source: LMA COL/CC/01/01/051, p. 143.

Table 8.2.1.3
Poll for candidates for Lord Mayor of London, 5 October 1710

Candidate	Votes received
RICHARD BEACHCROFT	5,092
GILBERT HEATHCOTE	2,878
Richard Hoare	2,506

Source: LMA COL/CC/01/01/053, fo 217.

Table 8.2.1.4
Poll for candidates for Lord Mayor of London, 3 October 1722

Candidate	Votes received	
	Poll	Scrutiny
GERARD CONYERS	3,217	2,942
PETER DELMÉ	3,172	2,907
George Merttins	1,349	1,242
Francis Forbes	1,334	1,228

Source: *Compleat set of St James's Journals*, 4 October 1722; LMA COL/CN/01/01/006, fo 150.

Table 8.2.1.5
Poll for candidates for Lord Mayor of London, 2 October 1739

Candidate	Votes received
JOHN SALTER	95
ROBERT GODSCHALL	90
George Champion	21

Source: Benjamin Robins, *A narrative of what passed in Common Hall* (1739), p. 6.

Table 8.2.1.6
Poll for candidates for Lord Mayor of London, 7 October 1756

Candidate	Votes received
MARSHE DICKINSON	1,615
Richard Glyn	528

Source: LMA COL/CN/01/01/008, fo 49; *Public Advertiser*, 7 October 1756.

Table 8.2.1.7
Poll for candidates for Lord Mayor of London, 10 October 1769

Candidate	Votes received
WILLIAM BECKFORD	1,967
BARLOW TRECOTHICK	1,911
Henry Bankes	676

Source: LMA COL/CN/01/01/008, fo 148.

Table 8.2.1.8
Poll for candidates for Lord Mayor of London, 28 June 1770

Candidate	Votes received
BARLOW TRECOTHICK	1,601
BRASS CROSBY	1,434
Henry Bankes	437

Source: LMA COL/CN/01/01/008, fo 155; *Public Advertiser*, 30 June 1770; *London Evening Post*, 28-30 June 1770.

Table 8.2.1.9
Poll for candidates for Lord Mayor of London, 8 October 1771

Candidate	Votes received
WILLIAM NASH	2,199
JOHN SAWBRIDGE	1,879
Brass Crosby (Lord Mayor)	1,795
Thomas Hallifax	846
James Townsend	152
Henry Bankes	36

Source: LMA COL/CN/01/01/008, fos 166-67; COL/CN/03/056.

Table 8.2.1.10
Poll for candidates for Lord Mayor of London, 24 October 1772

Candidate	Votes received
JOHN WILKES	2,301
JAMES TOWNSEND	2,278
Thomas Hallifax	2,126
John Shakespeare	1,912
Henry Bankes	2

Source: LMA COL/CN/01/01/008, fo 171; COL/CN/03/058; *Public Advertiser*, 7 October 1772.

Table 8.2.1.11
Poll for candidates for Lord Mayor of London, 8 October 1773

Candidate	Votes received
JOHN WILKES	1,690
FREDERICK BULL	1,655
John Sawbridge	1,178
Richard Oliver	1,094

Source: LMA COL/CN/01/01/008, fo 178; *Public Advertiser*, 7 October 1773.

Table 8.2.1.12
Poll for candidates for Lord Mayor of London, 8 October 1774

Candidate	Votes received
JOHN WILKES	1,957
FREDERICK BULL	1,923
James Esdaile	1,474
Brackley Kennet	1,410

Source: LMA COL/CN/01/01/008, fos 184-5; *Public Advertiser*, 7 October 1774.

Table 8.2.1.13
Poll for candidates for Lord Mayor of London, 7 October 1799

Candidate	Votes received
HARVEY C. COMBE	1,437
THOMAS SKINNER	1,153
William Staines	487

Source: LMA COL/CN/01/01/009, fo 108.

Table 8.2.1.14
Poll for candidates for Lord Mayor of London, 6 October 1800

Candidate	Votes received
WILLIAM STAINES	1,371
HARVEY C. COMBE (Lord Mayor)	1,007
William Newman	886

Source: LMA COL/CN/01/01/009, fos 124-5·

Table 8.2.1.15
Poll for candidates for Lord Mayor of London, 7 October 1804

Candidate	Votes received
PETER PERCHARD	1,781
JAMES SHAW	1,652
Charles Flower	687

Source: LMA COL/CN/01/01/009, fos 180-1.

Table 8.2.1.16
Poll for candidates for Lord Mayor of London, 7 October 1816

Candidate	Votes received
MATTHEW WOOD	2,656
HARVEY C. COMBE	2,416
Christopher Smith	1,055
John Atkins	11
Samuel Goodbehere	5

Source: LMA COL/CN/01/01/009, fos 345-6.

Table 8.2.1.17
Poll for candidates for Lord Mayor of London, 7 October 1817

Candidate	Votes received
CHRISTOPHER SMITH	2,273
JOHN ATKINS	1,586
Matthew Wood (Lord Mayor)	827
Samuel Goodbehere	763

Source: LMA COL/CN/01/01/010, pp. 37-9.

Table 8.2.1.18
Poll for candidates for Lord Mayor of London, 7 October 1819

Candidate	Votes received
GEORGE BRIDGES	3,069
JOHN THOMAS THORP	2,074
Matthew Wood	2,036
William Heygate	2

Source: LMA COL/CN/01/01/010, pp. 77-8.

Table 8.2.1.19
Poll for candidates for Lord Mayor of London, 7 October 1831

Candidate	Votes received
JOHN KEY (Lord Mayor)	3,268
JOHN THOMAS THORP	3,089
Peter Laurie	2,713
Charles Farebrother	16
Henry Winchester	2
William Taylor Copeland	1
Thomas Kelly	1

Source: LMA COL/CN/01/01/010, pp. 308-10; COL/CN/03/117.

Table 8.2.1.20
Poll for candidates for Lord Mayor of London, 21 October 1831

Candidate	Votes received	
WILLIAM THOMPSON	2,577	
JOHN KEY (Lord Mayor)	2,476	
Peter Laurie	486	
Robert Waithman	36	
Charles Farebrother	2	
Henry Winchester	2	
William Taylor Copeland	2	

Source: LMA COL/CN/01/01/010, pp. 314-16.

Table 8.2.1.21
Poll for candidates for Lord Mayor of London, 2 November 1831

Candidate	Votes received	
JOHN KEY (Lord Mayor)	2,517	
THOMAS KELLY	2,311	
Charles Farebrother	684	
Peter Laurie	5	
Henry Winchester	2	
William Taylor Copeland	1	

Source: LMA COL/CN/01/01/010, pp. 318-20; COL/CN/03/117.

8.2.2 Sheriffs of London and Middlesex, 1700-1832: 32 polls
Poll for sheriffs of London and Middlesex, 3 July 1716
Elected by the London liverymen in Common Hall: for details, see Section 3.3.7

Table 8.2.2.1
Poll for sheriffs of London and Middlesex, 25 June 1701

Candidate	Votes received
WILLIAM WITHERS	
PETER FLOYER	
Nathaniel Long	

Source: LMA COL/CC/01/01/051, p. 28.

Table 8.2.2.2
Poll for sheriff of London and Middlesex, 6 February 1702

Candidate	Votes received
JAMES BATEMAN	2,446
Robert Beddingfield	2,225

Source: LMA COL/CC/01/01/051, p. 181.

Table 8.2.2.3
Poll for sheriffs of London and Middlesex, 27 June 1702

Candidate	Votes received
ROBERT BEDDINGFIELD	1,840
SAMUEL GARRARD	1,828
Joseph Woolf	1,518
John Buckworth	1,492

Source: LMA COL/CC/01/01/051, p. 412.

Table 8.2.2.4
Poll for sheriff of London and Middlesex, 4 July 1704

Candidate	Votes received
WILLIAM HUMPHRIES	1,183
Edward Bovey	704
Edward Bolitha	15

Source: LMA COL/CC/01/01/051, p. 673.

Table 8.2.2.5
Poll for sheriffs of London and Middlesex, 29 June 1711

Candidate	Votes received
JOHN CASS	2,022
HENRY LAMB	1,981
John Ward	1,536
Richard Gough	1,464

Source: LMA COL/CC/01/01/053, fo 250.

Table 8.2.2.6 Poll for sheriffs of London and Middlesex, 24 June 1713

Candidate	Votes received
JOSHUA SHARP	2,226
FRANCIS FORBES	2,214
John Chadwick	1,156
Randolph Knipe	1,148

Source: LMA COL/CC/01/01/054, fo 49.

Table 8.2.2.7
Poll for sheriff of London and Middlesex, 27 September 1714

Candidate	Votes received
RANDOLPH KNIPE	2,817
George Merttins	1,812

Source: LMA COL/CC/01/01/054, fo 136.

Table 8.2.2.8
Poll for sheriffs of London and Middlesex, 3 July 1716

Candidate	Votes received
GERARD CONYERS	1,941
CHARLES COOK	1,935
William Chambers	1,456
James Chambers	1,420

Source: LMA COL/CC/01/01/054, fo 231.

Table 8.2.2.9
Poll for sheriffs of London and Middlesex, 28 June 1720

Candidate	Votes received
GEORGE CASWALL	2,548
WILLIAM BILLERS	2,503
Edward Becher	2,046
George Merttins	2,037

Source: LMA COL/CN/01/01/006, fo 101.

Table 8.2.2.10
Poll for sheriffs of London and Middlesex, 27 June 1721

Candidate	Votes received
GEORGE MERTTINS	1,860
EDWARD BECHER	1,856
Robert Baylis	1,381
James Colebrook	1,369

Source: LMA COL/CN/01/01/006, fo 123.

Table 8.2.2.11
Poll for sheriffs of London and Middlesex, 5 July 1723

Candidate	Votes received	
	Poll	Scrutiny
RICHARD HOPKINS		3,248
FELIX FEAST		3,244
Richard Lockwood		3,191
John Williams		3,188

Source: LMA COL/CN/01/01/006, fo 177; Anon., *A true account of the proceedings* (1723), p. 7.

Table 8.2.2.12
Poll for sheriff of London and Middlesex, 28 March 1724

Candidate	Votes received	
	Poll	Scrutiny
EDWARD BELLAMY	3,102	2,868
John Williams	3,557	2,850

Source: LMA COL/CN/01/01/006, fo 182; COL/CN/03/014; *Daily Journal*, 28 March 1724.

Table 8.2.2.13
Poll for sheriff of London and Middlesex, 7 April 1726

Candidate	Votes received
JOHN THOMPSON	2,564
Richard Brocas	2,065

Source: LMA COL/CN/01/01/006, fos 326-7.

Table 8.2.2.14
Poll for sheriff of London and Middlesex, 28 September 1742

Candidate	Votes received
WILLIAM BENN	1,925
Joseph Hankey	1,371

Source: LMA COL/CN/03/028.

Table 8.2.2.15
Poll for sheriffs of London and Middlesex, 8 July 1746

Candidate	Votes received
ROBERT ALSOP	1,006
THOMAS WINTERBOTTOM	1,003
Jonathan Forward	402
Kenelm Fawkener	391

Source: LMA COL/CN/03/032; COL/CN/01/01/007, fo 337.

Table 8.2.2.16
Poll for sheriff of London and Middlesex, 8 September 1749

Candidate	Votes received
WILLIAM WHITAKER	659
Thomas Corbett	105

Source: LMA COL/CN/01/01/007, fo 354; *General Advertiser*, 12 September 1749.

Table 8.2.2.17
Poll for sheriff of London and Middlesex, 2 July 1751

Candidate	Votes received
MARSHE DICKINSON	699
John Bosworth	394

Source: LMA COL/CN/01/01/007, fo 368.

Table 8.2.2.18
Poll for sheriffs of London and Middlesex, 9 July 1754

Candidate	Votes received
ALEXANDER SHEAFE	1,020
GEORGE STREATFIELD	1,016
Samuel Fludyer	718
William Beckford	716

Source: LMA COL/CN/01/01/008, fos 21-2; COL/CN/03/040.

Table 8.2.2.19
Poll for sheriffs of London and Middlesex, 1 August 1755

Candidate	Votes received
IVO WHITBREAD	1,139
JOHN MARKHAM	1,115
John Porter	796
William Beckford	781

Source: LMA COL/CN/01/01/008, fo 32; *Public Advertiser*, 2 August 1755.

Table 8.2.2.20
Poll for sheriffs of London and Middlesex, 6 July 1756

Candidate	Votes received
WILLIAM BRIDGEN	1,166
WILLIAM STEPHENSON	1,166
Thomas Truman	664
Thomas Whately	664

Source: LMA COL/CN/01/01/008, fos 43-4; COL/CN/03/042.

Table 8.2.2.21
Poll for sheriffs of London and Middlesex, 1 July 1758

Candidate	Votes received
THOMAS TRUMAN	1,452
THOMAS WHATELEY	1,415
Joseph Hankey	1,051
Robert Kite	1,027

Source: LMA COL/CN/01/01/008, fo 63; COL/CN/03/044.

Table 8.2.2.22
Poll for sheriff of London and Middlesex, 8 August 1760

Candidate	Votes received
ROBERT KITE	232
William Butler	127

Source: LMA COL/CN/03/046; COL/CN/01/01/008, fo 80-1; *Public Advertiser*, 9 August 1760.

Table 8.2.2.23
Poll for sheriff of London and Middlesex, 24 July 1766

Candidate	Votes received
PHILIP STEPHENS	165
ROBERT DARLING	164
Richard Peers	14
William Cracraft	12

Source: *London Evening Post*, 24 July 1766.

Table 8.2.2.24
Poll for sheriffs of London and Middlesex, 3 July 1771

Candidate	Votes received
JOHN WILKES	2,315
FREDERICK BULL	2,194
John Kirkman	1,949
Samuel Plumbe	1,875
Richard Oliver	119

Source: LMA COL/CN/01/01/008, fo 161.

Table 8.2.2.25
Poll for sheriffs of London and Middlesex, 3 July 1772

Candidate	Votes received
RICHARD OLIVER	1,586
WATKIN LEWES	1,327
Samuel Plumbe	762

Source: LMA COL/CN/01/01/008, fo 170; *Public Advertiser*, 2 July 1772.

Table 8.2.2.26
Poll for sheriffs of London and Middlesex, 1 July 1774

Candidate	Votes received
JOHN HART	908
WILLIAM PLOMER	900
John Williams	312
George Grieve	309

Source: LMA COL/CN/01/01/008, fo 182; *Morning Chronicle*, 29 June 1774.

Table 8.2.2.27
Poll for sheriffs of London and Middlesex, 4 July 1775

Candidate	Votes received
GEORGE HAYLEY	328
NATHANIEL NEWNHAM	315
Walter Rawlinson	120
Nathaniel Thomas	117

Source: LMA COL/CN/01/01/008, fos 188-9; COL/CN/03/060; *Lloyd's Evening Post and British Chronicle*, 23 June 1775.

Table 8.2.2.28
Poll for sheriffs of London and Middlesex, 2 July 1800

Candidate	Votes received
JOHN PERRING	1,245
THOMAS CADELL	1,245
Robert Albion Cox	895
William Leighton	894

Source: LMA COL/CN/01/01/009, fos 121-2; COL/CN/03/086.

Table 8.2.2.29
Poll for sheriffs of London and Middlesex, 3 July 1811

Candidate	Votes received
SAMUEL BIRCH	1,369
WILLIAM HEYGATE	653
Richard Sanderson	310
Christopher Magnay	302
George Bridges	45
John Gray	3
Christopher Taddy	1
William Cass	1
Michael Hoy	1
Thomas Foster	1
Andrew Jordaine	1
Philip Booth	1

Source: LMA COL/CN/01/01/009, fos 265-6; COL/CN/03/097.

Table 8.2.2.30
Poll for sheriffs of London and Middlesex, 4 July 1821

Candidate	Votes received
JOHN GARRATT	1,667
WILLIAM VENABLES	1,425
James Crook	423

Source: LMA COL/CN/01/01/010, pp. 121-2; COL/CN/03/107.

Table 8.2.2.31
Poll for sheriffs of London and Middlesex, 4 July 1825

Candidate	Votes received
JOHN CROWDER	945
THOMAS KELLY	872
John Fowler Dove	455
Philip Hurd	287
Robert Humphrey Marten	137
John Woolley	86

Source: LMA COL/CN/01/01/010, pp. 186-8; COL/CN/03/111.

Table 8.2.2.32
Poll for sheriffs of London and Middlesex, 3 July 1830

Candidate	Votes received
CHAPMAN MARSHALL	978
WILLIAM HENRY POLAND	859
Thomas Flight	273
Robert Humphrey Marten	127
Archdale Palmer	24
William Flower	15
John Woolley	8
Henry Fellowes	6
Isaac Bird	4
John Addinell	3
John Scott	3

Source: LMA COL/CN/01/01/010, pp. 268-71; COL/CN/03/116.

8.2.3 Chamberlains of London, 1700-1832: 14 polls

Elected by the London liverymen in Common Hall: for details, see Section 3.3.6. John Wilkes featured in five of these elections, winning the post at his fifth attempt.

Table 8.2.3.1
Poll for chamberlain of London, 21 January 1703

Candidate	Votes received
WILLIAM FAZACKERLEY	411
Thomas Eyre	283
Thomas Amy	218

Source: *Daily Courant*, 22 January 1703.

Table 8.2.3.2
Poll for chamberlain of London, 3 July 1716

Candidate	Votes received
WILLIAM FAZAKERLEY	1,799
Samuel Westall	721

Source: LMA COL/CC/01/01/054, fo 231.

Table 8.2.3.3
Poll for chamberlain of London, 3 July 1718

Candidate	Votes received
GEORGE LUDLAM	3,273
Samuel Westall	2,591

Source: *Daily Courant*, 28 June 1718.

Table 8.2.3.4
Poll for chamberlain of London, 10 February 1728

Candidate	Votes received
SAMUEL ROBINSON	3,058
Samuel Trench	2,250

Source: *Daily Journal*, 10 February 1728.

Table 8.2.3.5
Poll for chamberlain of London, 4 May 1734

Candidate	Votes received	
	Poll	Scrutiny
JOHN BOSWORTH	3,326	3,212
William Selwin	3,320	3,208

Source: LMA COL/CN/01/01/007, fo 201.

Table 8.2.3.6
Poll for chamberlain of London, 7 May 1751

Candidate	Votes received
THOMAS HARRISON	1,938
Richard Glover	1,358
Robert Pycroft	542
James Hodges	474

Source: LMA COL/CN/01/01/007, fo 367.

Table 8.2.3.7
Poll for chamberlain of London, 22 January 1765

Candidate	Votes received
STEPHEN THEODORE JANSSEN	1,316
Samuel Turner	1,202
Stracey Till	250
Francis Ellis	229
Samuel Freeman	180
Thomas Long	0

Source: LMA COL/CN/01/01/008, fo 124; COL/CN/03/050.

Table 8.2.3.8
Poll for chamberlain of London, 1 March 1776

Candidate	Votes received
BENJAMIN HOPKINS	2,887
John Wilkes	2,710

Source: LMA COL/CN/01/01/008, fo 199; COL/CN/03/061; *Daily Advertiser*, 28 February 1776.

Table 8.2.3.9
Poll for chamberlain of London, 4 July 1776

Candidate	Votes received
BENJAMIN HOPKINS	2,869
John Wilkes	1,673

Source: LMA COL/CN/01/01/008 fo 200; COL/CN/03/1776.

Table 8.2.3.10
Poll for chamberlain of London, 4 July 1777

Candidate	Votes received
BENJAMIN HOPKINS	2,132
John Wilkes	1,228

Source: LMA COL/CN/01/01/008, fo 205; *Morning Chronicle and London Advertiser*, 2 July 1777.

Table 8.2.3.11
Poll for chamberlain of London, 3 July 1778

Candidate	Votes received
BENJAMIN HOPKINS	1,216
John Wilkes	287

Source: LMA COL/CN/01/01/008, fo 211; COL/CN/03/063; *Morning Chronicle and London Advertiser*, 2 July 1778.

Table 8.2.3.12
Poll for chamberlain of London, 1 December 1779

Candidate	Votes received
JOHN WILKES	2,343
William James	370

Source: LMA COL/CN/01/01/008, fo 217.

Table 8.2.3.13
Poll for chamberlain of London, 9 January 1798

Candidate	Votes received
RICHARD CLARKE	558
Watkin Lewes	50

Source: LMA COL/CN/01/01/009, fo 95.

Table 8.2.3.14
Poll for chamberlain of London, 29 January 1831

Candidate	Votes received
JAMES SHAW	3,447
Robert Waithman	2,007

Source: LMA COL/CN/01/01/010, pp. 290-1; COL/CN/03/117.

8.2.4 Bridge Masters of London Bridge, 1709-1832: 25 polls

Elected by the London liverymen in Common Hall: for details, see Section 3.3.3.

Table 8.2.4.1
Poll for Bridge Master of London Bridge, 24 June 1709

Candidate	Votes received
ROBERT SWANN	1,046
Joseph Fossey	772

Source: *Daily Courant*, 25 June 1709.

Table 8.2.4.2
Poll for Bridge Master of London Bridge, 3 July 1718

Candidate	Votes received
HENRY OWEN	
Thomas Reynolds	

Source: LMA COL/CC/01/01/054, fo 311; *Daily Courant*, 25 June 1718.

Table 8.2.4.3
Poll for Bridge Master of London Bridge, 28 June 1725

Candidate	Votes received
MATTHEW SNABLIN	1,109
John Webb	679

Source: LMA COL/CN/03/015; COL/CN/01/01/006, fos 322-3.

Table 8.2.4.4
Poll for Bridge Master of London Bridge, 2 July 1729

Candidate	Votes received
JOHN LUND	2,350
Joseph Billers	1,759

Source: LMA COL/CN/01/01/007, fo 110.

Table 8.2.4.5
Poll for Bridge Master of London Bridge, 2 July 1734

Candidate	Votes received
THOMAS HYDE	1,652
William Davey	1,325
Thomas Toone	146
Thomas Mercer	132

Source: *Daily Journal*, 29 June 1734.

Table 8.2.4.6
Poll for Bridge Master of London Bridge, 1 July 1740

Candidate	Votes received
THOMAS PIDDINGTON	2,217
William Marsland	1,788

Source: LMA COL/CN/01/01/007, fo 283.

Table 8.2.4.7
Poll for Bridge Master of London Bridge, 29 June 1744

Candidate	Votes received
WILLIAM MINGAY	2,037
John Grant	1,645
Samuel Keynton	182
Thomas Hyde	117

Source: *Penny London Morning Advertiser*, 29 June – 2 July 1744; LMA COL/CN/01/01/007, fo 321.

Table 8.2.4.8
Poll for Bridge Master of London Bridge, 4 December 1750

Candidate	Votes received
HUGH ROSSITER	1,460
Edward Boxley	1,141
Sellers Thornberry	266
William Barton	243
Thomas Chance	179
Cornelius Herbert	44

Source: LMA COL/CN/03/036; COL/CN/01/01/007, fo 364.

Table 8.2.4.9
Poll for Bridge Master of London Bridge, 1 May 1759

Candidate	Votes received
WILLIAM SMITH	1,952
Edmund Stevens	1,701
Thomas Chance	71

Source: LMA COL/CN/01/01/008, fo 72.

Table 8.2.4.10
Poll for Bridge Master of London Bridge, 22 December 1760

Candidate	Votes received
EDMUND STEVENS	1,376
John Young	854
Peter Melling	72
Thomas Chance	57

Source: LMA COL/CN/01/01/008, fos 87-8.

Table 8.2.4.11
Poll for Bridge Master of London Bridge, 30 July 1761

Candidate	Votes received
JOHN SHEWELL	1,782
John Young	1,554

Source: LMA COL/CN/01/01/008, fo 93.

Table 8.2.4.12
Poll for Bridge Master of London Bridge, 1 July 1765

Candidate	Votes received
JOHN NICHOLLS	1,334
John Tovey	1,073

Source: LMA COL/CN/01/01/008, fo 126; *Gazetteer and New Daily Advertiser*, 27 June 1765.

Table 8.2.4.13
Poll for Bridge Master of London Bridge, 27 September 1771

Candidate	Votes received
THOMAS BORWICK	1,503
John Townsend	1,307
Thomas Parker	102
John Jefferson	98
John Garnons	55
William Dell	43
John Blake	35
Joseph Bowler	12

Source: LMA COL/CN/01/01/008, fos 165-6.

Table 8.2.4.14
Poll for Bridge Master of London Bridge, 1 December 1779

Candidate	Votes received
DAVID BUFFAR	1,305
John Taylor	260
Luckyn Betts	244

Source: LMA COL/CN/01/01/008, fo 218.

Table 8.2.4.15
Poll for Bridge Master of London Bridge, 13 February 1781

Candidate	Votes received
ROBERT HAZELFOOT GARRARD	1,914
Joseph Dixon	1,741
Edward Aldridge	314
Luckyn Betts	294
John Taylor	227
George Fewkes	199

Source: LMA COL/CN/03/066.

Table 8.2.4.16
Poll for Bridge Master of London Bridge, 1 May 1783

Candidate	Votes received
JOSEPH DIXON	2,093
Henry Gretton	1,760

Source: LMA COL/CN/03/068; COL/CN/01/01/8, fo 239; *Morning Herald*, 2 May 1783.

Table 8.2.4.17
Poll for Bridge Master of London Bridge, 5 July 1784

Candidate	Votes received
JOHN BURBANK	1,482
John Taylor	736
George Maynard	163
George Fewkes	72

Source: LMA COL/CN/03/069; COL/CN/01/01/008, fos 249-50; *Public Advertiser*, 2 July 1784.

Table 8.2.4.18
Poll for Bridge Master of London Bridge, 8 May 1787

Candidate	Votes received
JOSEPH SPECK	967
Arthur Scaife	463
Kendal	10

Source: *World and Fashionable Advertiser*, 11 May 1787.

Table 8.2.4.19
Poll for Bridge Master of London Bridge, 28 June 1792

Candidate	Votes received
JOHN REDHEAD	1,196
Arthur Scaife	1,893
Charles Wright	80

Source: LMA COL/CN/03/077; COL/CN/01/01/009, fo 31.

Table 8.2.4.20
Poll for Bridge Master of London Bridge, 22 September 1796

Candidate	Votes received
JOHN WILLIAM GALABIN	1,516
Edward Wilson	1,509
Thomas Wooley	855
Richard Yeoward	163

Source: LMA COL/CN/01/01/009, fos 65-6.

Table 8.2.4.21
Poll for Bridge Masters of London Bridge, 1 July 1802

Candidate	Votes received
JOHN WILLIAM GALABIN	3,078
SAMUEL MARRIOTT	2,277
Richard Yeoward	1,894

Source: LMA COL/CN/01/01/009 fo 150.

Table 8.2.4.22
Poll for Bridge Master of London Bridge, 1 March 1808

Candidate	Votes received
RICHARD YEOWARD	1,853
Samuel Thodey	1,603
Thomas Holland	110

Source: *Morning Chronicle*, 4 March 1808.

Table 8.2.4.23
Poll for Bridge Master of London Bridge, 27 November 1822

Candidate	Votes received
LEWIS LEWIS	2,086
James Norton	1,406
Gawen Shotter	43

Source: LMA COL/CN/01/01/10, pp. 153-4.

Table 8.2.4.24
Poll for Bridge Master of London Bridge, 28 September 1824

Candidate	Votes received
WILLIAM GILLMAN	2,174
William Hainworth	1,210
Sparkes Moline	55

Source: LMA COL/CN/01/01/010, pp. 173-4; COL/CN/03/110.

Table 8.2.4.25
Poll for Bridge Master of London Bridge, 11 February 1831

Candidate	Votes received	
JOSEPH WATSON	2,127	
David Gibbs	1,224	
Thomas Moulden	714	
William Hainworth	296	
Thomas Dale	11	
John Fryer Smallman	7	
Edward Sage	1	
Peter Houghton	1	
Henry Clark	1	

Source: LMA COL/CN/01/01/010, pp. 292-3; COL/CN/03/117.

8.2.5 Auditors of London, 1700-1832: one poll

Elected by the London liverymen in Common Hall: for details, see Section 3.3.3.

Table 8.2.5.1
Poll for auditors of London, 27 June 1786

Candidate	Votes received
SAMUEL THORNE	153
WILLIAM WILSON	153
J. Tomlins	128
Thomas Loveland	123
William Stock	66
Nettleship	65

Source: *Morning Chronicle*, 28 June 1786.

8.3 WARDMOTE POLLS

Note (1): See section 3.3.2 for a discussion of the wardmote freeman householder franchise and the quasi-wardmote householder franchise.

Note (2): The data available vary from election to election and are often incomplete as indicated variously below by null fields, Notes and other devices. The intention has been to record all surviving data for each election.

Note (3): The names of those recorded as elected are in SMALL CAPITALS and the names of unsuccessful candidates are in lower case.

8.3.1 Aldersgate, 1734-1830: 28 polls

(8 common councilmen; 251 freeman householders in 1833)

Table 8.3.1.a
Precincts in Aldersgate

Code	Precinct
1st Out	1st Without
2nd Out	2nd Without
3rd Out	3rd Without
4th Out	4th Without
A & A	St Ann & St Agnes
Leonard	St Leonard
Staining	St Mary Staining
Zachary	St John Zachary

Note: All electors in the ward were entitled to choose from among all the candidates but, in the larger wards, those elected as common councilmen were taken to represent specific precincts, which were electoral sub-divisions of the ward (whose boundaries, confusingly, did not automatically match the parish ecclesiastical boundaries).

Table 8.3.1.1
Poll for common councilmen of Aldersgate, 8 January 1734

Forename	Surname	Precinct	Livery	Votes received
RICHARD	BAYLEY			240
JOHN	WILLKINS			240
EDWARD	CHOWNE			239
SAMUEL	BALLARD			233
SAMUEL	SMITH			231
JOHN	SNART			227
GEORGE	JAMES			227
THOMAS	SKIPP			227
Richard	Scarr			117
Samwell	Knight			114

Source: *Grub Street Journal*, 27 December 1733.

Table 8.3.1.2
Poll for common councilmen of Aldersgate, 8 January 1739

Forename	Surname	Precinct	Livery	Votes received
NATHANIEL	MACCASCREE			N
Charles	Kemp			(N-2)

Source: *London Daily Post*, 25 December 1738.

Table 8.3.1.3
Poll for common councilmen of Aldersgate, 9 January 1749

Forename	Surname	Precinct	Livery	Votes received
SAMUEL	READ			202
ROBERT	EVANS			143
SAMUEL	BALLARD			141
RICHARD	REILY			140
ROBERT	HENSHAW			136
JOSEPH	ROSE			117
RICHARD	BAILEY			112
JOHN	UNDERWOOD			107
Samuel	Bates			98

Source: *London Evening Post*, 20-22 December 1748.

Table 8.3.1.4
Poll for common councilmen of Aldersgate, 7 January 1751

Forename	Surname	Precinct	Livery	Votes received
RICHARD	BAILEY			200
JOHN	UNDERWOOD			197
ROBERT	EVANS			196
JOSEPH	ROSE			189
SAMUEL	READ			178
SAMUEL	BALLARD			187
ROBERT	HENSHAW			184
RICHARD	REILY			181
Charles	Kemp			124

Source: *London Evening Post*, 22-25 December 1750.

Table 8.3.1.5
Poll for common councilmen of Aldersgate, 9 January 1764

Forename	Surname	Precinct	Livery	Votes received
WILLIAM	TYSER			160
ANDREW	JORDAINE			158
GEORGE LEWIS	CARR			157
SAMUEL	BATES			155
SAMUEL	JACAM			153
SAMUEL	READ			150
CHARLES	RIVINGTON			149
JOSEPH	ROSE			126
Jeremiah	Percy		Plu	72

Source: *London Evening Post*, 20-22 December 1763.

Table 8.3.1.6
Poll for common councilmen of Aldersgate, 7 January 1771

Forename	Surname	Precinct	Livery	Votes received
CHARLES	RIVINGTON			113
Benjamin	Maud		Gol	100

Source: *General Evening Post*, 22-26 December 1770; *London Evening Post*, 20-22 December 1770.

Table 8.3.1.7
Poll for common councilmen of Aldersgate, 6 January 1772

Forename	Surname	Precinct	Livery	Votes received
WILLIAM	FOUCH	Out	Joi	211
PHILIP	ORIEL	Out	Met	197
JEREMIAH	PERCY	Within	Plu	167
JOHN	ROBINS	Out	Gol	160
JAMES	BROGDEN	Out	Gol	158
ROBERT	FISHER	Within	Gol	149
BENJAMIN	MAUD	Within	Gol	140
SAMUEL	MANNING	Within		129
Thomas	Isherwood			124
Charles	Rivington			113
Samuel	Read			104

Source: *General Evening Post*, 21-24 December 1771; *Bingley's Journal*, 21-28 December 1771; *Craftsman*, 28 December 1771.

Table 8.3.1.8
Poll for common councilmen of Aldersgate, 11 January 1773

Forename	Surname	Precinct	Livery	Votes received	
				Poll	Scrutiny
JOHN	ROBINS		Gol	184	
JEREMIAH	PERCY		Plu	179	
ROBERT	FISHER		Gol	176	
WILLIAM	FOUCH		Joi	167	
JAMES	BROGDEN		Gol	165	
PHILIP	ORIEL		Met	152	
SAMUEL	MANNING			146	
BENJAMIN	MAUD		Gol	143	133
Charles	Aldridge		Gol	116	
Charles	Rivington			111	103

Source: *London Evening Post*, 14-15 January 1773.

Table 8.3.1.9
Poll for common councilmen of Aldersgate, 10 January 1774

Forename	Surname	Precinct	Livery	Votes received
ROBERT	FISHER		Gol	195
JEREMIAH	PERCY		Plu	194
WILLIAM	FOUCH		Joi	186
JAMES	BROGDEN		Gol	164
BENJAMIN	MAUD		Gol	163
JOHN	ROBINS		Gol	153
NATHANIEL	WRIGHT		Car	137
PHILIP	ORIEL		Met	136
Charles	Aldridge			133
Samuel	Manning			127

Source: *Lloyd's Evening Post*, 22-24 December 1773.

Table 8.3.1.10
Poll for common councilmen of Aldersgate, 9 January 1775

Forename	Surname	Precinct	Livery	Votes received	
				Poll	Scrutiny
WILLIAM	FOUCH	1st Out	Joi	185	
JEREMIAH	PERCY	Staining	Plu	175	
ROBERT	FISHER	Zachary	Gol	174	
BENJAMIN	MAUD	A & A	Gol	148	
JAMES	BROGDEN	2nd Out	Gol	140	
CHARLES	ALDRIDGE	Leonard	Gol	130	
NATHANIEL	WRIGHT	3rd Out	Car	118	
EDWARD	YATES	4th Out	Car	115	
Philip	Oriel		Met	110	
Samuel	Manning			110	
John	Robins			108	

Source: *Gazetteer and New Daily Advertiser*, 13 January 1775; *St James's Chronicle*, 12-14 January 1775; *Craftsman*, 14 January 1775.

Table 8.3.1.11
Poll for common councilmen of Aldersgate, 6 January 1783

Forename	Surname	Precinct	Livery	Votes received
GEORGE	SEDDON		Joi	248
CHARLES	ALDRIDGE		Gol	225
JOHN	BAILEY		Joi	221
THOMAS	ISHERWOOD		Sta	214
JOHN	MOTT		Inn	209
NATHANIEL	WRIGHT		Car	206
JEREMIAH	PERCY		Plu	186
BENJAMIN	MAUD		Gol	184
James	Brogden		Gol	180

Source: *Morning Chronicle*, 24 December 1782; *London Packet*, 23-25 December 1782.

Table 8.3.1.12
Poll for common councilmen of Aldersgate, 9 January 1786

Forename	Surname	Precinct	Livery	Votes received
JEREMIAH	PERCY		Plu	194
JOHN	BAILEY		Joi	168
CHARLES	ALDRIDGE		Gol	166
NATHANIEL	WRIGHT		Car	160
JOHN	MOTT		Inn	154
GEORGE	SEDDON		Joi	150
BENJAMIN	MAUD		Gol	134
THOMAS	ISHERWOOD		Sta	125
	Wilson			93

Source: *Whitehall Evening Post*, 22-24 December 1785.

Table 8.3.1.13
Poll for common councilmen of Aldersgate, 9 January 1792

Forename	Surname	Precinct	Livery	Votes received
CHARLES	ALDRIDGE		Gol	218
JOHN	DENZILOE		Gol	195
JOHN	ROWLATT		Glo	193
JOHN	BAILEY		Joi	172
THOMAS	LOVELAND		Bak	168
GEORGE	SEDDON		Joi	164
JOHN	MOTT		Inn	164
GEORGE	SMITH		Dis	152
Thomas	Denham		Iro	143
Charles	De Grave		Bla	129

Source: *Lloyd's Evening Post*, 23-26 December 1791.

Table 8.3.1.14
Poll for beadle of Aldersgate, 30 August 1792

Forename	Surname	Precinct	Livery	Votes received	
				Poll	Scrutiny
	MEEK			206	143
	Maddox			206	137

Source: *St James's Chronicle*, 4-7 August 1792; 30 August – 1 September 1792.

Table 8.3.1.15
Poll for common councilmen of Aldersgate, 11 January 1796

Forename	Surname	Precinct	Livery	Votes received
ROBERT ALBION	COX		Gol	212
CHARLES	ALDRIDGE		Gol	211
ROBERT	FISHER		Gol	200
JOHN	MOTT		Inn	172
THOMAS	LOVELAND		Bak	163
CHARLES	DE GRAVE		Bla	152
JOHN	DENZILOE		Gol	145
JOHN	ROWLATT		Glo	140
George	Seddon		Joi	135
Richard	Welch		Glo	125
	Willan			115

Source: *Morning Chronicle*, 24 December 1795.

Table 8.3.1.16
Poll for common councilmen of Aldersgate, 12 January 1802

Forename	Surname	Precinct	Livery	Votes received
CHARLES	ALDRIDGE		Gol	89
ROBERT ALBION	COX		Gol	86
HENRY	KING		Vin	86
ROBERT	FISHER		Gol	85
JOHN	DENZILOE		Gol	82
GEORGE	KING		Vin	76
THOMAS	LOVELAND		Bak	73
JOHN	ROWLATT		Glo	65
	Hopkins			37

Source: *Morning Chronicle*, 23 December 1801.

Table 8.3.1.17
Poll for common councilmen of Aldersgate, 10 January 1803

Forename	Surname	Precinct	Livery	Votes received
ROBERT	FISHER		Gol	>100
JOHN	DENZILOE		Gol	>100
ROBERT ALBION	COX		Gol	>100
CHARLES	ALDRIDGE		Gol	>100
HENRY	KING		Vin	>100
GEORGE	KING		Vin	>100
JOHN	ROWLATT		Glo	>100
THOMAS	LOVELAND		Bak	>100
	Hopkins			33

Note: Press reports stated that Hopkins withdrew with a tally of 33 votes, against over 100 votes for each of the other candidates.
Source: *Morning Chronicle*, 23 December 1802.

Table 8.3.1.18
Poll for common councilmen of Aldersgate, 9 January 1804

Forename	Surname	Precinct	Livery	Votes received
THOMAS	LOVELAND		Bak	222
HENRY	KING		Vin	215
CHARLES	ALDRIDGE		Gol	211
GEORGE	KING		Vin	208
JAMES	TURNER		Gwd	203
JOHN	ROWLATT		Glo	201
ROBERT	FISHER		Gol	157
JOHN	DUNKIN		Far	154
John	Denziloe		Gol	150
	Dare			39

Source: *Morning Chronicle*, 24 December 1803.

Table 8.3.1.19
Poll for common councilmen of Aldersgate, 8 January 1810

Forename	Surname	Precinct	Livery	Votes received
GEORGE	KING		Vin	203
CHARLES	ALDRIDGE		Gol	191
ROBERT	FISHER		Gol	187
JOSEPH	TURNER		Gwd	187
JOHN	BETTS		Lor	170
SAMUEL	THOMAS		Whe	170
ERRINGTON	PAXTON		Inn	167
JOHN	ROWLATT		Glo	146
Thomas	Loveland		Bak	96

Source: *Morning Chronicle*, 25 December 1809.

Table 8.3.1.20
Poll for common councilmen of Aldersgate, 7 January 1811

Forename	Surname	Precinct	Livery	Votes received
GEORGE	KING	4th Out	Vin	172
JOSEPH	TURNER	2nd Out	Gwd	171
SAMUEL	ROLLS	1st Out	Cur	162
ROBERT	FISHER	Staining	Gol	155
STEPHEN	ADAMS	Leonard	Gol	156
SAMUEL	THOMAS	3rd Out	Whe	153
JOHN	BETTS	A & A	Lor	150
ERRINGTON	PAXTON	Zachary	Inn	149
Thomas	Loveland		Bak	40

Source: *Morning Chronicle*, 25 December 1810.

Table 8.3.1.21
Poll for common councilmen of Aldersgate, 6 January 1812

Forename	Surname	Precinct	Livery	Votes received
GEORGE	KING		Vin	204
JOSEPH	TURNER		Gwd	194
SAMUEL	ROLLS		Cur	187
ROBERT	FISHER		Gol	184
ERRINGTON	PAXTON		Inn	173
STEPHEN	ADAMS		Gol	172
JAMES	ROSE		Lor	166
SAMUEL	THOMAS		Whe	160
Daniel	Kay		Whe	109

Source: *Morning Chronicle*, 25 December 1811.

Table 8.3.1.22
Poll for common councilmen of Aldersgate, 10 January 1814

Forename	Surname	Precinct	Livery	Votes received
GEORGE	KING		Vin	19
SAMUEL	ROLLS		Cur	19
STEPHEN	ADAMS		Gol	18
ERRINGTON	PAXTON		Inn	18
DANIEL	KAY		Whe	17
THOMAS LISTER	FORREST		Hab	17
JOSEPH	TURNER		Gwd	17
ROBERT	FISHER		Gol	17
	Dacre			5

Source: *St James's Chronicle*, 21-23 December 1813.

Table 8.3.1.23
Poll for common councilmen of Aldersgate, 8 January 1816

Forename	Surname	Precinct	Livery	Votes received
SAMUEL	ROLLS		Cur	147
GEORGE	KING		Vin	141
ERRINGTON	PAXTON		Inn	137
DANIEL	KAY		Whe	131
ROBERT	FISHER		Gol	129
JOSEPH	TURNER		Gwd	127
JOHN	LORKIN		Bak	115
THOMAS LISTER	FORREST		Hab	113
	Helluson			91
Stephen	Adams		Gol	77

Source: *Morning Chronicle*, 25 December 1815.

Table 8.3.1.24
Poll for common councilman of Aldersgate, 7 June 1821

Forename	Surname	Precinct	Livery	Votes received
WILLIAM	WALTON		Gol	124
John	Diggens		Sta	114

Source: *Morning Chronicle*, 8 June 1821.

Table 8.3.1.25
Poll for common councilmen of Aldersgate, 7 January 1822

Forename	Surname	Precinct	Livery	Votes received
SAMUEL	ROLLS		Cur	185
WILLIAM	MATTHEWS		Inn	185
ROBERT	FISHER		Gol	184
JOHN	DIGGENS		Sta	183
THOMAS LISTER	FORREST		Hab	169
ERRINGTON	PAXTON		Inn	173
JOHN	LORKIN		Bak	162
WILLIAM	WALTON		Gol	151
	Corbould			74

Source: *Morning Chronicle*, 25 December 1821.

Table 8.3.1.26
Poll for common councilmen of Aldersgate, 9 January 1826

Forename	Surname	Precinct	Livery	Votes received
WILLIAM	MATTHEWS	Within	Inn	139
ROBERT	FISHER	Within	Gol	130
THOMAS LISTER	FORREST	Out	Hab	128
WILLIAM	WALTON	Out	Gol	125
JOHN	DIGGINS	Within	Sta	124
JOHN	LORKIN	Out	Bak	124
ERRINGTON	PAXTON	Within	Inn	124
THOMAS	LLOYD	Out	Whe	118
Edward	Mottram		Sta	57
	Hume			26

Source: *St James's Chronicle*, 22-24 December 1825.

Table 8.3.1.27
Poll for common councilmen of Aldersgate, 8 January 1827

Forename	Surname	Precinct	Livery	Votes received
WILLIAM	MATTHEWS		Inn	199
ROBERT	FISHER		Gol	194
JOHN	DIGGENS		Sta	189
JOHN	LORKIN		Bak	186
WILLIAM	WALTON		Gol	183
ERRINGTON	PAXTON		Inn	181
THOMAS LISTER	FORREST		Hab	181
JOHN	ROLLS		Cur	119
Edward	Mottram		Sta	107

Source: *St James's Chronicle*, 23-26 December 1826.

Table 8.3.1.28
Poll for common councilmen of Aldersgate, 10 January 1831

Forename	Surname	Precinct	Livery	Votes received
JOHN	ROLLS	Out	Cur	159
JOHN	LORKIN	Out	Bak	156
WILLIAM	MATTHEWS	Within	Inn	155
EDWARD	MOTTRAM	Within	Sta	154
WILLIAM	WALTON	Out	Gol	150
EDWARD	GODSON	Within	Bla	148
THOMAS	SUMMERS	Out	Gol	125
ROBERT	FISHER	Within	Gol	120
John	Diggens			46

Source: *Morning Chronicle*, 24 December 1830.

8.3.2 Aldgate, 1717-1809: 16 polls

(6 common councilmen; 307 freeman householders in 1833)

Table 8.3.2.1
Poll for common councilmen of Aldgate, 7 January 1717

Forename	Surname	Precinct	Livery	Votes received	
				Poll	Scrutiny
ROBERT	HOLDITCH				
John	Staplehorn				

Source: LMA COL/CC/13/01/012, return dated 1 February 1717.

Table 8.3.2.2
Poll for common councilmen of Aldgate, 10 January 1726

Forename	Surname	Precinct	Livery	Votes received	
				Poll	Scrutiny
WILLIAM	SMITH			146	
JOHN	WHITEHORN			145	
THOMAS	BODICOAT			139	
JOHN	THOMSON			133	
WILLIAM	SHEPPARD			132	
SAVAGE	ATWOOD			131	
John	Staplehorn			127	
Thomas	Fludyer			132	
	Potter			126	
	Goodfellow			125	
	Parry			124	
William	Dawson			122	

Source: *London Journal*, 22 January 1726.

Table 8.3.2.3
Poll for common councilman of Aldgate, 17 March 1732

Forename	Surname	Precinct	Livery	Votes received	
				Poll	Scrutiny
RICHARD	SMITH			121	125
Thomas	Fludyer			118	118

Source: *Daily Courant*, 21 March 1732; 7 April 1732.

Table 8.3.2.4
Poll for beadle of Aldgate, 22 March 1732

Forename	Surname	Votes received
	RASH	235
Arthur	Joyce	149

Source: *Daily Journal*, 23 March 1732.

Table 8.3.2.5
Poll for common councilmen of Aldgate, 12 January 1737

Forename	Surname	Precinct	Livery	Votes received	
				Poll	Scrutiny
DANIEL	LAMBERT			212	
EDWARD	SANDERSON			204	
THOMAS	SANDFORD			201	
FRANCIS	CARTER			184	
CHRISTOPHER	FULLAGAR			155	
CHARLES	CORDEROY			133	
Richard	Smith			118	
	Whitehorn			103	
	Thomas			55	

Source: *London Evening Post*, 21 December 1736.

Table 8.3.2.6
Poll for common councilman of Aldgate, 10 February 1737

Forename	Surname	Precinct	Livery	Votes received
THOMAS	FLUDYER			N
	Sharp			(N-45)

Source: *Old Whig*, 17 February 1737.

Table 8.3.2.7
Poll for common councilmen of Aldgate, 9 January 1738

Forename	Surname	Precinct	Livery	Votes received	
				Poll	Scrutiny
RALPH	MARSH				N
	Sharp				(N-79)

Source: *London Evening Post*, 12 January 1738.

Table 8.3.2.8
Poll for alderman of Aldgate, 8 January 1747

Forename	Surname	Livery	Votes received
WILLIAM	SMITH	Wax	118
Thomas	Page	Sta	96

Source: Beaven, i, p. 14.

Table 8.3.2.9
Poll for common councilmen of Aldgate, 6 January 1752

Forename	Surname	Precinct	Livery	Votes received
CHRISTOPHER	FULLAGER			174
STRACEY	TILL			150
THOMAS	COCKSAYE			146
JOHN	PLATT			134
WILLIAM	ROGERS			129
JOHN	HALL			114
Joseph	Stibbs			113
John	Hill			105

Source: *General Evening Post*, 21 December 1751.

Table 8.3.2.10
Poll for alderman of Aldgate, 19 February 1767

Forename	Surname	Livery	Votes received	
			Poll	
			Scrutiny	
JOHN	SHAKESPEARE	Bro	132	106
John	Henniker	Gol	127	101

Source: *London Chronicle*, 20 January 1767; Beaven, i, p. 14.

Table 8.3.2.11
Poll for common councilman of Aldgate, 10 March 1772

Forename	Surname	Precinct	Livery	Votes received
SAMUEL	THORP		Tin	113
William	Townsend			63

Source: *Daily Advertiser*, 10 March 1772.

Table 8.3.2.12
Poll for alderman of Aldgate, 23 May 1775

Forename	Surname	Livery	Votes received
WILLIAM	LEE	Hab	73
William	Baker	Wea	40

Source: Beaven, i, p. 14.

Table 8.3.2.13
Poll for alderman of Aldgate, 14 January 1790

Forename	Surname	Precinct	Livery	Votes received
HARVEY C.	COMBE		Bre	77
Richard Carr	Glyn		Sal	18

Source: Beaven, i, p. 14.

Table 8.3.2.14
Poll for common councilmen of Aldgate, 11 January 1796

Forename	Surname	Precinct	Livery	Votes received
CHARLES	LINCOLN		Fle	143
PETER	DONKLEY		Car	145
RICHARD	HUMPHRIES		Mus	141
WILLIAM HENRY	DOUCE		Whe	141
SAMUEL	THORP		Tin	136
JAMES	TADDY		Gol	129
James	Danvers			20
Lancelot	Sharpe			14

Source: *Morning Post*, 23 December 1795.

Table 8.3.2.15
Poll for common councilmen of Aldgate, 24 December 1802

Forename	Surname	Precinct	Livery	Votes received
				Unopposed
CHARLES	LINCOLN		Fle	168
SAMUEL	WEDDELL		Dra	168
SAMUEL	THORP		Tin	167
JAMES	TADDY		Gol	165
JAMES	HIBBERT		Glo	165
William	Sharpe		Fis	111
Lancelot	Sharpe			101

Source: *The Times*, 24 December 1802.

Table 8.3.2.16
Poll for common councilmen of Aldgate, 24 December 1809

Forename	Surname	Precinct	Livery	Votes received
JAMES	TADDY		Gol	163
SAMUEL	WEDDELL		Dra	161
SAMUEL	THORP		Tin	158
JOHN	BICKERSTAFF		Hab	129
SAMUEL	FAVELL		Clo	120
CHARLES	DRUCE		Inn	114
	Robinson			75
	Taylor			Withdrew

Source: *Morning Chronicle*, 25 December 1809.

8.3.3 Bassishaw, 1731-1832: 18 polls

(4 common councilmen; freeman householders in 1833 unrecorded, but *c.* 50)

Table 8.3.3.1
Poll for common councilmen of Bassishaw, 11 January 1731

Forename	Surname	Precinct	Livery	Votes received
RICHARD	LONG			48
JOHN	SMITH			42
JOHN	WHEELER			42
WILLIAM	MONK			40
John	Shorey			33
Francis	Cooper			30

Source: *London Evening Post*, 19 December 1730.

Table 8.3.3.2
Poll for common councilman of Bassishaw, 19 June 1734

Forename	Surname	Precinct	Livery	Votes received
FRANCIS	COOPER			38
William	Calvert			20

Source: *London Journal*, 22 June 1734.

Table 8.3.3.3
Poll for common councilmen of Bassishaw, 6 January 1735

Forename	Surname	Precinct	Livery	Votes received
FRANCIS	COOPER			52
SAMUEL	FLUDYER			47
WILLIAM	COULTHURST			47
JOHN	WHEELER			47
Charles	Cutts			39
John	Smith			26
Richard	Stevenson			26
William	Calvert			25

Source: *Daily Journal*, 23 December 1734.

Table 8.3.3.4
Poll for common councilmen of Bassishaw, 12 January 1736

Forename	Surname	Precinct	Livery	Votes received	
				Poll	Scrutiny
JOHN	WHEELER			50	43
WILLIAM	COULTHURST			46	36
JAMES	REYNOLDS			43	36
FRANCIS	COOPER			45	35
Richard	Stevenson			39	32
Samuel	Fludyer			42	32
Richard	Smith			38	31
William	Baker			38	28

Note: Fludyer was returned on 16 November 1736, having petitioned against the return of Reynolds: LMA COL/CC/13/01/012.
Source: LMA CLC/W/GA/001/Ms. 02506/001.

Table 8.3.3.5
Poll for common councilmen of Bassishaw, 10 January 1737

Forename	Surname	Precinct	Livery	Votes received
WILLIAM	COULTHURST			49
SAMUEL	FLUDYER			48
FRANCIS	COOPER			47
WILLIAM	BAKER			47
John	Wheeler			40

Source: LMA CLC/W/GA/001/Ms. 02506/001.

Table 8.3.3.6
Poll for alderman of Bassishaw, 2 January 1739

Forename	Surname	Livery	Votes received
WILLIAM	BAKER	Wea	50
Edward	Elliston	Gol	32

Source: Beaven, i, p. 20.

Table 8.3.3.7
Poll for beadle of Bassishaw, 12 February 1742

Forename	Surname	Votes received
GEORGE	GREEN	
Richard	Stevenson	

Source: LMA CLC/W/GA/001/Ms. 02506/001.

Table 8.3.3.8
Poll for common councilmen of Bassishaw, 11 January 1762

Forename	Surname		Votes received
SAMUEL	ELLIS		37
JOHN	SAUNDERS	Met	32
JOHN	NICHOLSON	Clo	30
EDWARD	HEYLYN		26
Gabriel	Leekey	Ski	18

Source: LMA CLC/W/GA/001/Ms. 02506/001.

Table 8.3.3.9
Poll for common councilman of Bassishaw, 14 June 1774

Forename	Surname	Precinct	Livery	Votes received
JOHN	FIRTH		Glo	23
John	Bristow			14

Source: LMA CLC/W/GA/001/Ms. 02506/001.

Table 8.3.3.10
Poll for beadle of Bassishaw, 16 November 1785

Forename	Surname	Precinct	Livery	Votes received
GILES	HOLLOWAY			44
Stephen	Valliscure			46

Source: LMA CLC/W/GA/001/Ms. 02506/001.

Table 8.3.3.11
Poll for common councilman of Bassishaw, 25 June 1821

Forename	Surname	Precinct	Livery	Votes received
WILLIAM	LISTER		Sta	18
Henry	Hughes		But	17

Source: LMA CLC/W/GA/001/Ms. 02506/001.

Table 8.3.3.12
Poll for common councilman of Bassishaw, 26 July 1821

Forename	Surname	Precinct	Livery	Votes received
HENRY	HUGHES		But	19
William	Lister		Sta	17

Source: LMA CLC/W/GA/001/Ms. 02506/001.

Table 8.3.3.13
Poll for common councilmen of Bassishaw, 7 January 1822

Forename	Surname	Precinct	Livery	Votes received
HENRY	HUGHES		But	28
JAMES	FRISBY		Met	28
WILLIAM	LISTER		Sta	27
DANIEL	BRITTEN		Clo	26
William A.	Weguelin			23

Source: LMA CLC/W/GA/001/Ms. 02506/001.

Table 8.3.3.14
Poll for common councilmen of Bassishaw, 6 January 1823

Forename	Surname	Precinct	Livery	Votes received
HENRY	HUGHES		But	37
WILLIAM A.	WEGUELIN			34
WILLIAM	LISTER		Sta	31
James	Frisby		Met	27
Daniel	Britten		Clo	27

Note: Alderman Hunter, not being a householder, was unable to give a casting vote. He left the decision between Frisby and Britten to the Court of Aldermen. Frisby was unanimously selected by a later wardmote.
Source: LMA CLC/W/GA/001/Ms. 02504/001.

Table 8.3.3.15
Poll for common councilmen of Bassishaw, 12 January 1829

Forename	Surname	Precinct	Livery	Votes received
HENRY	HUGHES		But	38
JAMES	FRISBY		Met	36
JOHN FRYER	SMALLMAN		Joi	36
WILLIAM	LISTER		Sta	29
Samuel	Shirley		Spe	27
Nicholas	Richards			11

Source: LMA CLC/W/GA/001/Ms. 02504/001.

Table 8.3.3.16
Poll for common councilmen of Bassishaw, 11 January 1830

Forename	Surname	Precinct	Livery	Votes received
JAMES	FRISBY		Met	36
SAMUEL	SHIRLEY		Spe	36
JOHN EBENEZER	DAVIES		Cor	33
JAMES	SMITH		Cop	30
Nicholas	Richards			8
Jeremiah	Hodgson			7

Source: LMA CLC/W/GA/001/Ms. 02504/002.

Table 8.3.3.17
Poll for common councilmen of Bassishaw, 10 January 1831

Forename	Surname	Precinct	Livery	Votes received
JOHN EBENEZER	DAVIES		Cor	39
JAMES	FRISBY		Met	36
SAMUEL	SHIRLEY		Spe	36
DANIEL	BEVIS		Wea	29
Nicholas	Richards			13
Drew	Wood		Hab	0

Source: LMA CLC/W/GA/001/Ms. 02504/002.

Table 8.3.3.18
Poll for common councilmen of Bassishaw, 9 January 1832

Forename	Surname	Precinct	Livery	Votes received
JAMES	FRISBY		Met	32
JOHN EBENEZER	DAVIES		Cor	34
DANIEL	BEVIS		Wea	31
WILLIAM	BAKER		Pcm	31
Nicholas	Richards			12

Source: LMA CLC/W/GA/001/Ms. 02504/002.

8.3.4 Billingsgate, 1719-1821: 20 polls

(10 common councilmen; 206 freeman householders in 1833)

Table 8.3.4.a
Precincts in Billingsgate

Code	Precinct
Andrew	St Andrew Hubbard
Botolph	St Botolph Billingsgate
George	St George
Mary	St Mary at Hill
Pudding	Pudding Lane
Rood	Rood Lane

Note: All electors in the ward were entitled to choose from among all the candidates but, in the larger wards, those elected as common councilmen were then taken to represent specific precincts or ward electoral sub-divisions (whose boundaries, confusingly, did not automatically match the parish's ecclesiastical boundaries).

Table 8.3.4.1
Poll for common councilmen of Billingsgate, 12 January 1719

Forename	Surname	Precinct	Livery	Votes received	
				Poll	Scrutiny
EDWARD	BELLAMY		Fis		

Source: *Weekly Packet*, 3 January 1719.

Table 8.3.4.2
Poll for alderman of Billingsgate, 22 February 1723

Forename	Surname	Livery	Votes received
EDWARD	BELLAMY	Fis	166
John	Crowley		118

Source: Beaven, i, p. 31.

Table 8.3.4.3
Poll for common councilmen of Billingsgate, 10 January 1737

Forename	Surname	Precinct	Livery	Votes received
CHRYSOSTOM	WILKINS			77
John	Gregory			77

Note: The poll was declared invalid, the clerk not having been sworn in. Wilkins was elected as having had a majority on the show of hands.
Source: *London Evening Post*, 21 December 1736; 6 January 1737.

Table 8.3.4.4
Poll for common councilmen of Billingsgate, 9 January 1738

Forename	Surname	Precinct	Livery	Votes received	
				Poll	Scrutiny
	GROOM				
	Jackson				

Source: *London Evening Post*, 24 December 1737.

Table 8.3.4.5
Poll for common councilmen of Billingsgate, 12 January 1741

Forename	Surname	Precinct	Livery	Votes received	
				Poll	Scrutiny
THOMAS	WINTERBOTTOM	Andrew		114	105
CORNELIUS	OWEN	Pudding		109	101
Robert	Rossiter			110	99
	Marston			105	94

Source: *London Evening Post*, 20 December 1740; *London Evening Post*, 15 January 1741.

Table 8.3.4.6
Poll for common councilmen of Billingsgate, 11 January 1742

Forename	Surname	Precinct	Livery	Votes received
GEORGE	WOODS			96
Cornelius	Owen			59

Source: *London Evening Post*, 22 December 1741.

Table 8.3.4.7
Poll for common councilmen of Billingsgate, 7 January 1751

Forename	Surname	Precinct	Livery	Votes received
JOHN	GOODMAN			95
JAMES	ROSSITER			90
Charles	Easton			77
Stephen	Tyers			56

Source: *London Evening Post*, 20 December 1750.

Table 8.3.4.8
Poll for common councilmen of Billingsgate, 8 January 1770

Forename	Surname	Precinct	Livery	Votes received
JOHN	KITTERMASTER	Mary	Fis	
GEORGE	WARD	Mary	Fis	
THOMAS	FEST	Mary	Coo	
ROBERT	BARNEVELT	Botolph	Met	
STEPHEN	TYERS	Botolph	Coo	
CHARLES	EASTON	Andrew	Mus	
THOMAS	GORST	George	Coo	
JOHN	ROGERS	Pudding	Hab	
THOMAS	DUNNAGE	Rood	Cut	
CHARLES	MOTTLEY	Botolph	Whe	90
John	Read			65

Source: *Middlesex Journal*, 23 December 1769; LMA COL/AD/04/048.

Table 8.3.4.9
Poll for common councilmen of Billingsgate, 7 January 1771

Forename	Surname	Precinct	Livery	Votes received
JOHN	ROGERS		Hab	38
	Andrews			24

Source: *Middlesex Journal*, 20-2 December 1770.

Table 8.3.4.10
Poll for common councilmen of Billingsgate, 6 January1772

Forename	Surname	Precinct	Livery	Votes received
CHARLES	EASTON		Mus	105
STEPHEN	TYERS		Cop	103
ROBERT	BARNEVELT		Met	100
JOHN	KITTERMASTER		Fis	100
THOMAS	DUNNAGE		Cut	100
THOMAS	GORST		Cop	100
WILLIAM	OLIVER		Cop	88
GEORGE	WARD		Fis	87
ROBERT	ROSS		Sal	81
SAMUEL	HANSON		Joi	70
John	Rogers		Hab	47

Source: *Public Advertiser*, 25 December 1771.

Table 8.3.4.11
Poll for alderman of Billingsgate, 28 November 1778

Forename	Surname	Livery	Votes received
THOMAS	SAINSBURY	Bow	112
Josiah	Dornford	Cop	70

Source: Beaven, i, p. 31.

Table 8.3.4.12
Poll for common councilmen of Billingsgate, 11 January 1779

Forename	Surname	Precinct	Livery	Votes received
CHARLES	EASTON		Mus	89
JOSIAH	DORNFORD		Cop	87
THOMAS W.	PRESTON		Whe	86
THOMAS	GORST		Cop	86
SAMUEL	HANSON		Joi	86
WILLIAM	DEANE		Met	86
JOHN	KITTERMASTER		Fis	85
STEPHEN	TYERS		Cop	84
THOMAS	DUNNAGE		Cut	84
ROBERT	BARNEVELT		Met	73
James	Andrews			23

Source: *London Evening Post*, 22 December 1778.

Table 8.3.4.13
Poll for common councilmen of Billingsgate, 10 January 1785

Forename	Surname	Precinct	Livery	Votes received
SAMUEL	HANSON		Joi	66
WILLIAM	DEAN		Met	65
JAMES	ANDREWS		Clo	65
THOMAS	GORST		Cop	63
CHARLES	MOTLEY		Whe	62
JOHN	KITTERMASTER		Fis	59
JAMES RENAT	SYMS			59
JAMES	BARON		Iro	59
JOSIAH	DORNFORD		Cop	57
THOMAS	EDGLEY		Fis	53
Thomas	Phipps			18

Source: *Morning Chronicle*, 23 December 1784.

Table 8.3.4.14
Poll for common councilmen of Billingsgate, 8 January 1787

Forename	Surname	Precinct	Livery	Votes received
JOHN	KITTERMASTER		Fis	Unopposed
JAMES	ANDREWS		Clo	126
SAMUEL	HANSON		Joi	121
WILLIAM	DEAN		Met	118
THOMAS	EDGLEY		Fis	117
ALEXANDER	BRANDER		Whe	115
JOSIAH	DORNFORD		Cop	111
THOMAS	GORST		Cop	104
JAMES	BARON		Iro	102
HENRY	SHEPHARD		Met	98
James Renat	Syms			95

Source: *Morning Chronicle*, 25 December 1786.

Table 8.3.4.15
Poll for alderman of Billingsgate, 1 June 1799

Forename	Surname	Livery	Votes received
WILLIAM	CHAMPION	Gro	115
William	Leighton	Whe	92

Source: Beaven, i, p. 31.

Table 8.3.4.16
Poll for common councilmen of Billingsgate, 9 January 1804

Forename	Surname	Precinct	Livery	Votes received
WILLIAM	PASHLEY		Vin	133
HENRY	CRESSWELL		Fis	131
RICHARD	NOBLE		Fra	129
THEOPHILUS	HEARSEY		Glo	128
JOHN	ORD		Gol	123
ANTHONY	BROWN		Fis	119
TIMOTHY	BAXTER		Gro	116
THOMAS	RAMSEY		Vin	108
THOMAS	DORNFORD		Cop	102
EDWARD	HANSON		Joi	92
Thomas	Mankin		Pat	73
William	Beatson		Hab	44

Source: *Morning Chronicle*, 24 December 1803.

Table 8.3.4.17
Poll for common councilmen of Billingsgate, 8 January 1810

Forename	Surname	Precinct	Livery	Votes received
ANTHONY	BROWN		Fis	134
JOHN	ORD		Gol	131
MATTHEW	EDIS		Met	131
THOMAS	DORNFORD		Cop	125
THEOPHILUS	HEARSEY		Glo	108
EDWARD	HANSON		Joi	98
RICHARD JAMES	DICKENS		Whe	98
WILLIAM	DUNKLEY		Cop	96
JOHN	SUDLOW		Fis	94
WILLIAM	SAMPSON		Fra	88
William	Piper		Plu	63
James	Pickard			50
Samuel	Lovell			48
George Thomas	King		Vin	46

Source: *Morning Chronicle*, 25 December 1809.

Table 8.3.4.18
Poll for common councilman of Billingsgate, 15 April 1810

Forename	Surname	Precinct	Livery	Votes received
SAMUEL	WILSON		Dra	
William	Piper		Plu	

Source: LMA CLC/W/GB/001/Ms. 00051/001. No votes were recorded in these minutes, although there was a poll.

Table 8.3.4.19
Poll for common councilmen of Billingsgate, 7 January 1811

Forename	Surname	Precinct	Livery	Votes received
ANTHONY	BROWN	Botolph	Fis	134
JOHN	ORD	Mary	Gol	134
MATTHEW	EDIS	Rood	Met	131
THOMAS	DORNFORD	Andrew	Cop	125
THEOPHILUS	HEARSEY	Botolph	Glo	108
EDWARD	HANSON	Pudding	Joi	98
RICHARD JOSEPH	DICKENS	George	Whe	98
WILLIAM	DUNKLEY	Mary	Cop	96
JOHN	SUDLOW	Botolph	Fis	94
WILLIAM	SAMPSON	Mary	Fra	88
William	Piper		Plu	63
James	Pickard			50
Samuel	Lowell			48
George Thomas	King		Vin	46

Source: LMA CLC/W/GB/001/Ms. 00051/001; COL/AD/04/063.

Table 8.3.4.20
Poll for common councilmen of Billingsgate, 8 January 1821

Forename	Surname	Precinct	Livery	Votes received
EDWARD	HANSON	Pudding	Joi	86
ANTHONY	BROWN	Botolph	Fis	84
WILLIAM	AUSTIN	George	Inn	81
WILLIAM	CURLING	Botolph	Fis	81
WILLIAM	PIPER	Botolph	Plu	80
GEORGE THOMAS	KING	Rood	Vin	80
SAMUEL	WILSON	Mary	Dra	79
WILLIAM	SAMPSON	Mary	Fra	78
THOMAS	DORNFORD	Andrew	Cop	76
WILLIAM A.	RIDPATH	Mary	Pat	73
Henry	Francis		Cor	33

Source: LMA CLC/W/GB/001/Ms. 00051/001.

8.3.5 Bishopsgate, 1733-1832:41 polls

(14 common councilmen; 646 freeman householders in 1833)

Table 8.3.5.a
Precincts in Bishopsgate

Code	Precinct
All H	All Hallows
Botolph	St Botolph
Ethel	St Ethelburga
Helen	St Helen
Martin	St Martin
Peter	St Peter

Note: All electors in the ward were entitled to choose from among all the candidates but, in the larger wards, those elected as common councilmen were then taken to represent specific precincts or ward electoral sub-divisions (whose boundaries, confusingly, did not automatically match the parish's ecclesiastical boundaries).

Table 8.3.5.1
Poll for common councilmen of Bishopsgate, 8 January 1733

Forename	Surname	Precinct	Livery	Votes received
JOHN	POTT			Unopposed
JAMES	BARTLETT			Unopposed
JOHN	MAY			Unopposed
GEORGE	PEPYS			Unopposed
WILLIAM	POOL			Unopposed
JOHN	WEBB			Unopposed
PETER	ROBERTS			Unopposed
ROBERT	FAWDRY			Unopposed
HENRY	WILY			Unopposed
ROBERT	RAYMENT			Unopposed
WILLIAM	BENN			Unopposed
WILLIAM	NEWCOMBE			Unopposed
JAMES	DANSIE			324
CHARLES	COTTON			305
Daniel	West			237

Source: Anon., *A list of the names* (1733); *London Evening Post*, 21 December 1732.

Table 8.3.5.2
Poll for common councilmen of Bishopsgate, 12 January 1736

Forename	Surname	Precinct	Livery	Votes received	
				Poll	Scrutiny
JAMES	DANSIE			354	
CHARLES	COTTON			332	
DANIEL	DAVIES			326	
THOMAS	LONG			322	
Thomas	Cotton			259	
Charles	Sparrow			200	

Source: *London Evening Post*, 10 January 1736.

Table 8.3.5.3
Poll for common councilmen of Bishopsgate, 9 January 1738

Forename	Surname	Precinct	Livery	Votes received
	ALDRICH			N
	Gregman			(N-56)

Source: *London Evening Post*, 5 January 1738.

Table 8.3.5.4
Poll for common councilmen of Bishopsgate, 24 December 1739

Forename	Surname	Precinct	Livery	Votes received	
				Poll	Scrutiny
PETER	ROBERTS	Ethel		377	297
ROBERT	FAWDRY	Ethel		376 ▾	293
WILLIAM	BENN	Botolph		374	293
JACOB	LEE	Martin		373	294
JAMES	DANSIE	All H		373	293
HENRY	WILY	Botolph		370	292
JOHN	MAY	Martin		369	290
JOHN	WEBB	Helen		369	289
WILLIAM	POOL	Helen		368	290
JOHN	FORTY	Botolph		368	289
CHARLES	COTTON	All H		367	287
THOMAS	LONG	Peter		367	288
DANIEL	DAVIES	Peter		366	287
JOHN	HOLLAND	Botolph		366	288
Thomas	Cotton			329	246
Noah	Tittner			327	242
James	Carter			325	241
Arthur	Radcliff			322	239
James	Broughton			321	239
Peregrine	Phillips			319	237
Henry	Allen			319	236
William	Marsh			319	237
Charles	Ward			318	236
James	Allen			317	234
William	Seagood			317	234
Stephen	Hervey			316	234
George	Harrison			311	230
Samuel	Part			304	224

Source: LMA CLC/W/GC/001/Ms. 01428/001.

Table 8.3.5.5
Poll for common councilmen of Bishopsgate, 12 January 1741

Forename	Surname	Precinct	Livery	Votes received
JAMES	DANSIE			Unopposed
CHARLES	COTTON			Unopposed
DANIEL	DAVIES			Unopposed
THOMAS	LONG			Unopposed
JOHN	MAY			Unopposed
JACOB	LEE			Unopposed
WILLIAM	POOL			Unopposed
WALTER	BARNARD			Unopposed
PETER	ROBERTS			Unopposed
ROBERT	FAWDRY			Unopposed
JOHN	HOLLAND			317
HENRY	WILY			313
JOHN	FORTY			314
RICHARD	HEMING			309
Noah	Tittner			231
James	Boyte			186

Source: *London Evening Post*, 23 December 1740.

Table 8.3.5.6
Poll for beadle of Bishopsgate, 12 May 1746

Forename	Surname	Votes received	
		Poll	Scrutiny
JOHN	HODDELL	504	378
Jonathan	Flude	488	442

Source: LMA CLC/W/GC/001/Ms. 01428/001.

Table 8.3.5.7
Poll for beadle of Bishopsgate, 11 February 1750

Forename	Surname	Votes received	
		Poll	Scrutiny
THOMAS	HADDON	467	407
Christopher	Coverley	431	387

Source: LMA CLC/W/GC/001/Ms. 01428/001.

Table 8.3.5.8
Poll for common councilmen of Bishopsgate, 7 January 1754

Forename	Surname	Precinct	Livery	Votes received
GEORGE	WYLDE			Unopposed
SAMUEL	PALMER			Unopposed
THOMAS	LONG			Unopposed
WILLIAM	CRAMOND			Unopposed
SAMUEL	VICKERS			Unopposed
WILLIAM	MOTTERSHEAD			Unopposed
HENRY	HALL			Unopposed
JOHN	PEPYS			Unopposed
WILLIAM	HUSSEY			Unopposed
RICHARD	CHAPMAN			Unopposed
UPPINGTON	BRACEE	Botolph		288
JONATHAN	FARR	Botolph		287
JOHN	FORTY	Botolph		286
CALVERT	BENN	Botolph		269
James	Healy			193

Source: LMA CLC/W/GC/001/Ms. 01428/001.

Table 8.3.5.9
Poll for beadle of Bishopsgate, 24 December 1759

Forename	Surname	Votes received
WILLIAM	TEW	398
Benedict	Stout	143

Source: LMA CLC/W/GC/001/Ms. 01428/001.

Table 8.3.5.10
Poll for beadle of Bishopsgate, 24 December 1760

Forename	Surname	Votes received
WILLIAM	TEW	424
Thomas	Seamark	277

Source: LMA CLC/W/GC/001/Ms. 01428/001.

Table 8.3.5.11
Poll for common councilmen of Bishopsgate, 7 January 1765

Forename	Surname	Precinct	Livery	Votes received
JOHN	TRAVIS	All H		Unopposed
JOHN	TOWNSEND	All H		Unopposed
EDWARD	WIX	Peter		Unopposed
RICHARD	TOWNSEND	Peter		Unopposed
EDWARD	GEORGE	Martin		Unopposed
WILLIAM	WALKER	Helen		Unopposed
JAMES	STONE	Helen		Unopposed
JOHN	MILES	Ethel		Unopposed
WILLIAM	COOKE	Ethel		Unopposed
WILLIAM	ROGERS	Botolph		Unopposed
RICHARD	MUNDAY	Botolph		Unopposed
JOHN	WHITE	Botolph		Unopposed
THOMAS	PLESTOW	Botolph		Unopposed
THOMAS	COOPER	Martin		68
William	Reeves			48

Source: LMA CLC/W/GC/001/Ms. 01428/001.

Table 8.3.5.12
Poll for common councilmen of Bishopsgate, 7 January 1771

Forename	Surname	Precinct	Livery	Votes received
JOHN	TOWNSEND	All H		Unopposed
RICHARD	BLACKALL	All H	Mus	Unopposed
RICHARD	TOWNSEND	Peter		Unopposed
EDWARD	WIX	Peter	Tyl	Unopposed
EDWARD	GEORGE	Martin		Unopposed
JOHN	MERRY	Martin	Dna	Unopposed
HENRY	GEORGE	Helen	Wer	Unopposed
JOHN	FASSON	Helen		Unopposed
JOHN	MILES	Ethel		Unopposed
GEORGE	PAILLET	Botolph		Unopposed
WILLIAM	JUDD	Botolph	Joi	Unopposed
SAMUEL	PROVEY	Botolph	Clo	Unopposed
ROBERT	BULLCOCK	Botolph	Tin	Unopposed
EVAN	PUGH	Botolph		314
John	Austin			235

Source: LMA CLC/W/GC/001/Ms. 01428/001.

Table 8.3.5.13
Poll for common councilmen of Bishopsgate, 25 August 1775

Forename	Surname	Precinct	Livery	Votes received
RICHARD	DRAPER	Ethel	Glo	284
WILLIAM	COOK	Ethel	Bla	224
	Young			146
	Waghorne			60

Source: LMA CLC/W/GC/001/Ms. 01428/001.

Table 8.3.5.14
Poll for common councilmen of Bishopsgate, 7 January 1782

Forename	Surname	Precinct	Livery	Votes received
RICHARD	BLACKALL	All H	Mus	Unopposed
JOHN	PINHORN	All H	Wax	Unopposed
EDWARD	WIX	Peter	Tyl	Unopposed
MICHAEL	EATON	Peter	Met	Unopposed
WILLIAM	COOK	Ethel	Bla	Unopposed
RICHARD	DRAPER	Ethel	Glo	Unopposed
ROBERT	BULLCOCK	Botolph	Tin	Unopposed
WILLIAM	JUDD	Botolph	Joi	Unopposed
SAMUEL	PROVEY	Botolph	Clo	Unopposed
SAMUEL	NELME	Botolph	Vin	Unopposed
WILLIAM	FALKNER	Helen	Glo	299
JOHN	WARD	Martin	Clo	247
JOHN	MERRY	Martin	Dra	243
HENRY	GEORGE	Helen	Wea	235
John	Fasson			134
Edward	Eagleton			93

Source: LMA CLC/W/GC/001/Ms. 01428/001.

Table 8.3.5.15
Poll for common councilmen of Bishopsgate, 6 January 1783

Forename	Surname	Precinct	Livery	Votes received
EDWARD	WIX	Peter	Tyl	Unopposed
ROBERT	BULLCOCK	Botolph	Tin	Unopposed
WILLIAM	FALKNER		Glo	433
ARTHUR	WINDUS		Coa	407
WILLIAM	JUDD	Botolph	Joi	401
SAMUEL	NELME	Botolph	Vin	387
JOHN	PINHORN	All H	Wax	356
JOHN	WARD	Martin	Clo	349
SAMUEL	PROVEY	Botolph	Clo	329
JOHN	MERRY	Martin	Dra	318
RICHARD	BLACKALL	All H	Mus	313
MICHAEL	EATON	Peter	Met	308
THOMAS	GREENAWAY	Helen	Car	267
WILLIAM	BAMFORD	Helen	Cor	246
Edward	Eagleton			230
William	Gould		Uph	219
Henry	Ward		Fra	174

Source: LMA CLC/W/GC/001/Ms. 01428/001.

Table 8.3.5.16
Poll for common councilman of Bishopsgate, 5 August 1787

Forename	Surname	Precinct	Livery	Votes received
BOXELL	TARVER		Dye	271
Henry	Saffory			223

Source: LMA CLC/W/GC/001/Ms. 01428/001; *Morning Chronicle*, 25 December 1782.

Table 8.3.5.17
Poll for common councilmen of Bishopsgate, 12 January 1789

Forename	Surname	Precinct	Livery	Votes received
JOHN	MERRY	Martin	Dra	Unopposed
ROBERT	BULLCOCK	Botolph	Tin	Unopposed
RICHARD	SEXTON	Botolph	Bla	411
ARTHUR	WINDUS	Ethel	Coa	374
WILLIAM	COLLIER	Botolph	Bak	374
WILLIAM	RAWLINS		Uph	360
TOBIAS	MAYNARD	Ethel	Gro	358
JOHN	APPLETON		Pew	329
RICHARD	WOODYER	Botolph	Car	275
JOHN	BLEADEN	Martin	Vin	264
THOMAS	GREENAWAY	Helen	Car	263
WILLIAM	GOULD	All H	Uph	255
THOMAS	POYNDER	Peter	Tyl	243
HENRY	WARD	Helen	Fra	242
Michael	Eaton		Met	214
William	Fricker			158

Source: LMA CLC/W/GC/001/Ms. 01428/001.

Table 8.3.5.18
Poll for beadle of Bishopsgate, 1 May 1790

Forename	Surname	Votes received
JOHN	SEARS	465
William	Rutland	356

Source: LMA CLC/W/GC/001/Ms. 01428/001.

Table 8.3.5.19
Poll for common councilmen of Bishopsgate, 10 January 1791

Forename	Surname	Precinct	Livery	Votes received
ROBERT	BULLCOCK		Tin	326
RICHARD	SEXTON		Bla	325
ARTHUR	WINDUS		Coa	319
TOBIAS	MAYNARD		Gro	313
WILLIAM	COLLIER		Bak	312
JOHN	BLEADON		Vin	299
JOHN	MERRY		Dra	297
WILLIAM	RAWLINS		Uph	293
HENRY	WARD		Fra	282
RICHARD	WOODYER		Car	276
JOHN	APPLETON		Pew	273
THOMAS	GREENAWAY		Dra	261
THOMAS	POYNDER		Tyl	251
WILLIAM	GOULD		Uph	208
William	Fricker		Pou	190
Joseph	Gough		Mus	70

Source: LMA CLC/W/GC/001/Ms. 01428/001.

Table 8.3.5.20
Poll for common councilmen of Bishopsgate, 9 January 1792

Forename	Surname	Precinct	Livery	Votes received
ROBERT	BULLCOCK		Tin	408
ARTHUR	WINDUS		Coa	400
GEORGE	EADES		Coa	384
RICHARD	SEXTON		Bla	377
JOHN	MERRY		Dra	376
JOHN	BLEADON		Vin	332
WILLIAM	COLLIER		Bak	328
THOMAS	GREENAWAY		Dra	327
WILLIAM	GOULD		Uph	321
WILLIAM	FRICKER		Pou	294
THOMAS	DAVIS		Lea	288
THOMAS	POYNDER		Tyl	270
WILLIAM	RAWLINS		Uph	263
RICHARD	WOODYER		Car	230
John	Appleton		Pew	211
Henry	Ward		Fra	185

Source: LMA CLC/W/GC/001/Ms. 01428/001.

Table 8.3.5.21
Poll for common councilmen of Bishopsgate, 12 January 1795

Forename	Surname	Precinct	Livery	Votes received
ARTHUR	WINDUS		Coa	426
THOMAS	SMITH		Vin	423
JOHN	MERRY		Dra	395
WILLIAM	COLLIER		Bak	388
THOMAS	GREENAWAY		Dra	371
GEORGE	EADES		Coa	370
WILLIAM	RAWLINS		Uph	369
JOHN	BLEADON		Vin	358
THOMAS	POYNDER		Tyl	354
WILLIAM	FRICKER		Pou	328
WILLIAM	GOULD		Uph	321
ROBERT	BULLCOCK		Tin	287
RICHARD	WOODYER		Car	268
JOHN	APPLETON		Pew	263
J.J.	Cossart			243
Thomas	Davis		Lea	240
Joseph	Gough		Mus	208

Source: LMA CLC/W/GC/001/Ms. 01428/001.

Table 8.3.5.22
Poll for common councilman of Bishopsgate, 14 April 1797

Forename	Surname	Precinct	Livery	Votes received
THOMAS	FASSON		Pew	164
Alexander	Ross		Bar	122

Source: LMA CLC/W/GC/001/Ms. 01428/001.

Table 8.3.5.23
Poll for common councilmen of Bishopsgate, 11 January 1808

Forename	Surname	Precinct	Livery	Votes received
GEORGE	CLODE		Met	232
JOHN	DUEFFELL		Mas	202
ARTHUR	WINDUS		Coa	191
THOMAS	GREENAWAY		Dra	187
WILLIAM	RAWLINS		Uph	183
ALEXANDER	ROSS		Bar	174
SAMUEL	NASH		Sta	168
THOMAS	CLARK		Whe	160
RICHARD	KNIGHT		Fis	130
THOMAS	POYNDER		Tyl	117
JOSEPH	GOUGH		Mus	113
GEORGE	EADES		Coa	110
WILLIAM	GOULD		Uph	108
WILLIAM	FRICKER		Pou	98
David	Smith			65

Source: LMA CLC/W/GC/001/Ms. 01428/001.

Table 8.3.5.24
Poll for common councilmen of Bishopsgate, 9 January 1809

Forename	Surname	Precinct	Livery	Votes received
JOHN	DUEFFELL		Mas	239
GEORGE	CLODE		Met	237
THOMAS	RAWLINS		Uph	233
THOMAS	GREENAWAY		Dra	231
ARTHUR	WINDUS		Coa	225
EDWARD	WHITE		Inn	220
ALEXANDER	ROSS		Bar	220
SAMUEL	NASH		Sta	218
THOMAS	CLARK		Whe	197
RICHARD	WRIGHT		Fis	176
WILLIAM	FRICKER		Pou	161
JOSEPH	GOUGH		Mus	155
WILLIAM	GOULD		Uph	153
THOMAS	POYNDER		Tyl	152
John	Freeman			86

Source: LMA CLC/W/GC/001/Ms. 01428/001.

Table 8.3.5.25
Poll for common councilmen of Bishopsgate, 8 January 1810

Forename	Surname	Precinct	Livery	Votes received
WILLIAM	RAWLINS		Uph	403
GEORGE	CLODE		Met	386
JOHN	DUEFFELL		Mas	374
THOMAS	GREENAWAY		Dra	353
SAMUEL	NASH		Sta	343
ARTHUR	WINDUS		Coa	333
EDWARD	WHITE		Inn	332
ALEXANDER	ROSS		Bar	313
ISAAC	MARSH		Inn	304
JAMES	DAVIES		Cor	291
THOMAS	CLARK		Whe	283
WILLIAM	FRICKER		Pou	274
THOMAS	POYNDER		Tyl	268
RICHARD	KNIGHT		Fis	258
Thomas	Judkins		Bak	257
William	Gould		Uph	250
George	Blundell		Pat	247
William	Tilford			243
Joseph	Gough		Mus	238

Source: LMA CLC/W/GC/001/Ms. 01428/001.

Table 8.3.5.26
Poll for common councilmen of Bishopsgate, 6 April 1810

Forename	Surname	Precinct	Livery	Votes received
THOMAS	JUDKINS		Bak	264
William	Gould		Uph	208

Source: LMA CLC/W/GC/001/Ms. 01428/001.

Table 8.3.5.27
Poll for common councilmen of Bishopsgate, 7 January 1811

Forename	Surname	Precinct	Livery	Votes received
WILLIAM	RAWLINS		Uph	340
JOHN	DUEFFELL		Mas	338
GEORGE	CLODE		Met	338
EDWARD	WHITE		Inn	331
SAMUEL	NASH		Sta	314
THOMAS	JUDKINS		Bak	301
ISAAC	MARSH		Inn	292
JAMES	DAVIES		Cor	287
THOMAS	GREENAWAY		Dra	279
ARTHUR	WINDUS		Coa	271
ALEXANDER	ROSS		Bar	265
SAMUEL	BARTON		Tal	243
GEORGE	BLUNDELL		Pat	243
RICHARD	KNIGHT		Fis	208
Marshall	Spink			178

Source: LMA CLC/W/GC/001/Ms. 01428/001.

Table 8.3.5.28
Poll for common councilmen of Bishopsgate, 9 January 1815

Forename	Surname	Precinct	Livery	Votes received
THOMAS	GREENAWAY		Dra	354
WILLIAM	RAWLINS		Uph	350
JAMES	DAVIES		Cor	343
JOHN	DUEFFELL		Mas	335
THOMAS	GLOVER		Inn	335
ISAAC	VALE			334
EDWARD	WHITE		Inn	326
SAMUEL	NASH		Sta	318
JOHN	BUMSTED		Pat	314
THOMAS	JUDKINS		Bak	313
BENJAMIN	YATES		Cok	296
SAMUEL	BARTON		Tal	266
WILLIAM	DAY		Gro	261
DANIEL WHITTLE	HARVEY		Gir	235
John	Duddell		Gol	144
Richard	Hoare		Gla	136

Source: LMA CLC/W/GC/001/Ms. 01428/001.

Table 8.3.5.29
Poll for beadle of Bishopsgate, 7 March 1816

Forename	Surname	Votes received	
		Poll	Scrutiny
WILLIAM	TERRILL	377	356
Peter	Robinson	392	354

Source: LMA CLC/W/GC/001/Ms. 01428/001.

Table 8.3.5.30
Poll for common councilmen of Bishopsgate, 12 January 1818

Forename	Surname	Precinct	Livery	Votes received
THOMAS	GREENAWAY		Dra	297
WILLIAM	RAWLINS		Uph	287
ISAAC	VALE			283
JOHN	BUMSTED		Pat	270
JAMES	DAVIES		Cor	268
JOHN	DUEFFELL		Mas	266
SAMUEL	NASH		Sta	255
THOMAS	JUDKINS		Bak	252
DANIEL WHITTLE	HARVEY		Gir	248
THOMAS	GLOVER		Inn	247
BENJAMIN	YATES		Cok	245
CHARLES	PEARSON		Hab	240
WILLIAM	DAY		Gro	219
HENRY	SANFORD		Iro	197
Thomas J.	Wooller			174

Source: LMA CLC/W/GC/001/Ms. 01428/001.

Table 8.3.5.31
Poll for common councilmen of Bishopsgate, 11 January 1819

Forename	Surname	Precinct	Livery	Votes received
THOMAS	GREENAWAY		Dra	346
WILLIAM	RAWLINS		Uph	345
WILLIAM	DAY		Gro	333
WALTER	PEACOCK		Bak	332
JOHN	BUMSTED		Pat	330
SOLOMON	BENNETT		But	328
CHARLES	PEARSON		Hab	327
JAMES	DAVIES		Cor	315
SAMUEL	NASH		Sta	311
THOMAS	JUDKINS		Bak	310
THOMAS	GLOVER		Inn	297
HENRY	SANFORD		Iro	289
JOHN	DOWNES		Sal	245
THOMAS	RUDD		Met	244
John	Stirtevant		Fra	158
Thomas J.	Wooller			155

Source: LMA CLC/W/GC/001/Ms. 01428/001.

Table 8.3.5.32
Poll for common councilmen of Bishopsgate, 8 January 1821

Forename	Surname	Precinct	Livery	Votes received
THOMAS	GREENAWAY		Dra	349
WILLIAM	RAWLINS		Uph	338
SOLOMON	BENNETT		But	314
WILLIAM	JOHNSTON			310
WARWICK	WESTON		Cok	306
SAMUEL	NASH		Sta	299
WILLIAM	DAY		Gro	296
THOMAS	GLOVER		Inn	291
WALTER	PEACOCK		Bak	288
JAMES	DAVIES		Cor	287
BENJAMIN G.	WINDUS		Coa	278
JOHN	STIRTEVANT		Fra	271
RICHARD	HOARE		Glz	254
JOHN	DUDDELL		Gol	235
Charles	Pearson		Hab	226

Source: LMA CLC/W/GC/001/Ms. 01428/001.

Table 8.3.5.33
Poll for beadle of Bishopsgate, 12 February 1823

Forename	Surname	Votes received
JAMES	EVANS	297
Joseph	Wood	284

Source: LMA CLC/W/GC/001/Ms. 01428/001.

Table 8.3.5.34
Poll for common councilmen of Bishopsgate, 9 January 1826

Forename	Surname	Precinct	Livery	Votes received
THOMAS	GREENAWAY		Dra	262
WALTER A.	PEACOCK		Bak	260
WILLIAM	RAWLINS		Uph	256
SOLOMON	BENNETT		But	252
JABEZ	BEYNON		Nee	236
WILLIAM	DAY		Gro	234
JOHN	DUDDELL		Gol	225
THOMAS	GLOVER		Inn	223
BENJAMIN G.	WINDUS		Coa	220
WARWICK	WESTON		Cok	215
JOHN	DOWLER		Bow	211
NICHOLAS	PHENE		Sta	207
WILLIAM	STEVENS		Cop	188
JOHN	STIRTEVANT		Fra	178
Richard	Hoare		Glz	168

Source: LMA CLC/W/GC/001/Ms. 01428/001.

Table 8.3.5.35
Poll for beadle of Bishopsgate, 3 January 1827

Forename	Surname	Votes received
JOHN	HARPER	256
Samuel	Lench	153

Source: LMA CLC/W/GC/001/Ms. 01428/001.

Table 8.3.5.36
Poll for common councilmen of Bishopsgate, 8 January 1827

Forename	Surname	Precinct	Livery	Votes received
THOMAS	GREENAWAY		Dra	306
SOLOMON	BENNETT		But	294
WILLIAM	RAWLINS		Uph	292
JABEZ	BEYNON		Nee	290
THOMAS	WINDUS		Coa	281
WALTER A.	PEACOCK		Bak	281
JOHN	DOWLER		Bow	276
BENJAMIN G.	WINDUS		Coa	276
WILLIAM	DAY		Gro	269
WILLIAM	STEVENS		Cop	255
WARWICK	WESTON		Cok	246
JOHN	STIRTEVANT		Fra	242
THOMAS	GLOVER		Inn	236
JOHN	DUDDELL		Gol	229
Nicholas	Phene		Sta	211

Note: The clerk incorrectly dated this in the wardmote minutes as being the election of January 1826.
Source: LMA CLC/W/GC/001/Ms. 01428/001.

Table 8.3.5.37
Poll for common councilmen of Bishopsgate, 7 January 1828

Forename	Surname	Precinct	Livery	Votes received
SOLOMON	BENNETT		But	333
JOHN	DUDDELL		Gol	322
JOHN	DOWLER		Bow	319
THOMAS	GREENAWAY		Dra	318
WILLIAM	RAWLINS		Uph	311
WILLIAM	STEVENS		Cop	308
WALTER A.	PEACOCK		Bak	304
WARWICK	WESTON		Cok	299
WILLIAM	DAY		Gro	292
JABEZ	BEYNON		Nee	287
JOHN	STIRTEVANT		Fra	273
THOMAS	WINDUS		Coa	250
BENJAMIN G.	WINDUS		Coa	240
NATHANIEL	CLARK		Mer	237
Henry	Patten		Bar	212

Source: LMA CLC/W/GC/001/Ms. 01428/001.

Table 8.3.5.38
Poll for common councilmen of Bishopsgate, 12 January 1829

Forename	Surname	Precinct	Livery	Votes received
SOLOMON	BENNETT		But	289
WILLIAM	STEVENS		Coo	284
WALTER A.	PEACOCK		Bak	283
THOMAS	GREENAWAY		Dra	264
WILLIAM	RAWLINS		Uph	258
JOHN	DUDDELL		Gol	250
JABEZ	BEYNON		Nee	247
JOHN	DOWLER		Bow	246
WARWICK	WESTON		Cok	245
WILLIAM	DAY		Gro	245
JOHN	STIRTEVANT		Fra	237
THOMAS	WINDUS		Coa	236
BENJAMIN G.	WINDUS		Coa	235
NATHANIEL	CLARK		Mer	221
Charles	Pearson		Hab	205

Source: LMA CLC/W/GC/001/Ms. 01428/001

Table 8.3.5.39
Poll for alderman of Bishopsgate, 5 February 1829

Forename	Surname	Livery	Votes received
WILLIAM TAYLOR	COPELAND	Gol	280
John Fowler	Dove	Sta	230

Source: LMA CLC/W/GC/001/Ms. 01428/001; Beaven, i, p. 43.

Table 8.3.5.40
Poll for common councilman of Bishopsgate, 24 August 1831

Forename	Surname	Precinct	Livery	Votes received
WILLIAM H.	PILCHER		Hab	192
Benjamin D.	Springall			140

Source: LMA CLC/W/GC/001/Ms. 01428/001.

Table 8.3.5.41
Poll for common councilmen of Bishopsgate, 9 January 1832

Forename	Surname	Precinct	Livery	Votes received
THOMAS	GREENAWAY	Helen	Dra	273
WILLIAM	RAWLINS	Without	Uph	259
HENRY	PATTEN	Martin	Bar	300
WALTER A.	PEACOCK	Without	Bak	276
THOMAS	DAVIS		But	247
CHARLES	GIBSON	Ethel	Pat	207
SOLOMON	BENNETT	Without	But	291
WILLIAM H.	PILCHER		Hab	306
JABEZ	BEYNON	Peter	Nee	272
WARWICK	WESTON	All H	Coo	282
WILLIAM	DAY	Peter	Gro	258
WILLIAM	JONES		Woo	267
WILLIAM	STEVENS	Ethel	Coo	285
CHARLES	PEARSON		Hab	284
Benjamin G.	Windus		Coa	185
Thomas	Windus		Coa	180

Source: LMA CLC/W/GC/001/Ms. 01428/001.

8.3.6 Bread Street, 1715-1831: 35 polls

(12 common councilmen; 90 freeman householders in 1833)

Table 8.3.6.1
Poll for common councilmen of Bread Street, 10 January 1715

Forename	Surname	Precinct	Livery	Votes received	
				Poll	Scrutiny
WILLIAM	YERBERRY			151	
ROBERT	CARY			149	
JAMES	LUND			148	
THOMAS	BUTTERFIELD			147	
RICHARD	BROCAS			146	
BENJAMIN	WELLS			142	
Robert	Baylis			126	
Jerome	Knapp			118	
John	Wormlayton			117	
William	Billers			117	
Samuel	Marsh			116	
James	Church			115	

Source: *Post Boy*, 6 January 1715.

Table 8.3.6.2
Poll for common councilmen of Bread Street, 9 January 1716

Forename	Surname	Precinct	Livery	Votes received	
				Poll	Scrutiny
JAMES	LUND				
FRANCIS	GOVE				
RICHARD	BROCAS				
GEORGE	MILLS				
GEORGE	LUDLAM				
JAMES	CAREY				
JOHN	BEECHER				
WILLIAM	YERBURY				
ROBERT	CAREY				
ROBERT	ASTON				
BENJAMIN	WELLS				
JOHN	BARWICK				

Source: LMA COL/CC/13/01/012.

Table 8.3.6.3
Poll for common councilmen of Bread Street, 12 January 1719

Forename	Surname	Precinct	Livery	Votes received	
				Poll	Scrutiny
JEREMIAH	GOUGH				
GEORGE	LUDLAM				
WILLIAM	YERBURY				
JAMES	LUND				146
RICHARD	BROCAS		Gro		141
GEORGE	MILLS				142
ROBERT	CAREY				144
JAMES	CAREY				143
JOHN	BEECHER				146
ROBERT	ASTON				143
BENJAMIN	WELLS				141
JOHN	BARWICK				143
Robert	Baylis		Gro		141
William	Proctor				138
Richard	Waller				136
James	Church				136
Richard	Butterfield				135
Samuel	Marsh				135
John	Wormlayton				134
William	Billers				131
Jerome	Knapp				129

Source: LMA COL/CC/13/01/012.

Table 8.3.6.4
Poll for alderman of Bread Street, 3 March 1719

Forename	Surname	Livery	Votes received	
			Poll	Scrutiny
ROBERT	BAYLIS	Gro	140	125
Richard	Brocas	Gro	170	128

Note: Final tally never declared; 'scrutiny' figures were interim.
Source: Beaven, i, p. 53.

Table 8.3.6.5
Poll for common councilmen of Bread Street, 11 January 1720

Forename	Surname	Precinct	Livery	Votes received	
				Poll	Scrutiny
WILLIAM	BILLERS			159	
JEREMIAH	MURDEN			159	
ROBERT	ASHURST			159	
JAMES	CHURCH			158	
JAMES	TOWNSEND			158	
JOHN	WORMLAYTON			157	
RICHARD	READ			157	
JEROME	KNAPP			157	
JOHN	COGGS			157	
ROBERT	CADY			157	
JOHN	GIBBS			156	
SAMUEL	MARSH			156	
Charles	Whadcock			147	
Benjamin	Wells			145	
Thomas	Bristow			144	
Francis	Gore			144	
Spencer	Man			144	
Sellers	Thornbury			144	
John	Becher			144	
Robert	Cary			144	
John	Barwick			144	
James	Cary			143	
James	Lund			142	
Robert	Aston			142	

Source: *Weekly Journal*, 26 December 1719.

Table 8.3.6.6
Poll for common councilmen of Bread Street, 11 January 1725

Forename	Surname	Precinct	Livery	Votes received	
SAMUEL	VEWEY			Unopposed	
RICHARD	CHANCEY			Unopposed	
JAMES	COLEBROOK			Unopposed	
BENJAMIN	MAA			Unopposed	
GEORGE	FRYE			Unopposed	
ROBERT	BIRCHALL			Unopposed	
RICHARD	COOPE			Unopposed	
WILLIAM	TOWNSHEND			Unopposed	
ROBERT	KEYNTON			Unopposed	
				Poll	**Scrutiny**
JOHN	LEQUESNE			126	116
David	Meridith			124	107

Source: *Parker's Penny Post*, 12 January 1726.

Table 8.3.6.7
Poll for common councilmen of Bread Street, 7 January 1734

Forename	Surname	Precinct	Livery	Votes received	
				Poll	**Scrutiny**
JAMES	BUDGETT			97	
JOHN	SELWIN			92	
	Mann			93	
John	Champion			85	

Source: *Daily Post*, 25 December 1733.

Table 8.3.6.8
Poll for common councilmen of Bread Street, 6 January 1735

Forename	Surname	Precinct	Livery	Votes received
JOHN	SEDGWICK			118
JAMES	CHURCH			115
JOHN	BUDGETT			114
JOHN	COGGS			111
JOHN	SELWIN			109
JOHN	HOLMES			109
John	Champion			80
Henry	Stracey			78
George	Pochin			76
Henry	Symonds			76
Charles	Gearing			69
John	Ileff			64

Source: *London Journal*, 28 December 1734.

Table 8.3.6.9
Poll for common councilmen of Bread Street, 8 January 1739

Forename	Surname	Precinct	Livery	Votes received
THOMAS	HOLFORD			101
Henry	Symonds			90

Source: *London Evening Post*, 21-23 December 1738.

Table 8.3.6.10
Poll for common councilmen of Bread Street, 21 January 1741

Forename	Surname	Precinct	Livery	Votes received
JOHN	SEDGWICK			93
THOMAS	SMITH			91
Charles	Geering			90
Humphry	Payne			88

Source: *London Evening Post*, 22 January 1741.

Table 8.3.6.11
Poll for common councilmen of Bread Street, 9 January 1764

Forename	Surname	Precinct	Livery	Votes received
JOHN	RUSSELL		Whe	50
Edward	Robinson			25

Source: *London Evening Post*, 22-24 December 1763.

Table 8.3.6.12
Poll for common councilman of Bread Street, 26 April 1770

Forename	Surname	Precinct	Livery	Votes received
MAYNARD	TORIN		Wax	50
William	Hallier		Tin	47

Source: *London Evening Post*, 26 April 1770; LMA COL/AD/04/048.

Table 8.3.6.13
Poll for common councilmen of Bread Street, 6 January 1772

Forename	Surname	Precinct	Livery	Votes received	
				Poll	Scrutiny
JOHN	MOOREY		Sal	90	
LUKE	STAVELEY		Fra	74	64
EDWARD	POLHILL		Uph	73	64
JAMES	ARCHER		Fra	73	64
JOHN	PARTRIDGE		Inn	70	60
WILLIAM	SAXBY		Pai	70	61
THOMAS	DEVERELL		Hab	69	58
JOHN	HEMANS		Glo	68	57
MAYNARD	TORIN		Wax	67	59
JOHN	HENLOCK		Glo	66	57
EDWARD	BARWICK		Bow	64	61
JOHN	WALKER		Iro	63	58
Bignell	Potter			58	54
William	Tapp			57	53
John	Ewer			56	49
John	Payne			56	52
William	Hallier			56	
Anthony	Woolley			48	
Joseph	Chapman			48	
John	Briggs			43	
John	Walker, jnr			42	
John	Graham			21	

Source: *Public Advertiser*, 25 December 1771; 8 January 1772.

Table 8.3.6.14
Poll for common councilman of Bread Street, 12 November 1773

Forename	Surname	Precinct	Livery	Votes received
WILLIAM	SLATER			57
James	Chapman			31

Source: *Daily Advertiser*, 13 November 1773.

Table 8.3.6.15
Poll for common councilmen of Bread Street, 10 January 1774

Forename	Surname	Precinct	Livery	Votes received
JOHN	MOOREY		Sal	86
LUKE	STAVELEY		Fra	79
WILLIAM	SAXBY		Pai	78
JOHN	WALKER		Iro	74
EDWARD	POLHILL		Uph	73
JOHN	HEMANS		Glo	70
ROBERT	TURNER		Bow	70
JOHN	HENLOCK		Glo	69
THOMAS	DEVERELL		Hab	69
JAMES	ARCHER		Fra	69
BENJAMIN	BURNLEY		Inn	63
ROBERT	WATKINS		Tyl	60
William	Hallier			47

Source: *Middlesex Journal*, 21 December 1773; *Lloyd's Evening Post*, 22-24 December 1773.

Table 8.3.6.16
Poll for common councilmen of Bread Street, 6 January 1777

Forename	Surname	Precinct	Livery	Votes received
JOHN	MOOREY		Sal	78
ROBERT	TURNER		Bow	67
LUKE	STAVELEY		Fra	66
EDWARD	POLHILL		Uph	65
JOHN	HEMANS		Glo	63
WILLIAM	HALLIER		Tin	62
WILLIAM	SAXBY		Pai	60
JOHN	WALKER		Iro	57
THOMAS	WRIGHT		Inn	56
JOHN	EWER		Ski	47
JAMES	CHAPMAN		Gir	40
ROBERT	WATKINS		Ski	39
William	Bedford		Arm	34
Isaac	Nicholson			34
James	Archer			34

Source: *Gazetteer and New Daily Advertiser*, 26 December 1776.

Table 8.3.6.17
Poll for common councilmen of Bread Street, 11 January 1779

Forename	Surname	Precinct	Livery	Votes received
WILLIAM	SAXBY		Pai	Unopposed
WILLIAM	HALLIER		Tin	73
PETER JAMES	BENNETT		Gol	71
JOHN	WALKER		Iro	68
H.	PACKER			67
JOHN	HEMANS		Glo	67
THOMAS	WRIGHT		Inn	67
JOHN	MOOREY		Sal	63
JOHN	JAMES		Dyer	62
JAMES	CHAPMAN		Gir	62
JOHN	EWER		Ski	59
WILLIAM	BEDFORD		Arm	58
S.E.	Acton			26

Source: *London Evening Post*, 22 December 1778.

Table 8.3.6.18
Poll for common councilmen of Bread Street, 9 January 1786

Forename	Surname	Precinct	Livery	Votes received
JOHN	HEMANS		Glo	Unopposed
PETER JAMES	BENNETT		Gol	84
WILLIAM	HALLIER		Tin	82
ISAAC	HENSLEY		Vin	82
ARTHUR SKEER	LOFTIE		Sal	81
STEPHEN	LANGSTON		Joi	79
JAMES	CHAPMAN		Gir	78
CHARLES	HAMERTON		Tyl	78
JOHN	PAYNE		Gol	76
CHARLES	ILIFFE		Car	73
MOSES	WILLATTS		Pla	70
WILLIAM	BEDFORD		Arm	65
Roger	Shackleton		Gir	44

Source: *The Times*, 24 December 1785.

Table 8.3.6.19
Poll for common councilmen of Bread Street, 8 January 1787

Forename	Surname	Precinct	Livery	Votes received
ROGER	SHACKLETON		Gir	39
Samuel	Tomkins		Uph	10

Source: *General Advertiser*, 22 December 1786.

Table 8.3.6.20
Poll for common councilmen of Bread Street, 7 January 1788

Forename	Surname	Precinct	Livery	Votes received	
				Poll	Scrutiny
SAMUEL	TOMKINS		Uph	(N-1)	
	Croft			N	

Source: *World*, 24 December 1787.

Table 8.3.6.21
Poll for common councilmen of Bread Street, 10 January 1791

Forename	Surname	Precinct	Livery	Votes received	
				Poll	Scrutiny

Note: This election is counted as part of the total tally of contested elections, since the newspaper evidence makes it clear that there was both a poll and a scrutiny. Continuing research may in due course provide details of at least some candidates and the votes cast. **Source**: *The Times*, 7 January 1791.

Table 8.3.6.22
Poll for alderman of Bread Street, 10 November 1797

Forename	Surname	Precinct	Livery	Votes received
CHARLES	HAMERTON		Tyl	52
Samuel Ferrand	Waddington		Joi	28

Source: Beaven, i, p. 53.

Table 8.3.6.23
Poll for common councilmen of Bread Street, 6 January 1817

Forename	Surname	Precinct	Livery	Votes received
SAMUEL	HAYWARD		Glz	65
WILLIAM	MATHIE		Gro	60
WILLIAM	SOWERBY		Lea	59
THOMAS	COLMAN		Clo	57
ZACHARY	LANGTON		Ski	57
HENRY	DIBBIN		Inn	57
THOMAS	MOORE		Ski	56
WILLIAM	GILMAN		Fou	56
MATTHEW T.	GIBSON		Wea	55
JAMES	BATE		Sta	55
JOHN	ELLIOTT		Dra	54
JOHN	BLACKMORE		Cor	48
Samuel	Oliver			37

Source: *Morning Chronicle*, 25 December 1816.

Table 8.3.6.24
Poll for common councilmen of Bread Street, 12 January 1818

Forename	Surname	Precinct	Livery	Votes received
SAMUEL	HAYWARD		Glz	58
WILLIAM	SOWERBY		Lea	57
WILLIAM	GILLMAN		Fou	56
THOMAS	MOORE		Ski	53
HENRY	DIBBIN		Inn	52
JOHN	ELLIOTT		Dra	52
MATTHEW T.	GIBSON		Wea	52
WILLIAM	MATHIE		Gro	50
THOMAS	COLMAN		Clo	50
JOHN	BLACKMORE		Cor	46
ZACHARY	LANGTON		Ski	45
JAMES	BATE		Sta	44
Samuel	Oliver			22

Source: *Morning Chronicle*, 25 December 1817.

Table 8.3.6.25
Poll for common councilmen of Bread Street, 11 January 1819

Forename	Surname	Precinct	Livery	Votes received
SAMUEL	HAYWARD		Glz	72
WILLIAM	SOWERBY		Lea	72
HENRY	DIBBIN		Inn	71
WILLIAM	MATHIE		Gro	68
THOMAS	COLMAN		Clo	68
WILLIAM	GILLMAN		Fou	67
JOHN	ELLIOTT		Dra	65
MATTHEW T.	GIBSON		Wea	64
THOMAS	MOORE		Ski	62
BENJAMIN	BLAKESBY		Hab	61
JOHN	BLACKMORE		Cor	56
JAMES	BATE		Sta	53
Samuel	Oliver			27
Samuel	Tipper			19

Source: *Morning Chronicle*, 24 December 1818.

Table 8.3.6.26
Poll for common councilmen of Bread Street, 10 January 1820

Forename	Surname	Precinct	Livery	Votes received
SAMUEL	HAYWARD		Glz	85
WILLIAM	SOWERBY		Lea	88
THOMAS	COLMAN		Clo	79
JOHN	ELLIOTT		Dra	71
HENRY	DIBBIN		Inn	79
WILLIAM	GILLMAN		Fou	72
MATTHEW T.	GIBSON		Wea	70
WILLIAM	MATHIE		Gro	75
JOHN	HALLAM		Nee	67
BENJAMIN	BLAKESLEY		Hab	71
JONATHAN	CROCKER		Whe	68
JAMES	BRIDGE		Mus	59
Samuel	Tipper			33

Source: *Morning Chronicle*, 24 December 1819.

Table 8.3.6.27
Poll for common councilmen of Bread Street, 8 January 1821

Forename	Surname	Precinct	Livery	Votes received
SAMUEL	HAYWARD		Glz	73
WILLIAM	SOWERBY		Lea	68
WILLIAM	GILMAN		Fou	68
WILLIAM	MATHIE		Gro	67
THOMAS	COLMAN		Clo	65
HENRY	DIBBIN		Inn	64
BENJAMIN	BLAKESLEY		Hab	63
ROBERT	BURRA		Cut	63
MATTHEW T.	GIBSON		Wea	60
JONATHAN	CROCKER		Whe	58
JOHN	HALLAM		Nee	58
JAMES	BRIDGE		Mus	55
Samuel	Tipper			31

Source: *Morning Chronicle*, 25 December 1820.

Table 8.3.6.28
Poll for common councilmen of Bread Street, 7 January 1822

Forename	Surname	Precinct	Livery	Votes received
SAMUEL	HAYWARD		Glz	69
WILLIAM	MATHIE		Gro	63
THOMAS	COLMAN		Clo	63
HENRY	DIBBIN		Inn	63
MATTHEW T.	GIBSON		Wea	62
ROBERT	BURRA		Cut	62
BENJAMIN	BLAKESLEY		Hab	60
JONATHAN	CROCKER		Whe	59
JOHN SOUTHBY	BRIDGE		Mus	59
JOHN	HALLAM		Nee	59
JOHN	BIDEN		Hab	53
JOHN	DE GRAVE		Bla	52
	Webb			27
John	Bruckfield			8
William	Thomas, snr			8
Oliver	Hatch			7
Henry	Fulton			7
B.P.	Witts			7
Archibald	Corbett			7

Source: *Morning Chronicle*, 25 December 1821.

Table 8.3.6.29
Poll for common councilmen of Bread Street, 12 January 1824

Forename	Surname	Precinct	Livery	Votes received
SAMUEL	HAYWARD		Glz	57
WILLIAM	MATHIE		Gro	51
ROBERT	BURRA		Cut	51
MOSES EDWARD	LEGGE		Nee	49
MATTHEW T.	GIBSON		Wea	48
BENJAMIN	BLAKESLEY		Hab	48
JOHN SOUTHBY	BRIDGE		Mus	47
JOHN	HALLAM		Nee	47
JONATHAN	CROCKER		Whe	46
JOHN	DE GRAVE		Bla	44
JOHN	BIDEN		Hab	43
THOMAS	COLMAN		Clo	42
M.	Lawrence			18

Source: *St James's Chronicle*, 23-25 December 1823.

Table 8.3.6.30
Poll for common councilmen of Bread Street, 9 January 1826

Forename	Surname	Precinct	Livery	Votes received
WILLIAM	MATHIE		Gro	48
ROBERT	BURRA		Cut	47
THOMAS	COLMAN		Clo	46
JOHN SOUTHBY	BRIDGE		Mus	46
MOSES EDWARD	LEGGE		Nee	46
WILLIAM	DAVISON		Met	46
JOHN FRANCIS	DE GRAVE		Bla	46
JOHN	HALLAM		Nee	45
THOMAS	COPE		Pat	45
PETER POPE	FIRTH		Hab	44
HENRY	SCOTT		Met	42
WILLIAM C.	HOOPER		Gro	37
M.	Lawrence			17
	Shoobridge			12

Source: *St James's Chronicle*, 22-24 December 1825.

Table 8.3.6.31
Poll for common councilmen of Bread Street, 8 January 1827

Forename	Surname	Precinct	Livery	Votes received
WILLIAM	MATHIE		Gro	41
PETER POPE	FIRTH		Hab	39
THOMAS	COLMAN		Clo	38
MOSES EDWARD	LEGGE		Nee	38
JAMES SOUTHBY	BRIDGE		Mus	38
HENRY	SCOTT		Met	38
JOHN	HALLAM		Nee	38
ROBERT	BURRA		Cut	37
JOHN FRANCIS	DE GRAVE		Bla	37
WILLIAM	DAVISON		Met	37
THOMAS	COPE		Pat	36
WILLIAM C.	HOOPER		Gro	35
	Shoobridge			10

Source: *Morning Chronicle*, 25 December 1826.

Table 8.3.6.32
Poll for common councilmen of Bread Street, 7 January 1828

Forename	Surname	Precinct	Livery	Votes received
PETER POPE	FIRTH		Hab	37
WILLIAM	MATHIE		Gro	35
JOHN SOUTHBY	BRIDGE		Mus	34
JOHN	HALLAM		Nee	34
MOSES EDWARD	LEGG		Nee	34
HENRY	SCOTT		Met	34
ROBERT	BURRA		Cut	33
JOHN FRANCIS	DE GRAVE		Bla	33
THOMAS	COPE		Pat	33
THOMAS	COLMAN		Clo	32
WILLIAM	DAVISON		Met	32
WILLIAM C.	HOOPER		Gro	31
	Shoobridge			8

Source: *Morning Chronicle*, 25 December 1827.

Table 8.3.6.33

Poll for common councilmen of Bread Street, 12 January 1829

Forename	Surname	Precinct	Livery	Votes received
WILLIAM	MATHIE		Gro	37
THOMAS	COLMAN		Clo	33
JAMES SOUTHBY	BRIDGE		Mus	33
JOHN	HALLAM		Nee	33
ROBERT	BURRA		Cut	33
JOHN FRANCIS	DE GRAVE		Bla	33
MOSES EDWARD	LEGGE		Nee	33
THOMAS	COPE		Pat	33
PETER POPE	FIRTH		Hab	33
HENRY	SCOTT		Met	33
WILLIAM C.	HOOPER		Gro	33
WILLIAM	DAVISON		Met	32
	Shoobridge			5

Source: *Morning Chronicle*, 25 December 1828.

Table 8.3.6.34

Poll for common councilmen of Bread Street, 11 January 1830

Forename	Surname	Precinct	Livery	Votes received
MOSES EDWARD	LEGG		Nee	40
THOMAS	COLMAN		Clw	39
WILLIAM	MATHIE		Gro	39
JOHN	HALLAM		Nee	38
JOHN BRADLEY	SHUTTLEWORTH		Dye	38
DAVID	CRACKLOW		Clo	37
THOMAS	COPE		Pat	37
WILLIAM C.	HOOPER		Gro	37
JOHN FRANCIS	DE GRAVE		Bla	37
JAMES SOUTHBY	BRIDGE		Mus	37
WILLIAM	DAVISON		Met	37
ROBERT	BURRA		Cut	37
	Shoobridge			3

Source: *Morning Chronicle*, 24 December 1829.

Table 8.3.6.35
Poll for common councilmen of Bread Street, 10 January 1831

Forename	Surname	Precinct	Livery	Votes received
WILLIAM	MATHIE		Gro	80
MOSES EDWARD	LEGGE		Nee	76
THOMAS	COLMAN		Clo	73
JOHN BRADLEY	SHUTTLEWORTH		Dye	65
JAMES SOUTHBY	BRIDGE		Mus	60
JOHN	HALLAM		Nee	60
THOMAS	COPE		Pat	60
DAVID	CRACKLOW		Clo	60
ROBERT	BURRA		Cut	59
WILLIAM	KIPLING		Wax	58
WILLIAM	DAVISON		Met	58
JOHN FRANCIS	DE GRAVE		Bla	53
William C.	Hooper		Gro	46
John Pocock	Holmes		Wax	34
	Shoobridge			16

Source: *Morning Chronicle*, 24 December 1830.

8.3.7 Bridge, 1711-1832: 23 polls

(15 common councilmen; 135 freeman householders in 1833)

Table 8.3.7.1
Poll for aldermanic candidates of Bridge, 13 April 1711

Forename	Surname	Livery	Votes received
Henry	Furnese	Dra	172
Robert	Dunckley		172
Gilbert	Heathcote		168
John	Fleet		168
Francis	Child		159
William	Withers		159
John	Ladd		152

Source: *British Mercury*, 13 April 1711.

Table 8.3.7.2
Poll for alderman of Bridge, 7 November 1727

Forename	Surname	Livery	Votes received
THOMAS	PRESTON, JNR	Vin	150
John	Grosvenor	Coo	110

Source: Beaven, i, p. 61.

Table 8.3.7.3
Poll for common councilmen of Bridge, 10 January 1737

Forename	Surname	Precinct	Livery	Votes received	
				Poll	Scrutiny
JAMES	HEYWOOD			168	
JOHN	THOMAS			166	
EDWARD	ARCHER			164	
WILLIAM	MINGAY			163	
WILLIAM	KINLESIDE			158	
WILLIAM	SHELDON			155	
CORNELIUS	HERBERT			149	
JOHN	STEWART			147	
MAYHEW	MERRETT			145	
RICHARD	BAREFOOT			142	
MICHAEL	MERTINS			133	
JOHN	DUMELLO			131	
Joseph	Goodchild			130	
WILLIAM	NEWLAND			126	
OGLANDER	MYNGS			119	
BENJAMIN	TYSON			113	
Henry	King			99	
John	Cooper			80	

Note: Goodchild died before the declaration of the scrutiny.
Source: *London Evening Post*, 21 December 1736.

Table 8.3.7.4
Poll for common councilmen of Bridge, 9 January 1738

Forename	Surname	Precinct	Livery	Votes received
HENRY	KING			
Oglander	Myngs			

Source: *London Evening Post*, 22 December 1737.

Table 8.3.7.5
Poll for common councilmen of Bridge, 7 January 1740

Forename	Surname	Precinct	Livery	Votes received
GEORGE	HAYWARD			Unopposed
JOHN	DUMELLO			Unopposed
BENJAMIN	TYSON			Unopposed
RICHARD	CLAY			Unopposed
EDWARD	BRIGHT			Unopposed
SAMUEL	FENWICK			Unopposed
JOHN	COOPER			Unopposed
JOHN	THOMAS			Unopposed
JAMES	HAYWOOD			Unopposed
HENRY	KING			Unopposed
WILLIAM	SHELDON			Unopposed
JAMES	HODGES			Unopposed
WILLIAM	NEWLAND			Unopposed
WILLIAM	MINGAY			Unopposed
EDWARD	ARCHER			
John	Goodyer			

Source: *Daily Post*, 22 December 1739.

Table 8.3.7.6
Poll for common councilmen of Bridge, 12 January 1741

Forename	Surname	Precinct	Livery	Votes received
JAMES	HAYWOOD			162
JAMES	HODGES			159
SAMUEL	FENWICK			145
STEPHEN	COOPER			136
JOHN	STUART			120
MICHAEL	MERTINS			119
WILLIAM	WHITE			117
CORNELIUS	HERBERT			115
John	Dumello			114
Benjamin	Tyson			110
George	Hayward			97
Henry	King			86
John	Goodyer			86
James	Brock			65
Gabriel	Wright			59
James	Tew			59

Source: *London Evening Post*, 23 December 1740.

Table 8.3.7.7
Poll for common councilmen of Bridge, 16 July 1741

Forename	Surname	Precinct	Livery	Votes received
THOMAS	DURNFORD			114
CHRISTOPHER	TAYLOR			95
Benjamin	Tyson			84
Coles	Child			66

Source: *London Evening Post*, 16 July 1741.

Table 8.3.7.8
Poll for common councilman of Bridge, 6 January 1752

Forename	Surname	Precinct	Livery	Votes received
JOHN	WATHEN			90
	Silcock			70

Source: *London Daily Advertiser*, 23 December 1751.

Table 8.3.7.9
Poll for common councilmen of Bridge, 8 January 1770

Forename	Surname	Precinct	Livery	Votes received
SAMUEL	BAUGHAN		Dye	Unopposed
WILLIAM	POST		Bro	Unopposed
GEORGE	COOPER		Gol	Unopposed
OWEN	WILLIAMS		Fis	Unopposed
JACOB	WRENCH		Dra	Unopposed
MARMADUKE	THOMPSON		Fis	Unopposed
JOHN	VECK		Glz	Unopposed
JOSEPH	JENSON		Tur	Unopposed
ROBERT	FREELAND		Clw	Unopposed
WILLIAM	JEBSON		Fra	Unopposed
THOMAS	NORMAN		Whe	Unopposed
THOMAS	TURVILLE		Nee	Unopposed
CLEMENT	CORDEROY		Hab	81
THOMAS	HORNE		Fis	71
CHARLES	BARROW		Coo	63
Richard	Bristow			57
Charles	Bartrum			47
Henry	Dekar			23

Source: *Middlesex Journal*, 23 December 1769; LMA COL/AD/04/048.

Table 8.3.7.10
Poll for alderman of Bridge, 29 October 1774

Forename	Surname	Livery	Votes received	
			Poll	**Scrutiny**
JOHN	HART	Ski	99	84
William	Neate	Dra	95	95

Note: Election declared void by King's Bench.
Source: *Daily Advertiser*, 3 November 1774; *London Evening Post*, 24 November 1774; Beaven, i, p. 61.

Table 8.3.7.11
Poll for alderman of Bridge, 15 May 1776

Forename	Surname	Livery	Votes received	
			Poll	**Scrutiny**
THOMAS	WOOLDRIDGE	Mus	84	75
John	Hart	Ski	78	70

Source: Beaven, i, p. 61; *Morning Chronicle*, 8 June 1776.

Table 8.3.7.12
Poll for common councilmen of Bridge, 10 January 1780

Forename	Surname	Precinct	Livery	Votes received
GEORGE	COOPER		Gol	108
CLEMENT	CORDEROY		Hab	102
MARMADUKE	THOMPSON		Fis	102
JAMES	JEWSON		Tur	101
JOHN	COBB		Bar	100
WILLIAM	ANDERSON		Met	99
EDWARD	COSTER		Cop	98
WILLIAM	ROWLATT		Glo	97
COLES	CHILD		Wea	96
HENRY	CROSSLEY		Fra	96
JOHN	DOWLEY		Bla	96
SAMUEL	BAUGHAN		Dye	95
JOSEPH	BROWN		Whe	89
JACOB	WRENCH		Arm	87
JOHN	ROWLATT		Glo	75
B.J.	Cheale			63
James	Alldin		Bak	29

Source: *General Advertiser and Morning Intelligencer*, 24 December 1779.

Table 8.3.7.13
Poll for common councilmen of Bridge, 11 January 1796

Forename	Surname	Precinct	Livery	Votes received
JACOB	COPE		Fis	110
JACOB	WRENCH		Arm	101
BENJAMIN	BOVILL		Gol	97
WILLIAM	SUTHERLAND		Gro	97
JOSEPH	ALLDIN		Bar	93
COLES	CHILD		Wea	93
CHARLES	BARTRUM		Vin	84
JAMES	WILDE		Fis	80
SIMON	BARRATTY		Gol	79
WILLIAM	JACKSON		Fou	77
WILLIAM	ANDERSON		Met	75
JAMES	GURRY		Mus	75
JOHN	BROWNE		Coa	73
FENTON	ROBINSON		Gir	70
EDMUND	DARBY		Dra	69
Thomas	Flint			54
William	Rawlings			51
Robert	Robinson			49
Joseph	Martin			48
William	Ross			35

Source: *The Times*, 25 December 1795.

Table 8.3.7.14
Poll for common councilmen of Bridge, 7 January 1805

Forename	Surname	Precinct	Livery	Votes received
JACOB	WRENCH		Arm	96
THOMAS	ROBERTS		Car	95
CHARLES	BARTRAM		Vin	93
JACOB	COPE		Fis	93
WILLIAM	CHILD		Met	92
JOHN	GARRATT		Gol	89
ROBERT	BROWN		Fis	89
JOSEPH	ALLDIN		Bak	87
WILLIAM	JACKSON		Fou	87
JOHN	CLEUGH		Arm	86
ROLAND	MALTBY		Fis	86
JOHN	JOYNER		Hab	85
BENJAMIN	BOVILL		Gol	79
WILLIAM	ROSS		Gro	73
JAMES	LACY		Met	67
Robert	Dutton			55
James	Wilde			12

Source: *Morning Chronicle*, 25 December 1804.

Table 8.3.7.15
Poll for common councilmen of Bridge, 8 January 1810

Forename	Surname	Precinct	Livery	Votes received
WILLIAM	CHILD		Met	106
THOMAS	CARTWRIGHT		Tyl	104
PHILIP	GREEN		Iro	103
ROBERT	BROWN		Fis	102
NATHANIEL	SAUNDERS		Fis	102
THOMAS	ROBERTS		Car	101
CHARLES	BARTRUM		Vin	100
JAMES	LACEY		Met	96
MATTHIAS	ATTWOOD		Met	94
JOHN	CLEUGH		Arm	94
JOHN	JOYNER		Hab	88
JOHN	GARRATT		Gol	87
BENJAMIN	BOVILL		Gol	87
ROBERT	DUTTON		Apo	87
JOHN	ALLDIN		Vin	70
John	Locke			44
John	Smallpiece			23

Source: *Morning Chronicle*, 25 December 1809.

Table 8.3.7.16
Poll for common councilmen of Bridge, 6 January 1812

Forename	Surname	Precinct	Livery	Votes received
WILLIAM	CHILD		Met	118
PHILIP	GREEN		Iro	116
THOMAS	ROBERTS		Car	115
JOHN	JOYNER		Hab	115
ROBERT	BROWN		Fis	113
THOMAS	CARTWRIGHT		Tyl	112
NATHANIEL	SAUNDERS		Fis	112
JAMES	LACY		Met	111
JOHN	ALLDIN		Vin	110
MATTHIAS	ATTWOOD		Met	109
ROBERT	DUTTON		Apo	96
M. WELLS	DEANE		Clo	89
JACOB	COPE		Fis	89
JOHN	LOCKE		Pai	79
BENJAMIN	BOVILL		Gol	79
	Betts			56
John	Sharp			32

Source: *Morning Chronicle*, 25 December 1811.

Table 8.3.7.17
Poll for common councilmen of Bridge, 8 January 1821

Forename	Surname	Precinct	Livery	Votes received
WILLIAM	CHILD		Met	122
PHILIP	GREEN, SNR		Iro	120
WILLIAM W.	COPE		Fis	120
NATHANIEL	SAUNDERS		Fis	119
BENJAMIN	BOVILL		Gol	116
THOMAS	CARTWRIGHT		Tyl	115
JOHN	LOCKE		Pai	112
FREDERICK	GYE		Iro	111
JAMES	HARRIS		Joi	110
PHILIP	GREEN, JNR		Vin	106
WILLIAM R.	CHILD, JNR		Met	105
JOHN	DICKSON		Hab	101
JOHN	JOYNER		Hab	97
JOHN	SMALLPIECE		Met	96
THOMAS	FLINT		Mus	87
John	Sharpe			80
	Beddome			57

Source: *Morning Chronicle*, 25 December 1820.

Table 8.3.7.18
Poll for alderman of Bridge, 10 March 1821

Forename	Surname	Livery	Votes received
JOHN	GARRATT	Gol	87
James	Williams	Gol	81

Source: Beaven, i, p. 61.

Table 8.3.7.19
Poll for common councilmen of Bridge, 8 January 1827

Forename	Surname	Precinct	Livery	Votes received
JOHN	JOYNER		Hab	103
WILLIAM	CHILD, SNR		Met	102
WILLIAM U.	SMITH		Gun	102
THOMAS	CARTWRIGHT		Tyl	101
PHILIP	GREEN		Vin	100
WILLIAM R.	CHILD		Met	99
JOHN	LOCKE		Pai	99
NATHANIEL	SAUNDERS		Fis	98
CHARLES	CHATFIELD		Pat	97
DAVID	VOSS		Bak	94
THOMAS	PEWTRESS		Sta	92
BENJAMIN	BOVILL		Gol	91
JOHN	SMALLPIECE		Met	85
WILLIAM	JONES		Glo	78
WILLIAM	KNOTT		Hab	74
Stephen	Ponder			42
Joseph York	Hatton			40

Source: *Morning Chronicle*, 25 December 1826.

Table 8.3.7.20
Poll for common councilmen of Bridge, 7 January 1828

Forename	Surname	Precinct	Livery	Votes received
WILLIAM	CHILD		Met	40
PHILIP	GREEN		Vin	40
DAVID	VOSS		Bak	41
WILLIAM U.	SMITH		Gun	42
JOHN	JOYNER		Hab	40
THOMAS	CARTWRIGHT		Tyl	38
NATHANIEL	SAUNDERS		Fis	37
JOHN	LOCKE		Pai	42
WILLIAM R.	CHILD		Met	38
BENJAMIN	BOVILL		Gol	37
CHARLES	CHATFIELD		Pat	35
WILLIAM	KNOTT		Hab	35
JOHN	SMALLPIECE		Met	34
WILLIAM	JONES		Glo	34
THOMAS	PEWTRESS		Sta	32
Joseph York	Hatton			23

Source: *Morning Chronicle*, 24 December 1827.

Table 8.3.7.21
Poll for common councilmen of Bridge, 12 January 1829

Forename	Surname	Precinct	Livery	Votes received
WILLIAM U.	SMITH		Gun	109
JOHN	JOYNER		Hab	107
PHILIP	GREEN		Vin	105
THOMAS	CARTWRIGHT		Tyl	104
WILLIAM	KNOTT		Hab	101
JOHN	LOCKE		Pai	101
BENJAMIN	BOVILL		Gol	100
NATHANIEL	SAUNDERS		Fis	99
CHARLES	CHATFIELD		Pat	98
THOMAS	PEWTRESS		Sta	96
DAVID	VOSS		Bak	95
JOHN	SMALLPIECE		Met	89
WILLIAM	JONES		Glo	84
THOMAS	THORNHILL		Fou	80
GEORGE	BOUSFIELD		Clw	51
Stephen	Ponder			40
Orlando	Stone			40
Joseph York	Hatton			32

Source: *Morning Chronicle*, 25 December 1828.

Table 8.3.7.22
Poll for common councilmen of Bridge, 10 January 1831

Forename	Surname	Precinct	Livery	Votes received
WILLIAM U.	SMITH		Gun	84
THOMAS	THORNHILL		Fou	84
THOMAS	CARTWRIGHT		Tyl	82
WILLIAM	KNOTT		Hab	81
GEORGE	BOUSFIELD		Clw	80
ORLANDO	STONE		Hab	79
JOHN	LOCK		Pai	79
THOMAS	PEWTRESS		Sta	76
CHARLES	CHATFIELD		Pat	75
PHILIP	GREEN		Iro	75
GREGORY	JARMAN		Tin	75
JOHN	SHARP		Clo	71
JOHN	ALBERT		Inn	67
THOMAS	GATES		Gol	61
JOHN	HILL		Nee	47
David	Voss		Bak	40
Joseph York	Hatton			22

Source: *St James's Chronicle*, 23-25 December 1830.

Table 8.3.7.23
Poll for common councilmen of Bridge, 9 January 1832

Forename	Surname	Precinct	Livery	Votes received
WILLIAM U.	SMITH		Gun	76
THOMAS	THORNHILL		Fou	80
THOMAS	CARTWRIGHT		Tyl	80
JOHN	LOCKE		Pai	80
CHARLES	CHATFIELD		Pat	77
WILLIAM	KNOTT		Hab	80
GEORGE	BOUSFIELD		Clw	77
PHILIP	GREEN		Iro	79
THOMAS	COOPER		Pew	68
ORLANDO	STONE		Hab	77
JOHN	SHARP		Clm	75
THOMAS	PEWTRESS		Sta	76
JOHN	HILL		Nee	71
GREGORY	JARMAN		Tin	72
JAMES	LOW		Sta	62
John	Albert		Inn	44

Source: *St James's Chronicle*, 22-24 December 1831.

8.3.8 Broad Street, 1711-1831: 22 polls

(10 common councilmen; 220 freeman householders in 1833)

Table 8.3.8.a
Precincts in Broad Street

Code	Precinct
All H	All Hallows
Bart L	St Bartholomew Lower
Bart U	St Bartholomew Upper
Benet L	St Benet Fink Lower
Benet U	St Benet Fink Upper
Chrisr	St Christopher
Margt	St Margaret
Martin	St Martin
Mildred	St Mildred
Peter	St Peter le Poor

Note: All electors in the ward were entitled to choose from among all the candidates but, in the larger wards, those elected as common councilmen were then taken to represent specific precincts or ward electoral sub-divisions (whose boundaries, confusingly, did not automatically match the parish's ecclesiastical boundaries).

Table 8.3.8.1
Poll for aldermanic candidates of Broad Street, 27 October 1711

Forename	Surname	Livery	Votes received	
			Poll	Scrutiny
John	Houblon		229	154
Samuel	Stanier		229	154
John	Scott		233	156
Gerard	Conyers		231	156
William	Withers		238	151
William	Lewin		238	151
George	Newland		242	154
Robert	Dunckley		240	152

Source: Anon., *Tory partiality detected* (1712).

Table 8.3.8.2
Poll for common councilmen of Broad Street, 10 January 1732

Forename	Surname	Precinct	Livery	Votes received
THOMAS	RUTTY			141
JOHN	KELLAWAY			119
Henry	Soames			106
Thomas	Dyer			100

Source: *Grub Street Journal*, 30 December 1731.

Table 8.3.8.3
Poll for alderman of Broad Street, 30 October 1735

Forename	Surname	Precinct	Livery	Votes received
JOHN	LEQUESNE		Gro	191
William	Chapman		Mer	103

Source: Beaven, i, p. 78.

Table 8.3.8.4
Poll for common councilmen of Broad Street, 12 January 1736

Forename	Surname	Precinct	Livery	Votes received	
SAMUEL	NEWEY			Unopposed	
THOMAS	RUTTY			Unopposed	
NATHANIEL	TOWNSEND			Unopposed	
JOHN	CURRIER			Unopposed	
JOHN	KNIGHT			Unopposed	
DAVID	LEQUESNE			Unopposed	
JAMES	FORDHAM			Unopposed	
				Poll	**Scrutiny**
TIMOTHY	WALDO			159	
JOHN	MANSHIP			157	
WILLIAM	STAPLES, JNR			157	
William	Bedell			141	
John	Clarke			140	
Richard	Lucas			129	

Source: *London Evening Post*, 20 December 1735; *Daily Post*, 15 January 1736.

Table 8.3.8.5
Poll for common councilmen of Broad Street, 10 January 1737

Forename	Surname	Precinct	Livery	Votes received
EDWARD	GROSE			135
John	Clarke			122

Source: *London Evening Post*, 21 December 1736.

Table 8.3.8.6
Poll for alderman of Broad Street, 10 April 1741

Forename	Surname	Livery	Votes received	
			Poll	Scrutiny
Charles	Ewer		146	117
Charles	Egleton		132	117

Note: Election declared void; Ewer returned unopposed at second wardmote.

Source: Beaven, i, pp. 78-9.

Table 8.3.8.7
Poll for beadle of Broad Street, 21 December 1741

Forename	Surname	Votes received
	TUDMAN	208
	Boseley	195

Source: *London Evening Post*, 22 December 1741.

Table 8.3.8.8
Poll for alderman of Broad Street, 8 December 1769

Forename	Surname	Livery	Votes received
JAMES	ROSSETER	Fel	143
Frederick	Bull	Sal	93

Source: Beaven, i, p. 78.

Table 8.3.8.9
Poll for common councilmen of Broad Street, 8 January 1770

Forename	Surname	Precinct	Livery	Votes received	
				Poll	Scrutiny
HENRY	KENT		Ski	164	
JOHN	POULTNEY		Inn	156	
PETER N.	FRISQUET		Hab	145	
JOHN	ELLIS		Scr	137	
JOHN	STEPHENS		Met	139	
JOHN	COTTERELL		Gls	138	
NATHANIEL	BURROUGH		Gro	136	
RICHARD	WINDSOR		Mer	135	
BENJAMIN	BONNET		Scr	130	
Charles	Wenman		Hab	122	
JOHN	SEALLY		Gro	112	
John	Dodson		Tin	20	

Source: *St James's Chronicle*, 23 December 1769; LMA COL/AD/04/048.

Table 8.3.8.10
Poll for beadle of Broad Street, 20 July 1782

Forename	Surname	Votes received
JOHN	BREACH	221
Francis	Pearson	189

Source: LMA CLC/W/GF/001/Ms. 01229/001.

Table 8.3.8.11
Poll for beadle of Broad Street, 28 March 1793

Forename	Surname	Votes received
ALEXANDER	STEWART	166
John	Pickett	67

Source: LMA CLC/W/GF/001/Ms. 01229/001.

Table 8.3.8.12
Poll for common councilman of Broad Street, 11 January 1796

Forename	Surname	Precinct	Livery	Votes received
JAMES	ARTHUR	Mildred	Wea	Unopposed
JOHN	UPWARD	Margt	Hab	Unopposed
JOSEPH	HEARN	Bart U	Clw	Unopposed
THOMAS	MARRIOTT	Bart L	Arm	Unopposed
RICHARD	CAUSTON	Benet U	Ski	Unopposed
HENRY	BLAXLAND	Benet L	Uph	Unopposed
WILLIAM	WATLINGTON	Peter	Glo	Unopposed
GEORGE	SHARP	Martin	Gir	Unopposed
ROBERT	CHAPMAN	All H	Joi	Unopposed
WILLIAM	COTTERELL	Chrisr	Gls	83
James	Duthoit			38

Source: LMA CLC/W/GF/001/Ms. 01229/001.

Table 8.3.8.13
Poll for common councilmen of Broad Street, 7 January 1799

Forename	Surname	Precinct	Livery	Votes received
THOMAS	MARRIOTT	Bart L	Arm	105
JOSEPH	HEARN	Bart U	Clw	105
GEORGE	SHARP	Martin	Gir	104
JOHN	UPWARD	Margt	Hab	104
HENRY	BLAXLAND	Benet L	Uph	103
JAMES	ARTHUR	Mildred	Wea	103
ROBERT	CHAPMAN	All H	Joi	102
RICHARD	CAUSTON	Benet U	Ski	101
WILLIAM	COTTERELL	Chrisr	Gls	100
WILLIAM	SHARP	Peter	Wax	20
James	Benwell			88

Note: Benwell apparently declined the poll.
Source: LMA CLC/W/GF/001/Ms. 01229/001.

Table 8.3.8.14
Poll for common councilman of Broad Street, 3 December 1801

Forename	Surname	Precinct	Livery	Votes received
JOHN	STUART	Peter	Cok	75
John	Duddell			68
Thomas	Clarke, jnr		Met	22

Source: LMA CLC/W/GF/001/Ms. 01229/001.

Table 8.3.8.15
Poll for beadle of Broad Street, 27 March 1804

Forename	Surname	Votes received
WILLIAM	SMITH	122
Giles	Hanwell	62

Source: LMA CLC/W/GF/001/Ms. 01229/001.

Table 8.3.8.16
Poll for common councilman of Broad Street, 26 May 1808

Forename	Surname	Precinct	Livery	Votes received
JOHN	PATERSON		Met	37
Thomas	Clarke		Met	18

Source: LMA CLC/W/GF/001/Ms. 01229/001.

Table 8.3.8.17
Poll for common councilman of Broad Street, 1 November 1809

Forename	Surname	Precinct	Livery	Votes received
THOMAS	CROCKATT		Fis	91
Thomas	Clarke		Met	41

Source: LMA CLC/W/GF/001/Ms. 01229/002.

Table 8.3.8.18
Poll for common councilmen of Broad Street, 8 January 1810

Forename	Surname	Precinct	Livery	Votes received
THOMAS	MARRIOTT		Arm	103
THOMAS	CROCKATT		Fis	95
HENRY	BLAXLAND		Uph	94
THOMAS	CLARKE		Met	89
JOHN	PATERSON		Met	81
JAMES	ARTHUR		Wea	81
JOSEPH	HEARN		Clw	75
GEORGE	SHARP		Gir	74
NATHANIEL	ATCHESON		Dra	73
ROBERT	CHAPMAN		Joi	72
Richard	Causton		Ski	33
William	Cotterell		Gls	14

Source: LMA CLC/W/GF/001/Ms. 01229/002.

Table 8.3.8.19
Poll for common councilmen of Broad Street, 11 January 1813

Forename	Surname	Precinct	Livery	Votes received
THOMAS	MARRIOTT		Arm	161
HENRY	BLAXLAND		Uph	155
THOMAS	CROCKATT		Fis	143
JOSEPH	HEARN		Clw	141
JOHN	PATTERSON		Met	127
THOMAS	CLARKE		Met	126
CHARLES	FOSTER		Gol	119
JOHN	DESHONS		Dra	117
WILLIAM	PEPPERCORN		Met	111
NATHANIEL	ATCHESON		Dra	99
Joseph	Patience			86
Richard Webb	Jupp		Car	79

Source: *Morning Chronicle*, 24 December 1812.

Table 8.3.8.20
Poll for common councilmen of Broad Street, 12 January 1818

Forename	Surname	Precinct	Livery	Votes received
THOMAS	CROCKATT		Fis	123
RICHARD WEBB	JUPP		Car	122
FRANCIS	WAKEFIELD		Dra	119
JOHN	COWAN		Wax	118
JAMES	SMITH		Cop	117
JOHN	DESHONS		Dra	117
CHARLES	FOSTER		Gol	115
WILLIAM	PEPPERCORN		Met	115
JOHN	PATERSON		Met	106
RICHARD H.	PIGEON		Met	96
Thomas	Clarke		Met	70

Source: *Morning Chronicle*, 24 December 1817.

Table 8.3.8.21
Poll for common councilmen of Broad Street, 12 January 1829

Forename	Surname	Precinct	Livery	Votes received
THOMAS	CROCKATT		Fis	156
RICHARD WEBB	JUPP		Car	153
JOHN	PATTERSON		Met	143
RICHARD H.	PIGEON		Met	143
FRANCIS	WAKEFIELD		Dra	142
JOHN	DESHONS		Dra	140
WILLIAM	PEPPERCORN		Inn	136
JOHN	COWAN		Wax	133
GEORGE	STEWART		Met	130
THOMAS	CORNEY		Dra	120
	Weller			110

Source: *Morning Chronicle*, 25 December 1828.

Table 8.3.8.22
Poll for alderman of Broad Street, 7 February 1831

Forename	Surname	Livery	Votes received
JAMES	COWAN	Wax	82
Thomas	Ward	Shi	30

Source: Beaven, i, p. 78.

8.3.9 Candlewick, 1728-1829: seven polls

(8 common councilmen; 118 freeman householders in 1833)

Table 8.3.9.1
Poll for common councilmen of Candlewick, 8 January 1728

Forename	Surname	Precinct	Livery	Votes received	
				Poll	Scrutiny
RICHARD	VICKERS				
EDWARD	COCKAYNE				
WILLIAM	WILCOX				
Nathaniel	Arnold				
William	Clark				
Joseph	Thompson				

Source: LMA COL/CC/13/01/012, return dated 25 January 1728.

Table 8.3.9.2
Poll for alderman of Candlewick, 12 May 1807

Forename	Surname	Precinct	Livery	Votes received	
				Poll	Scrutiny
SAMUEL	BIRCH		Coo	69	62
John	Atkins		Met	61	51

Source: Beaven, i, p. 87.

Table 8.3.9.3
Poll for common councilmen of Candlewick, 11 January 1808

Forename	Surname	Precinct	Livery	Votes received
JOHN	WALTER		Cor	86
JOHN	GALE		Gol	84
JOHN RYLAND	MANDER		Tin	84
JOSEPH	WELCH		Gir	84
DANIEL	FOSSICK		Tin	76
JOHN	PLATT		Vin	74
THOMAS	PALMER		Pla	71
ROBERT	KIRBY		Nee	61
Joseph	Humpleby		Plu	55
John	Groombridge		Met	16

Source: LMA CLC/W/HA/001/Ms. 08534/001.

Table 8.3.9.4
Poll for common councilmen of Candlewick, 8 January 1810

Forename	Surname	Precinct	Livery	Votes received
JOHN	WALTER		Cor	111
ROBERT	KIRBY		Nee	93
JOSEPH	HUMPLEBY		Plu	82
JOSEPH	WELCH		Gir	73
JOHN	GALE		Gol	72
JOHN	PLATT		Vin	70
WILLIAM	WHITBY		Arm	70
JOHN RYLAND	MANDER		Tin	69
Daniel	Fossick		Tin	66
John	Groombridge		Met	63

Source: LMA CLC/W/HA/001/Ms. 08534/001.

Table 8.3.9.5
Poll for common councilmen of Candlewick, 9 January 1815

Forename	Surname	Precinct	Livery	Votes received
JOSEPH	EATON, SNR		Fis	97
ROBERT	KIRBY		Nee	93
JOSEPH	WELCH		Gir	92
JOHN	WALTER		Cor	92
JOSEPH	HUMPLEBY		Plu	91
JOHN	PLATT		Vin	86
JOHN	GALE		Gol	70
JOHN RYLAND	MANDER		Tin	62
Edward	Collinson		Tin	61

Source: LMA CLC/W/HA/001/Ms. 08534/001.

Table 8.3.9.6
Poll for beadle of Candlewick, 23 December 1815

Forename	Surname	Votes received
EDWARD	LEWIS	82
John George	Walker	72

Source: LMA CLC/W/HA/001/Ms. 08534/001.

Table 8.3.9.7
Poll for common councilmen of Candlewick, 12 January 1829

Forename	Surname	Precinct	Livery	Votes received
JOHN	WALTER		Cor	55
JOHN	PLATT		Vin	55
JOHN	SAUNDERS		Fis	55
THOMAS	BOND		Fis	53
JOHN	DOWNES		Sal	54
JEREMIAH	EVANS		Fru	55
WILLIAM	WHITE		Bla	55
SAMUEL	BRADLEY		Pat	49
John Ryland	Mander		Tin	7

Source: LMA CLC/W/HA/001/Ms. 08534/001.

8.3.10 Castle Baynard, 1722-1832: 28 polls

(10 common councilmen; 234 freeman householders in 1833)

Table 8.3.10.a
Precincts in Castle Baynard

Code	Precinct
Andrew	St Andrew
Benet	St Benet
Faith	St Faith
Gregory	St Gregory
Mary	St Mary Magdalen

Note: All electors in the ward were entitled to choose from among all the candidates but, in the larger wards, those elected as common councilmen were then taken to represent specific precincts or ward electoral sub-divisions (whose boundaries, confusingly, did not automatically match the parish's ecclesiastical boundaries).

Table 8.3.10.1
Poll for alderman of Castle Baynard, 19 March 1722

Forename	Surname	Livery	Votes received
JOHN	BARBER	Sta	229
Robert	Ladbroke	Gro	191

Source: Beaven, i, p. 96.

Table 8.3.10.2
Poll for common councilmen of Castle Baynard, 10 January 1726

Forename	Surname	Precinct	Livery	Votes received
JOHN	PEACHEY			134
JOHN	WHITE			130
Edward	Woodward			122
Samuel	Williams			121

Source: *Daily Journal*, 23 December 1725.

Table 8.3.10.3
Poll for common councilmen of Castle Baynard, 10 January 1732

Forename	Surname	Precinct	Livery	Votes received	
JOHN	BATEMAN			Unopposed	
JOHN	TOWNSEND			Unopposed	
WILLIAM	LORD			Unopposed	
ROBERT	TERRITT			Unopposed	
JOHN	CORDWELL			Unopposed	
				Poll	**Scrutiny**
VALENTINE	GRIMSTEAD			153	140
JOHN	BELCHIER			153	139
SAMUEL	WILLIAMS			147	133
RICHARD	TRUBEY			146	133
WILLIAM	INNYS			143	129
	Perkins			128	110
John	Peachey			123	105
	Williamson			114	107
	Cleare			111	95
	Atkinson			110	94

Source: *London Evening Post*, 18 January 1732; *Daily Courant*, 10 February 1732.

Table 8.3.10.4
Poll for beadle of Castle Baynard, 21 December 1736

Forename	Surname	Votes received
	ATKINS	N
	Delander	(N-84)
	Ray	
	Atkinson	

Source: *London Evening Post*, 21-23 December 1736.

Table 8.3.10.5
Poll for beadle of Castle Baynard, 10 January 1738

Forename	Surname	Votes received
GEORGE	DUNN	228
John	Delander	89

Source: *London Evening Post*, 10 January 1738.

Table 8.3.10.6
Poll for common councilmen of Castle Baynard, 8 January 1739

Forename	Surname	Precinct	Livery	Votes received	
				Poll	Scrutiny
ROBERT	LADBROKE			215	
WILLIAM	HUNT			214	
NICHOLAS	SMITH			176	
JOHN	CORDWELL			169	
VALENTINE	GRIMSTEAD			168	
WILLIAM	INNYS			166	
ROBERT	TERRITT			157	
WILLIAM	LORD			157	
JOHN	TOWNSEND			156	
JOHN	BATEMAN			150	
John	Belchier			145	
Samuel	Williams			123	

Source: *London Evening Post*, 21-23 December 1738; *Daily Gazetteer*, 2 March 1739.

Table 8.3.10.7
Poll for common councilmen of Castle Baynard, 7 January 1740

Forename	Surname	Precinct	Livery	Votes received
ROBERT	LADBROKE			195
	AUSTEN			194
NICHOLAS	SMITH			193
WILLIAM	HUNT			191
CHARLES	HITCH			185
NATHANIEL	NASH			184
JOHN	TOWNSEND			183
ROBERT	TERRITT			180
JOHN	WINDER			178
WILLIAM	INNYS			145
William	Lord			143
John	Cordwell			143

Source: *London Daily Post*, 22 December 1739.

Table 8.3.10.8
Poll for common councilmen of Castle Baynard, 12 January 1741

Forename	Surname	Precinct	Livery	Votes received	
				Poll	Scrutiny
WILLIAM	LORD				137
JOHN	CORDWELL				134
Benjamin	Crook				61

Note: This was a rare example of a by-election with two vacant seats and two candidates returned.
Source: *London Evening Post*, 13 January 1741; *Daily Post*, 15 January 1741; *London Daily Post and General Advertiser*, 15 January 1741; *Weekly Miscellany*, 17 January 1741.

Table 8.3.10.9
Poll for common councilmen of Castle Baynard, 8 January 1759

Forename	Surname	Precinct	Livery	Votes received
JOHN	HOPKINS			131
GEORGE	BELLAS			131
ROBERT	WILLIS			125
HENRY	MAJOR			123
WILLIAM	GYLES			122
JOHN	WILSON			121
JOHN	PITTWAY			120
PHILIP	BELL			118
BENJAMIN	CROOK			117
JOHN	JORDAINE			82
John	Willis			

Source: *London Evening Post*, 21 December 1758.

Table 8.3.10.10
Poll for common councilmen of Castle Baynard, 8 January 1770

Forename	Surname	Precinct	Livery	Votes received
GEORGE	BELLAS	Andrew	Car	164
JOHN	JORDAINE	Gregory	Tal	153
PHILIP	BELL	Gregory	Vin	142
HENRY	MAJOR	Benet	Hab	142
JOHN	PITTWAY	Benet	Fis	139
THOMAS	HARRISON	Mary	Sta	138
JOHN	HOPKINS	Faith	Gro	130
RICHARD	MACHELL	Mary	Plu	125
ROBERT	HARRIS	Gregory	Tin	114
WILLIAM	HURFORD	Benet	Hab	107
Midford	Young		Tin	102
John	Wilson			79

Source: *Independent Chronicle*, 25 December 1769.

Table 8.3.10.11
Poll for common councilman of Castle Baynard, 17 June 1784

Forename	Surname	Precinct	Livery	Votes received
JAMES	GRIFFITHS		Joi	89
John	Smith		Fis	36

Source: LMA CLC/W/HB/001/Ms. 05644/001.

Table 8.3.10.12
Poll for common councilmen of Castle Baynard, 10 January 1785

Forename	Surname	Precinct	Livery	Votes received
THOMAS	HARRISON	Mary	Sta	Unopposed
JAMES	GRIFFITHS	Gregory	Joi	205
WILLIAM	BOX	Andrew	Apo	192
TIPPING	RIGBY	Gregory	Dra	173
MIDFORD	YOUNG	Benet	Tin	172
HENRY	MAJOR	Gregory	Hab	170
SAMUEL	THOMPSON	Faith	Shi	165
ROBERT	SMITH	Mary	Vin	161
WILLIAM	STONE	Andrew	Bar	154
JOHN	WILLOUGHBY	Benet	Tal	121
Thomas	Morris		Whe	116
John	Smith		Fis	100

Source: LMA CLC/W/HB/001/Ms. 05644/001.

Table 8.3.10.13
Poll for common councilman of Castle Baynard, 26 April 1787

Forename	Surname	Precinct	Livery	Votes received
GEORGE	HUDSON		Far	101
Thomas	Morris		Whe	53

Source: LMA CLC/W/HB/001/Ms. 05644/001.

Table 8.3.10.14
Poll for common councilman of Castle Baynard, 22 December 1787

Forename	Surname	Precinct	Livery	Votes received
GEORGE	HUDSON		Far	123
Thomas	Morris		Whe	96

Source: LMA CLC/W/HB/001/Ms. 05644/001.

Table 8.3.10.15
Poll for common councilmen of Castle Baynard, 7 January 1793

Forename	Surname	Precinct	Livery	Votes received
MIDFORD	YOUNG	Benet	Tin	Unopposed
WILLIAM	BOX	Andrew	Apo	170
JAMES	GRIFFITHS	Gregory	Joi	169
SAMUEL	THOMPSON	Faith	Shi	159
JOHN	WILLOUGHBY	Benet	Tal	159
TIPPING	RIGBY	Gregory	Dra	158
ROBERT	SLADE	Gregory	Iro	155
WILLIAM	HERNE	Andrew	Vin	150
THOMAS	WHEELER	Mary	Glz	147
ROBERT	SMITH	Mary	Vin	144
Thomas	Simpson		Gol	64
Thomas	Farrance		Cok	17

Source: LMA CLC/W/HB/001/Ms. 05644/001.

Table 8.3.10.16
Poll for common councilmen of Castle Baynard, 11 January 1796

Forename	Surname	Precinct	Livery	Votes received
MIDFORD	YOUNG	Benet	Tin	Unopposed
RICHARD	HOWELL	Faith	Nee	170
JAMES	GRIFFITHS	Gregory	Joi	169
ROBERT	SLADE	Gregory	Iro	148
THOMAS	WHEELER	Mary	Glz	146
WILLIAM	BOX	Andrew	Apo	141
PERROT	FENTON	Mary	Wea	138
JOHN	WILLOUGHBY	Benet	Tal	127
TIPPING	RIGBY	Gregory	Dra	119
WILLIAM	HERNE	Andrew	Vin	117
Robert	Smith		Vin	115

Source: LMA CLC/W/HB/001/Ms. 05644/001.

Table 8.3.10.17
Poll for alderman of Castle Baynard, 20 October 1796

Forename	Surname	Livery	Votes received
WILLIAM	HERNE	Vin	124
John	Crickitt	Sta	58

Source: LMA CLC/W/HB/001/Ms. 05644/001; Beaven, i, p. 97.

Table 8.3.10.18
Poll for common councilmen of Castle Baynard, 9 January 1797

Forename	Surname	Precinct	Livery	Votes received
MIDFORD	YOUNG	Benet	Tin	169
JAMES	GRIFFITHS	Gregory	Joi	164
RICHARD	HOWELL	Faith	Vin	164
THOMAS	WHEELER	Mary	Glz	160
WILLIAM	BOX	Andrew	Apo	159
ROBERT	SLADE	Gregory	Iro	146
PERROT	FENTON	Mary	Wea	144
JOHN	WILLOUGHBY	Benet	Tal	142
TIPPING	RIGBY	Gregory	Dra	142
THOMAS	FARRANCE	Andrew	Cok	120
W.	Sharpe			96
John	Treacher			96

Source: *Oracle and Public Advertiser*, 23 December 1796.

Table 8.3.10.19
Poll for common councilmen of Castle Baynard, 12 January 1807

Forename	Surname	Precinct	Livery	Votes received
JAMES	HURCOMBE	Gregory	Whe	172
JAMES	GRIFFITHS	Gregory	Joi	170
WILLIAM	BOX	Andrew	Apo	169
RICHARD	HOWELL	Faith	Vin	169
JOHN	TREACHER	Benet	Whe	167
JAMES	HURLOCK	Benet	Apo	166
PERROT	FENTON	Mary	Wea	163
ROBERT	SLADE	Gregory	Iro	158
THOMAS	FARRANCE	Andrew	Cok	157
JAMES	PEARCE	Mary	Vin	96
James Edward	Pownell		Sta	67
Joseph	Vere		Bak	65

Source: *Morning Chronicle*, 25 December 1806.

Table 8.3.10.20
Poll for beadle of Castle Baynard, 20 June 1807

Forename	Surname	Votes received
HENRY	KERRIDGE	173
Henry	Brooker	135

Source: LMA CLC/W/HB/001/Ms. 05644/001

Table 8.3.10.21
Poll for common councilmen of Castle Baynard, 11 January 1808

Forename	Surname	Precinct	Livery	Votes received
JAMES	GRIFFITHS	Gregory	Joi	144
RICHARD	HOWELL	Faith	Nee	142
WILLIAM	BOX	Andrew	Apo	141
JOHN	TREACHER	Benet	Whe	133
JAMES	HURLOCK	Benet	Apo	137
JAMES	HURCOMBE	Gregory	Whe	134
PERROT	FENTON	Mary	Wea	125
ROBERT	SLADE	Gregory	Iro	124
THOMAS	FARRANCE	Andrew	Cok	109
JAMES EDWARD	POWNELL	Mary	Sta	97
James	Welch			89

Source: LMA CLC/W/HB/001/Ms. 05644/001.

Table 8.3.10.22
Poll for common councilmen of Castle Baynard, 8 January 1810

Forename	Surname	Precinct	Livery	Votes received
JAMES	GRIFFITHS	Gregory	Joi	162
JAMES	HURCOMBE	Gregory	Whe	152
RICHARD	HOWELL	Faith	Nee	150
PERROT	FENTON, JNR	Mary	Wea	144
JOHN	TREACHER	Benet	Whe	143
WILLIAM	BOX	Andrew	Apo	143
ROBERT	SLADE	Gregory	Iro	136
JAMES EDWARD	POWNELL	Mary	Sta	136
THOMAS	FARRANCE	Andrew	Cok	133
JAMES	HURLOCK	Benet	Apo	103
John	Pearson		Dra	100
James	Welch			47

Source: LMA CLC/W/HB/001/Ms. 05644/001.

Table 8.3.10.23
Poll for common councilmen of Castle Baynard, 8 January 1816

Forename	Surname	Precinct	Livery	Votes received
JAMES	GRIFFITHS	Gregory	Joi	177
JAMES	HURCOMBE	Gregory	Whe	174
JOHN	PEARSON	Faith	Dra	172
WILLIAM	BOX	Andrew	Apo	168
JAMES	HURLOCK	Benet	Apo	168
PERROT	FENTON, JNR	Mary	Wea	167
THOMAS	FARRANCE	Andrew	Cok	164
ROBERT	SLADE	Gregory	Iro	158
JOHN	TREACHER	Benet	Whe	149
JAMES	VERE	Mary	Bak	127
William	Pulley			111

Source: LMA CLC/W/HB/001/Ms. 05644/001.

Table 8.3.10.24
Poll for common councilmen of Castle Baynard, 12 January 1818

Forename	Surname	Precinct	Livery	Votes received
JOHN	PEARSON	Faith	Dra	136
JOSEPH	HURCOMBE	Gregory	Whe	134
ROBERT	SLADE	Gregory	Iro	124
JOHN	TREACHER	Benet	Whe	124
JOSEPH	HURLOCK	Benet	Apo	123
JAMES	GRIFFITHS	Gregory	Joi	122
PERROT	FENTON, JNR	Mary	Wea	122
WILLIAM	BOX	Andrew	Apo	122
THOMAS	FARRANCE	Andrew	Cok	119
JAMES	WELCH	Mary	Arm	105
James	Vere		Bak	65

Source: LMA CLC/W/HB/001/Ms. 05644/001.

Table 8.3.10.25
Poll for common councilman of Castle Baynard, 11 February 1820

Forename	Surname	Precinct	Livery	Votes received
THOMAS	HAMILTON	Faith	Lor	116
William	Pulley		Wax	99

Source: LMA CLC/W/HB/001/Ms. 05644/001.

Table 8.3.10.26
Poll for common councilmen of Castle Baynard, 8 January 1827

Forename	Surname	Precinct	Livery	Votes received
SAMUEL	LOVEGROVE	Gregory	Joi	161
THOMAS	FARRANCE	Andrew	Cok	152
APSLEY	PELLATT	Mary	Iro	149
PERROT	FENTON, JNR	Mary	Wea	149
JAMES	HOPPE	Benet	Gol	148
JAMES	NEWBON	Mary	Bak	147
JOHN	EVANS	Gregory	Cut	146
ROBERT	SLADE	Gregory	Iro	141
JAMES	TOPLIS	Faith	Uph	138
WILLIAM DAVID	JENNINGS	Benet	Scr	102
William	Pritchard		Met	101

Source: LMA CLC/W/HB/001/Ms. 05644/001.

Table 8.3.10.27
Poll for common councilmen of Castle Baynard, 11 January 1830

Forename	Surname	Precinct	Livery	Votes received
THOMAS	FARRANCE	Andrew	Coo	106
SAMUEL	LOVEGROVE	Gregory	Joi	105
ROBERT	SLADE	Gregory	Iro	104
JOHN	EVANS	Gregory	Cut	104
JAMES	TOPLIS	Faith	Uph	103
PERROT	FENTON, JNR	Mary	Wea	103
WILLIAM	PRITCHARD	Benet	Met	103
APSLEY	PELLATT	Mary	Iro	103
JAMES	HOPPE	Benet	Gol	97
RICHARD	HICKS	Andrew	But	82
John	Crookes			54

Source: LMA CLC/W/HB/001/Ms. 05644/001.

Table 8.3.10.28
Poll for common councilmen of Castle Baynard, 9 January 1832

Forename	Surname	Precinct	Livery	Votes received
RICHARD	HICKS	Andrew	But	124
JOHN	EVANS	Gregory	Cut	117
SAMUEL	LOVEGROVE	Gregory	Joi	116
WILLIAM	PRITCHARD	Benet	Met	115
JAMES	HOPPE	Benet	Gol	115
ROBERT	SLADE		Iro	114
PERROT	FENTON	Mary	Wea	114
APSLEY	PELLATT	Mary	Iro	111
JAMES	TOPLIS		Uph	110
JAMES	SMITH	Faith	Bak	106
James	Hardy		Gol	60

Source: LMA CLC/W/HB/001/Ms. 05644/002; *The Times*, 24 December 1831.

8.3.11 Cheap, 1713-1829: 22 polls

(12 common councilmen; 157 freeman householders in 1833)

Table 8.3.11.1
Poll for common councilmen of Cheap, 12 January 1713

Forename	Surname	Precinct	Livery	Votes received	
				Poll	Scrutiny
HENRY	COLCHESTER				
JOHN	YOUNG				
SAMUEL	SPRAGG				
JOHN	MOORE				
JOHN	BUSFIELD				
ROBERT	SMITHSON				
BENJAMIN	HILL				
ROBERT	NORRIS				
HENRY	CORNISH				
WILLIAM	HOBDAY				
CHRISTOPHER	WHITE				

Source: LMA COL/CC/013/01/020.

Table 8.3.11.2
Poll for common councilmen of Cheap, 9 January 1716

Forename	Surname	Precinct	Livery	Votes received	
				Poll	Scrutiny
JOHN	HERON				
JOHN	YOUNG				
JOHN	MORGAN				
JONAH	CRYNES				
ROBERT	KEYNTON				
JOHN	SPILLET				
HENRY	COLCHESTER				
BENJAMIN	HILL				
GEORGE	WILCOX				
ROBERT	NORRIS				
TIMOTHY	PERRY				
CHRISTOPHER	WHITE				

Source: LMA COL/CC/013/01/012, return dated 16 January 1716.

Table 8.3.11.3
Poll for common councilmen of Cheap, 7 January 1717

Forename	Surname	Precinct	Livery	Votes received	
				Poll	**Scrutiny**
JOHN	MORGAN				156
JOHN	HERON				151
ROBERT	NORRIS				151
JONAH	CRYNES				150
GEORGE	WILCOX				150
TIMOTHY	PERRY				150
JOHN	SPILLET				149
HENRY	COLCHESTER				149
JOHN	YOUNG				148
ROBERT	KEYNTON				147
BENJAMIN	HILL				146
CHRISTOPHER	WHITE				143
Thomas	Smith				131
Robert	Pead				122
Richard	Russell				120
John	Vanham				120
Robert	Fotherby				119
William	Maxey				118
Thomas	Bearcliffe				118
John	White				117
Thomas	Fothergill				117
William	Beecher				116
Miles	Whitworth				116
John	Eyloe				111

Source: LMA COL/CC/13/01/012.

Table 8.3.11.4
Poll for common councilmen of Cheap, 6 January 1718

Forename	Surname	Precinct	Livery	Votes received
THOMAS	SMITH			171
ROBERT	FOTHERBY			171
JOSHUA	SHARP			170
THOMAS	FOTHERGILL			170
EDWARD	TAY			169
WILLIAM	MAXEY			169
WILLIAM	TRUBSHAW			168
RICHARD	LAWRENCE			168
JOSEPH	WEBB			166
JOHN	WHITE			166
JOHN	HERON			166
GEORGE	WILCOX			160
John	Young			163
John	Morgan			163
Jonah	Crynes			163
Richard	Bridgman			161
Christopher	White			161
Timothy	Perry			160
Henry	Colchester			160
John	Spillet			159
Robert	Norris			159
John	Shorey			156
Robert	Norris			147

Source: *Post Boy*, 26 December 1717.

Table 8.3.11.5
Poll for common councilmen of Cheap, 12 January 1719

Forename	Surname	Precinct	Livery	Votes received	
				Poll	Scrutiny
JOHN	HERON				
JOHN	YOUNG				
JOHN	MORGAN				
JONAH	CRYNES				
JOHN	SHOREY				
JOHN	SPILLET				
RICHARD	BRIDEMAN				
WILLIAM	SCRIMSHIRE				
THOMAS	HALSEY				
FREDERICK	STANTON				
TIMOTHY	PERRY				
WILLIAM	BILL				

Source: *Whitehall Evening Post*, 15 January 1719.

Table 8.3.11.6
Poll for common councilmen of Cheap, 10 January 1732

Forename	Surname	Precinct	Livery	Votes received
THOMAS	WRIGHT			145
GEORGE	ARNOLD			127
JOHN	SPILLET			126
THOMAS	PORTE			125
WILLIAM	DAVIES			125
JOHN	HANBURY			125
SAMUEL	ASHURST			124
ROBERT	KENDAL			124
EDWARD	TAY			124
JOSEPH	BOURNE			123
FREDERICK	STANTON			122
HENRY	WATTS			116
Allen	Webb			98
George	Verney			89

Source: *Daily Post*, 22 December 1731.

Table 8.3.11.7
Poll for alderman of Cheap, 27 January 1733

Forename	Surname	Livery	Votes received	
			Poll	Scrutiny
ROBERT	KENDAL	Fis	135	
Robert	Westley	Met	105	

Source: Beaven, i, p. 105.

Table 8.3.11.8
Poll for common councilmen of Cheap, 6 January 1735

Forename	Surname	Precinct	Livery	Votes received
ROBERT	WATE			N
				(N-13)

Source: *Daily Courant*, 24 December 1734.

Table 8.3.11.9
Poll for common councilmen of Cheap, 10 January 1737

Forename	Surname	Precinct	Livery	Votes received
JOHN	SMITH			245
JOHN	SPILLET			216
SAMUEL	SEDGWICK			206
RICHARD	SCRAFTON			158
GEORGE	ARNOLD			148
WALTER	HAYTER			146
ALLEN	WEBB			144
ROBERT	WAITE			141
HENRY	CLARKE			141
THOMAS	WRIGHT			134
JOHN	HANBURY			132
FREDERICK	STANTON			126
John	Skinner			122
Leonard	Pead			121
Joseph	Lewin			116
Samuel	Crisp			115
John	Picton			114

Source: *London Evening Post*, 21 December 1736.

Table 8.3.11.10
Poll for alderman of Cheap, 3 January 1739

Forename	Surname	Livery	Votes received	
			Poll	Scrutiny
JOSEPH	EYLES	Hab	137	125
Richard	Hoare	Gol	136	116

Source: Beaven, i, p. 105.

Table 8.3.11.11
Poll for common councilmen of Cheap, 7 January 1754

Forename	Surname	Precinct	Livery	Votes received
	'OLD LIST'			N
	Wickes			(N-31)

Source: *London Evening Post*, 20-22 December 1753; *Public Advertiser*, 22 December 1753.

Table 8.3.11.12
Poll for common councilmen of Cheap, 6 January 1772

Forename	Surname	Precinct	Livery	Votes received
PATRICK	CAWDROW			109
THOMAS	BURFORD		Pew	105
JOHN	SMITH		Iro	100
STEPHEN	CAMM		Mus	99
ROBERT	SIDDALL		Mus	98
JOHN	FULLER		Met	96
SAMUEL	DALE		Gol	94
RICHARD	BRISTOW		Gol	94
THOMAS	BODDINGTON		Clo	92
THOMAS	PRESTON		Fis	88
JOHN	MARLAR		Hab	82
JOHN	SALT		Gro	79
Nicholas	Forster			43
Samuel	Clarke			34

Source: *Middlesex Journal*, 24 December 1771; *London Evening Post*, 20-22 December 1753; and *Public Advertiser*, 22 December 1753.

Table 8.3.11.13
Poll for common councilmen of Cheap, 9 January 1786

Forename	Surname	Precinct	Livery	Votes received
JOHN	SMITH		Iro	127
JOHN	HINDE		Gro	117
WILLIAM	ELLIS		Whe	117
EDWARD	PEARSON		Gol	115
THOMAS B.	PRATT		Gol	114
THOMAS	TAYLOR		Gir	113
JOHN	WITHERS		Tyl	112
RICHARD	BRISTOW		Gol	108
NICHOLAS	FORSTER		Met	104
JOHN	COWLEY		Clw	90
SAMUEL	MARRIOTT		Vin	87
JOHN	READ		Met	86
	Danvin			76
Francis	Naizon		Nee	70

Source: *The Times*, 24 December 1785.

Table 8.3.11.14
Poll for common councilmen of Cheap, 7 January 1788

Forename	Surname	Precinct	Livery	Votes received
BENJAMIN	FIGGINS		Pai	70
SAMUEL	GOODBEHERE		Nee	67
SAMUEL	MARRIOTT		Vin	66
JOHN THOROLD	DARWIN		Mus	66
THOMAS	TAYLOR		Gir	66
WILLIAM	ELLIS		Whe	66
THOMAS B.	PRATT		Gol	65
JOHN	READE		Met	64
JOHN	SMITH		Iro	63
NICHOLAS	FORSTER		Met	55
RICHARD	BRISTOW		Gol	54
JOHN	COWLEY		Clw	43
John	Withers		Tyl	26
John	Hinde		Gro	23
	Andrews			15
	Hudson			11

Source: *Whitehall Evening Post*, 22 December 1787.

Table 8.3.11.15
Poll for common councilmen of Cheap, 11 January 1796

Forename	Surname	Precinct	Livery	Votes received
WILLIAM	ELLIS		Whe	134
JOHN THOROLD	DARWIN		Mus	123
THOMAS	TAYLOR		Gir	118
THOMAS A.	LOXLEY		Tyl	116
BENJAMIN	FIGGINS		Pai	105
ISAAC	WORLEY		Fis	103
SAMUEL	GOODBEHERE		Nee	101
WILLIAM	CASS		Whe	94
SAMUEL	HALE		Vin	91
SAMUEL	MARRIOTT		Vin	88
GEORGE	FOURNIER		Vin	85
EDWARD	WIGAN		Gol	85
William Edward	Smith		Iro	83
Matthew	Simpson			83
John	Cowley		Clw	81
Ebenezer	Bourne			76
William	Andrews			68
Edward	Gibbons			66
	Hanson			61
Thomas B.	Pratt		Gol	59

Source: *Morning Post*, 24 December 1795.

Table 8.3.11.16
Poll for alderman of Cheap, 5 June 1809

Forename	Surname	Precinct	Livery	Votes received
SAMUEL	GOODBEHERE		Nee	81
William	Heygate		Met	49

Source: Beaven, i, p. 105.

Table 8.3.11.17
Poll for common councilmen of Cheap, 8 January 1810

Forename	Surname	Precinct	Livery	Votes received
EDWARD	WIGAN		Gol	122
THOMAS A.	LOXLEY		Tyl	118
WILLIAM	CUMMINS		Nee	118
JOHN	WRIGHT		Dra	116
RICHARD	CHEESEWRIGHT		Tur	113
JOHN	SMITH		Fis	111
GEORGE	FOURNIER		Vin	94
SAMUEL	HALE		Vin	93
HENRY	FARR		Hab	91
THOMAS	SWIFT		Uph	89
JOHN	WILLIAMS		Glz	88
JOSEPH	MAWMAN		Sta	87
	Dolman			86

Source: *Morning Chronicle*, 25 December 1809.

Table 8.3.11.18
Poll for common councilmen of Cheap, 7 January 1811

Forename	Surname	Precinct	Livery	Votes received
THOMAS A.	LOXLEY		Tyl	119
EDWARD	WIGAN		Gol	117
RICHARD	CHEESEWRIGHT		Tur	109
RICHARD	ROTHWELL		Fis	109
SAMUEL	HALE		Vin	105
JOHN	WRIGHT		Dra	105
HENRY	FARR		Hab	105
WILLIAM	CUMMINS		Nee	104
JOSEPH	MAWMAN		Sta	103
GEORGE	FOURNIER		Vin	98
JOHN	SMITH		Fis	98
THOMAS	SWIFT		Uph	94
William	Street			78

Source: *Morning Chronicle*, 25 December 1810; LMA COL/AD/04/063.

Table 8.3.11.19
Poll for common councilmen of Cheap, 12 January 1818

Forename	Surname	Precinct	Livery	Votes received
THOMAS A.	LOXLEY		Tyl	104
RICHARD	ROTHWELL		Fis	96
JAMES	KEATS		Fel	94
EUGENIUS	FENNING		Vin	94
JOHN	SMITH		Fis	92
RICHARD	CHEESEWRIGHT		Tur	91
JOHN	PERRELL		Wea	91
WILLIAM E.	SMITH		Iro	89
RICHARD	BROOKE		Gol	89
SAMUEL	JERRAM		Gir	88
ROBERT	JENNINGS		Sta	80
SAMUEL	JONES		Pat	74
Thomas	Swift		Uph	66

Source: *Morning Chronicle*, 25 December 1817.

Table 8.3.11.20
Poll for common councilmen of Cheap, 11 January 1819

Forename	Surname	Precinct	Livery	Votes received
THOMAS A.	LOXLEY		Tyl	105
JOHN	SMITH		Fis	98
EUGENIUS	FENNING		Vin	98
JOSEPH	KEATS		Fel	96
SAMUEL	JERRAM		Gir	96
JOHN	PERRELL		Wea	96
JOHN	JAMES		Pat	95
RICHARD	BROOK		Gol	95
SAMUEL	JONES		Pat	93
WILLIAM E.	SMITH		Iro	91
ROBERT	JENNINGS		Sta	91
GEORGE	LEDGER		Sta	91
David	Weatherspoon			43

Source: *Morning Chronicle*, 24 December 1818.

Table 8.3.11.21
Poll for common councilmen of Cheap, 8 January 1821

Forename	Surname	Precinct	Livery	Votes received
THOMAS A.	LOXLEY		Tyl	89
GEORGE	LEDGER		Sta	89
CHARLES	BLEADEN		Vin	89
SAMUEL	JONES		Pat	87
EUGENIUS	FENNING		Vin	82
RICHARD	BROOK		Gol	76
JOHN	PERRELL		Wea	76
WILLIAM E.	SMITH		Iro	75
ROBERT	JENNINGS		Sta	75
JOHN	JAMES		Pat	75
GEORGE E.	SHUTTLEWORTH		Ski	59
DAVID	WEATHERSPOON			41
Thomas	Tegg			18

Source: *Morning Chronicle*, 25 December 1820.

Table 8.3.11.22
Poll for common councilmen of Cheap, 12 January 1829

Forename	Surname	Precinct	Livery	Votes received
RICHARD	BROOK		Gol	104
CHARLES	BLEADON		Vin	98
EUGENIUS	FENNING		Vin	97
SAMUEL	JONES		Pat	97
WILLIAM	STEVENS		Pat	96
GEORGE	LEDGER		Sta	96
EDWIN	CUTHBERT		Lea	94
GEORGE E.	SHUTTLEWORTH		Ski	89
JAMES	BURRA		Bro	86
RICHARD P.	GANTHONY		Clm	85
JAMES	GRANT		Gol	82
THOMAS A.	LOXLEY		Tyl	78
J.S.	Rigge			41

Source: *Morning Chronicle*, 25 December 1828.

8.3.12 Coleman Street, 1718-1829: 21 polls

(6 common councilmen; 176 freeman householders in 1833)

Table 8.3.12.1
Poll for alderman of Coleman Street, 13 November 1718

Forename	Surname	Precinct	Livery	Votes received
HARCOURT	MASTER		Hab	165
Samuel	Clarke			135

Source: Beaven, i, p. 112.

Table 8.3.12.2
Poll for common councilmen of Coleman Street, 8 January 1722

Forename	Surname	Precinct	Livery	Votes received	
				Poll	Scrutiny
SIMON	ANDREWS			228	
THOMAS	PESTELL			144	130
JOHN	MARTYN			140	126
RICHARD	WRIGHT			136	121
JAMES	NUTCHER			132	116
ZOROBABEL	CROUCH			125	109
Thomas	Wilkenson			121	105
	Walburge			4	

Source: Anon., *A true account of the total of the poll for common councilmen for the ward of Coleman Street* [London, 1722].

Table 8.3.12.3
Poll for common councilmen of Coleman Street, 10 January 1737

Forename	Surname	Precinct	Livery	Votes received	
				Poll	Scrutiny
JOHN	LLOYD			124	N
	Markham			102	(N-11)

Source: *Old Whig*, 23 December 1736; *Read's Weekly Journal*, 22 January 1737.

Table 8.3.12.4
Poll for common councilman of Coleman Street, 24 October 1758

Forename	Surname	Precinct	Livery	Votes received
FRANCIS	BAKER			65
William	Bishop			36

Source: *Whitehall Evening Post*, 24 October 1758.

Table 8.3.12.5
Poll for common councilmen of Coleman Street, 8 January 1759

Forename	Surname	Precinct	Livery	Votes received
JAMES	KETTILBY		APO	118
ROGER	STAPLES			114
FRANCIS	BAKER			109
HENRY	WHITRIDGE			106
RICHARD	STRATTON			102
WILLIAM	BISHOP			95
John	Saffory		Hab	78

Source: *London Evening Post*, 21 December 1758.

Table 8.3.12.6
Poll for common councilmen of Coleman Street, 7 January 1765

Forename	Surname	Precinct	Livery	Votes received
JAMES	KETTILBY		Apo	114
JOHN	SAFFORY		Hab	113
ROBERT	SHANK		Scr	107
DAVID	MORRIS			107
THOMAS	SMITH		Dis	105
FRANCIS	BAKER			100
William	Bishop		Sad	97
William	Hanscomb			58

Source: *London Chronicle*, 22 December 1764.

Table 8.3.12.7
Poll for beadle of Coleman Street, 24 December 1765

Forename	Surname	Votes received	
		Poll	Scrutiny
JOHN	TOWNSEND	134	128
Joseph	Williams	139	121

Source: *Gazetteer and New Daily Advertiser*, 23 December 1765.

Table 8.3.12.8 Poll for alderman of Coleman Street, 5 November 1773

Forename	Surname	Livery	Votes received
ROBERT	PECKHAM		112
Stephen	Sayre		37

Source: Beaven, i, p. 112.

Table 8.3.12.9
Poll for common councilmen of Coleman Street, 10 January 1785

Forename	Surname	Precinct	Livery	Votes received
THOMAS	RUSSELL		Car	37
WILLIAM	CHAPMAN		Arm	37
ROBERT	WINBOLT		Gol	34
HENRY	COTHERY		Inn	33
WILLIAM	LEWIS		Car	31
DAVID	BALDY		Glo	30
John	Jacobs		Joi	18

Source: *Gazetteer and New Daily Advertiser*, 22 December 1784

Table 8.3.12.10
Poll for common councilmen of Coleman Street, 7 January 1788

Forename	Surname	Precinct	Livery	Votes received
WILLIAM	CHAPMAN		Arm	84
THOMAS	RUSSELL		Car	84
HENRY	COTHERY		Inn	67
THOMAS	PEAKE		Plu	67
DAVID	BALDY		Glo	59
WILLIAM	BOLTON		Dye	55
Thomas	Hurd			38

Source: *Whitehall Evening Post*, 22 December 1787.

Table 8.3.12.11
Poll for common councilmen of Coleman Street, 10 January 1791

Forename	Surname	Precinct	Livery	Votes received
THOMAS	RUSSELL		Car	122
WILLIAM	ROLFE		Gol	120
SAMUEL	DRAPER		Plu	116
RICHARD	DONNE		Met	115
WILLIAM	CHAPMAN		Arm	112
JOHN	RUSSELL		Glo	95
Henry	Cothery		Inn	74
David	Baldy		Glo	43
William	Bolton			33

Source: *Whitehall Evening Post*, 23 December 1790.

Table 8.3.12.12
Poll for common councilmen of Coleman Street, 9 January 1792

Forename	Surname	Precinct	Livery	Votes received
WILLIAM	CHAPMAN		Arm	141
THOMAS	RUSSELL		Car	136
SAMUEL	DRAPER		Plu	127
WILLIAM	ROLFE		Gol	123
RICHARD	DONNE		Met	140
JOHN	RUSSELL		Glo	101
Henry	Cothery		Inn	87
David	Baldy		Glo	28

Source: *Lloyd's Evening Post*, 24-26 December 1791.

Table 8.3.12.13
Poll for common councilmen of Coleman Street, 11 January 1796

Forename	Surname	Precinct	Livery	Votes received
RICHARD	DONNE		Met	95
HENRY	SOAMES		Tal	92
THOMAS	RUSSELL		Car	91
SAMUEL	DRAPER		Plu	91
WILLIAM	CHAPMAN		Arm	85
JONATHAN	SADLER		Pai	76
David	Baldy		Glo	51

Source: *Oracle and Public Advertiser*, 24 December 1795.

Table 8.3.12.14
Poll for common councilmen of Coleman Street, 9 January 1797

Forename	Surname	Precinct	Livery	Votes received	
				Poll	Scrutiny
RICHARD	DONNE		Met		
HENRY	SOAMES		Tal		
SAMUEL	DRAPER		Plu		
JONATHAN	SADLER		Pai		
WILLIAM	EDWARDS		Fis		
JOHN	WEST		Gir		
William	Chapman		Arm		
Thomas	Russell		Car		

Source: *Oracle and Public Advertiser*, 9 January 1797.

Table 8.3.12.15
Poll for common councilmen of Coleman Street, 11 January 1802

Forename	Surname	Precinct	Livery	Votes received
RICHARD	DONNE		Met	137
NATHANIEL	DAVIES		Mus	135
FRANCIS	PAYNTER		Nee	130
JONATHAN	SADLER		Pai	125
JOHN	WEST		Gir	117
WILLIAM	EDWARDS		Fis	96
William	Chapman		Arm	90

Source: *Morning Chronicle*, 24 December 1801.

Table 8.3.12.16
Poll for common councilmen of Coleman Street, 10 January 1803

Forename	Surname	Precinct	Livery	Votes received
FRANCIS	PAYNTER		Nee	146
RICHARD	DONNE		Met	141
NATHANIEL	DAVIES		Mus	139
JOHN	WEST		Gir	135
JONATHAN	SADLER		Pai	131
WILLIAM	EDWARDS		Fis	103
William	Chapman		Arm	99

Source: *The Times*, 24 December 1802.

Table 8.3.12.17
Poll for alderman of Coleman Street, 28 May 1808

Forename	Surname	Livery	Votes received
WILLIAM	PLOMER	Vin	88
Richard	Phillips	Sta	54

Source: Beaven i, p. 112.

Table 8.3.12.18
Poll for common councilmen of Coleman Street, 8 January 1816

Forename	Surname	Precinct	Livery	Votes received
FRANCIS	PAYNTER		Nee	107
JOHN	WEST		Gir	102
NATHANIEL	DAVIES		Mus	101
JOHN	LETTS		Met	101
WILLIAM	MERCER		Gol	97
WILLIAM	CHAPMAN		Arm	70
Charles	Walker		Sta	32

Source: *Morning Chronicle*, 25 December 1815.

Table 8.3.12.19
Poll for common councilmen of Coleman Street, 9 January 1826

Forename	Surname	Precinct	Livery	Votes received
WILLIAM	HUNTER		Uph	147
JOHN	WEST		Gir	135
JEREMIAH	CARTER		Cop	133
WARREN STORMS	HALE		Tal	109
JOHN	BLEADEN		Sta	102
DAVID	ALLEN		Pai	98
James	Griffiths		Pai	78
	Jones			49

Source: *St James's Chronicle*, 22-24 December 1825.

Table 8.3.12.20
Poll for common councilmen of Coleman Street, 8 January 1827

Forename	Surname	Precinct	Livery	Votes received
WILLIAM	HUNTER		Uph	121
JEREMIAH	CARTER		Cop	115
WILLIAM STORMS	HALE		Tal	110
JOHN	WEST		Gir	107
DAVID	ALLEN		Pai	104
JAMES	GRIFFITHS		Pai	87
John	Bleaden		Sta	75

Source: *Morning Chronicle*, 25 December 1826.

Table 8.3.12.21
Poll for common councilmen of Coleman Street, 12 January 1829

Forename	Surname	Precinct	Livery	Votes received
JEREMIAH	CARTER		Cop	173
WILLIAM	HUNTER		Uph	171
THOMAS HENRY	HALL		Fel	169
WARREN STORMS	HALE		Tal	159
DAVID	ALLEN		Pai	146
JOHN	BLEADEN		Sta	133
	Peck			127
	Brachin			66

Source: *Morning Chronicle*, 25 December 1828.

8.3.13 Cordwainer, 1716-1832: 14 polls

(8 common councilmen; 140 freemen householders in 1833)

Table 8.3.13.1
Poll for common councilmen of Cordwainer, 9 January 1716

Forename	Surname	Precinct	Livery	Votes received
JOHN	BROWNE			
JOHN	CASBIRD			
HENRY	CLARKE			

Source: LMA COL/CC/13/01/012, return dated 15 January 1716.

Table 8.3.13.2
Poll for common councilmen of Cordwainer, 12 January 1741

Forename	Surname	Precinct	Livery	Votes received
JOSIAH	COLEBROOK			98
RICHARD	BLUNT			92
JOHN	DAY			92
JOHN	LANCASHIRE			91
WILLIAM	PARKINS			91
GEORGE	BOHEEM			87
JOSHUA	MARRIOTT			84
ROUND	LAMPARD			77
George	Smith			76
Francis	Grizell			75
Henry	Spencer			73
John	Major			72
Nehemiah	Ringe			71
William	Soden			67
Abraham	Winterbottom			64
Percival	Pott			64

Source: *London Evening Post*, 23 December 1740.

Table 8.3.13.3
Poll for common councilmen of Cordwainer, 8 January 1770

Forename	Surname	Precinct	Livery	Votes received
WILLIAM	POOLE		Wea	116
THOMAS	BAKER		Gro	108
WILLIAM	KIRKMAN		Sal	93
LAKE	YOUNG		Gla	90
MATTHEW	HOWARD		Mer	81
GEORGE	HAYTER		Sal	78
JOHN	GUY		Dis	78
CLEMENT S.	STRONG		Sal	68
	Hanning			65
	Yates			56
	Board			51
	Peart			47
	Middleditch			46

Source: *St James's Chronicle*, 25 December 1769.

Table 8.3.13.4
Poll for election of alderman of Cordwainer, 22 July 1774

Forename	Surname	Precinct	Livery	Votes received
GEORGE	HAYLEY		Arm	76
John	Hart		Ski	31

Source: Beaven, i, p. 120.

Table 8.3.13.5
Poll for common councilmen of Cordwainer, 8 January 1776

Forename	Surname	Precinct	Livery	Votes received
WILLIAM	POOLE		Cor	45
WILLIAM	STONE		Joi	45
LAKE	YOUNG		Glz	45
JOHN	PEART		Uph	44
SAMUEL	HANNING		Car	44
THOMAS	BOARD			43
STEPHEN	YATES			42
JOHN	CHAPMAN			39
Sainsbury	Sibley			8

Source: *London Chronicle*, 21 December 1775.

Table 8.3.13.6
Poll for alderman of Cordwainer, 1 September 1781

Forename	Surname	Livery	Votes received
BERNARD	TURNER	Mus	57
William	Pickett	Gol	22

Source: Beaven, i, p. 120.

Table 8.3.13.7
Poll for common councilmen of Cordwainer, 11 January 1808

Forename	Surname	Precinct	Livery	Votes received
JOHN	HARWOOD			180
WILLIAM	ROW		Ski	180
EDWARD	KEMBLE		Sal	100
CHARLES W.	HICK		Fel	100
GUSTAVE A.	SMITH		Fis	92
JAMES	TRIMBEY		Dra	81
RICHARD	ABBEY		Pat	74
SAMUEL	JONES			68
Thomas	Templeman		Wax	66
Aaron	Watson		Whe	65
William	Jones		Gir	55
	Blake			52

Source: *Morning Chronicle*, 24 December 1807.

Table 8.3.13.8
Poll for common councilmen of Cordwainer, 9 January 1809

Forename	Surname	Precinct	Livery	Votes received
JOHN	HAMMAN		Gir	105
EDWARD	KEMBLE		Sal	105
GUSTAVE A.	SMITH		Fis	103
WILLIAM	ROW		Ski	100
RICHARD	ABBEY		Pat	91
AARON	WATSON		Whe	90
JAMES	TRIMBEY		Dra	86
CHARLES W.	HICK		Fel	79
William	Jones		Gir	56
	Blake			44

Source: *Morning Chronicle*, 24 December 1808.

Table 8.3.13.9
Poll for common councilmen of Cordwainer, 8 January 1810

Forename	Surname	Precinct	Livery	Votes received
GUSTAV ADOLPH	SMITH		Fis	117
CHARLES W.	HICK		Fel	115
EDWARD	KEMBLE		Sal	102
JOHN	HAMMAN		Gir	100
WILLIAM	ROW		Ski	94
RICHARD	ABBEY		Pat	92
WILLIAM	JONES		Gir	83
JAMES	TRIMBEY		Dra	81
William	Watson		Whe	70
Thomas	Bedder			66
	Blake			47
William	Jones		Gir	30
	Gardner			27
	Smith			20

Source: *Morning Chronicle*, 25 December 1809.

Table 8.3.13.10
Poll for common councilman of Cordwainer, 26 May 1812

Forename	Surname	Precinct	Livery	Votes received
AARON	WATSON		Whe	57
Thomas	Bedder			47

Source: LMA CLC/W/HE/001/Ms. 08634/001.

Table 8.3.13.11
Poll for common councilmen of Cordwainer, 10 January 1820

Forename	Surname	Precinct	Livery	Votes received
JOHN	HAMMAN		Gir	91
WILLIAM	ROW		Ski	88
CHARLES W.	HICK		Fel	87
GEORGE	STEVENSON		Sta	87
GUSTAV A.	SMITH		Fis	85
AARON	WATSON		Whe	83
RICHARD	ABBEY		Pat	78
JAMES	TRIMBEY		Dra	73
	Wood			42

Source: LMA CLC/W/HE/001/Ms. 08634/001.

Table 8.3.13.12
Poll for common councilmen of Cordwainer, 8 January 1821

Forename	Surname	Precinct	Livery	Votes received
RICHARD	ABBEY		Pat	91
GEORGE	STEVENSON		Sta	90
WILLIAM	ROW, SNR		Ski	89
JOHN	HAMMAN		Gir	87
WILLIAM	ROW, JNR		Ski	77
WILLIAM	WATSON		Whe	76
CHARLES W.	HICK		Fel	74
JAMES	TRIMBEY		Dra	71
Nathaniel	Ainger		Met	51

Source: LMA CLC/W/HE/001/Ms. 08634/001.

Table 8.3.13.13
Poll for common councilmen of Cordwainer, 10 January 1831

Forename	Surname	Precinct	Livery	Votes received
JOHN	HAMMAN		Gir	108
WILLIAM	ROW		Ski	100
NATHANIEL	AINGER		Met	106
THOMAS	WOOD		Fra	106
GEORGE	LAMB		Gls	102
WILLIAM T.	HEATH		Gol	91
SAMUEL	HALL		Hab	81
JAMES	CULVERWELL		Wax	69
Thomas George	Williams		Nee	57

Source: LMA CLC/W/HE/001/Ms. 08634/001.

Table 8.3.13.14
Poll for common councilmen of Cordwainer, 9 January 1832

Forename	Surname	Precinct	Livery	Votes received
JOHN	HAMMAN		Gir	92
THOMAS	WOOD		Fra	90
SAMUEL	HALL		Hab	85
GEORGE	LAMB		Gls	82
JAMES	CULVERWELL		Wax	80
WILLIAM T.	HEATH		Gol	80
THOMAS G.	WILLIAMS		Nee	71
HENRY	PHILLIPS		Iro	57
William	Croucher		Glz	50
Thomas	Lott		Bak	32

Source: LMA CLC/W/HE/001/Ms. 08634/001.

8.3.14 Cornhill, 1712-1820: nine polls

(6 common councilmen; 101 freeman householders in 1831)

Table 8.3.14.1
Poll for aldermanic candidates of Cornhill, 14 January 1712

Forename	Surname	Precinct	Livery	Votes received
JOHN	WARD			88
THOMAS	SCAWEN		Fis	88
Richard	Hoare			74
Samuel	Ongley			74

Source: LMA COL/WD/03/040; Beaven, ii, p. 123.

Table 8.3.14.2
Poll for common councilmen of Cornhill, 11 January 1720

Forename	Surname	Precinct	Livery	Votes received
MATTHEW	SNABLIN			108
HENRY	BOWATER			108
THOMAS	RILEY			107
JOHN	COX			107
WILLIAM	HYDE			106
EDWARD	DODD			104
Richard	Chauncey			84
John	Wood			83
	Blunt			82
	Goddard			81
	Pate			80
	Elwick			77

Source: *Post Boy*, 22 December 1719.

Table 8.3.14.3
Poll for common councilman of Cornhill, 11 February 1737

Forename	Surname	Precinct	Livery	Votes received
JOHN	SHIPTON			60
John	Young			35

Source: *London Evening Post*, 12 February 1737.

Table 8.3.14.4
Poll for common councilmen of Cornhill, 8 January 1770

Forename	Surname	Precinct	Livery	Votes received
WILLIAM	DAWSON		Met	77
HENRY	PARKER		Sta	66
FRANCIS	ELLIS		Gro	64
THOMAS	COGAN		Pla	63
JAMES	WALTON		Met	60
WILLIAM	SHENTON		Met	59
Joseph	Vaux			30
Joseph	Heylin			29
Arthur George	Farr			28
James	Champneys			26
John	Seaber			24

Source: *Middlesex Journal*, 21 December 1769.

Table 8.3.14.5
Poll for alderman of Cornhill, 17 May 1782

Forename	Surname	Livery	Votes received
WILLIAM	PICKETT	Gol	62
William	Nicholson	Nee	52

Source: Beaven, i, p. 126.

Table 8.3.14.6
Poll for common councilmen of Cornhill, 6 January 1783

Forename	Surname	Precinct	Livery	Votes received
SAMUEL	BIRCH		Cok	101
HENRY	PARKER		Sta	98
JOHN	LODGE		Clw	82
WILLIAM	SHENTON		Met	77
JACOB	BIRD		Glo	64
JAMES	BATE		Sta	63
William	Angel		Clw	54
	Turner			13

Source: *Morning Chronicle*, 24 December 1782.

Table 8.3.14.7
Poll for common councilmen of Cornhill, 6 January 1806

Forename	Surname	Precinct	Livery	Votes received
SAMUEL	BIRCH		Cok	67
WILLIAM	ANGEL		Clw	55
JAMES	JACKS		Met	60
CHARLES	CHAPMAN		Cor	59
THOMAS	BLUNT		Nee	57
PAUL PHILIP	BARRAUD		Clm	59
Joseph	Norville			35
William	Costeker			22

Source: *Morning Chronicle*, 25 December 1805.

Table 8.3.14.8
Poll for common councilmen of Cornhill, 6 January 1817

Forename	Surname	Precinct	Livery	Votes received
CHARLES	CHAPMAN		Cor	70
LUCAS	BIRCH		Cok	67
THOMAS	BLUNT		Nee	65
WILLIAM	ANGEL		Clw	63
PAUL PHILIP	BARRAUD		Clm	60
JAMES	JACKS		Met	59
Edward	Eyton		Inn	32
	Nicholson			29

Source: *Morning Chronicle*, 25 December 1816.

Table 8.3.14.9
Poll for common councilmen of Cornhill, 10 January 1820

Forename	Surname	Precinct	Livery	Votes received
CHARLES	CHAPMAN		Cor	65
LUCAS	BIRCH		Cok	64
JOHN	MAUND		Lor	77
JAMES	JACKS		Met	60
WILLIAM	ANGEL		Clw	63
EDWARD	EYTON		Inn	64
Thomas	Blunt		Nee	44
	Allerston			44
G.	Garrell			39

Source: *Morning Chronicle*, 24 December 1819.

8.3.15 Cripplegate Within, 1723-1831: 26 polls

(8 common councilmen; 222 freeman householders in 1831)

Table 8.3.15.1
Poll for alderman of Cripplegate, 2 May 1723

Forename	Surname	Precinct	Livery	Votes received	
				Poll	Scrutiny
FELIX	FEAST		Bra	623	
John	Williams		Mer	597	

Source: Beaven, i, p. 134.

Table 8.3.15.2
Poll for common councilmen of Cripplegate Within, 7 January 1745

Forename	Surname	Precinct	Livery	Votes received
JOHN	KNIGHT	St Peter		181
Robert	Coverly			140

Source: *Daily Advertiser*, 22 December 1744.

Table 8.3.15.3
Poll for common councilmen of Cripplegate Within, 7 January 1754

Forename	Surname	Precinct	Livery	Votes received
ROBERT	ELLIOTT			238
THOMAS	ATKINS			234
EDWARD	SADLER			231
JOHN	KNIGHT			228
JOHN	CARTWRIGHT			228
RICHARD	MOLINEUX			228
ROBERT	MARKLAND			224
HOLLES	BULL			220
Peter	Moulson			141
	Ford			101

Source: *Public Advertiser*, 22 December 1753.

Table 8.3.15.4
Poll for common councilmen of Cripplegate Within, 7 January 1760

Forename	Surname	Precinct	Livery	Votes received
PETER	MOULSON			N
	Garrard			(N-9)

Source: *Whitehall Evening Post*, 20-22 December 1759.

Table 8.3.15.5
Poll for common councilmen of Cripplegate Within, 7 January 1782

Forename	Surname	Precinct	Livery	Votes received
WILLIAM	GIFFORD		Lea	157
RICHARD	MATHEWS		Cop	153
HENRY	WHITE		Fis	152
EDWARD	DOWLING		Cut	152
JAMES	SIMPSON		Glz	151
ISAAC	MATHER		Plu	149
THOMAS	VALLANCE		Sta	140
JAMES	BIRT		Uph	137
William	Brookes			108

Source: *Morning Chronicle*, 25 December 1781.

Table 8.3.15.6
Poll for common councilmen of Cripplegate Within, 11 January 1796

Forename	Surname	Precinct	Livery	Votes received
WILLIAM	HARDY		Gol	162
WILLIAM	GIFFORD		Lea	160
JAMES	BIRT		Uph	159
CHARLES	HIGDEN		Cur	159
HENRY	WHITE		Fis	152
THOMAS	VALLANCE		Sta	147
WILLIAM	SIMPSON		Glz	138
JONATHAN	DELVER		Fle	135
Edward	Dowling, snr		Cut	84
Edward	Dowling, jnr		Cut	58
	Robinson			48
	Thomas			44

Source: LMA CLC/W/HH/001/Ms. 01561/001; *Oracle and Public Advertiser*, 24 December 1795; *Morning Post*, 24 December 1795; and *Lloyd's Evening Post*, 23 December 1795.

Table 8.3.15.7
Poll for common councilmen of Cripplegate Within, 7 January 1799

Forename	Surname	Precinct	Livery	Votes received
WILLIAM	HARDY		Gol	130
JONATHAN	DELVER		Fle	117
CHARLES	HIGDEN		Cur	117
JAMES	BIRT		Uph	113
HENRY	WHITE		Fis	111
THOMAS	VALLANCE		Sta	108
GEORGE	SMITH		Gol	107
EDWARD	DOWLING, JNR		Cut	78
William	Simpson		Glz	69

Source: *True Briton*, 24 December 1798.

Table 8.3.15.8
Poll for common councilmen of Cripplegate Within, 6 January 1800

Forename	Surname	Precinct	Livery	Votes received
WILLIAM	HARDY		Gol	159
HENRY	WHITE		Fis	155
JAMES	BIRT		Uph	152
CHARLES	HIGDEN		Cur	152
JONATHAN	DELVER		Fle	150
GEORGE	SMITH		Gol	147
THOMAS	VALLANCE		Sta	145
EDWARD	DOWLING, JNR		Cut	100
James	Simpson		Glz	80

Source: *Morning Post*, 25 December 1799.

Table 8.3.15.9
Poll for common councilmen of Cripplegate Within, 10 January 1803

Forename	Surname	Precinct	Livery	Votes received
WILLIAM	HARDY		Gol	128
THOMAS	VALLANCE		Sta	125
JAMES	BIRT		Uph	122
JONATHAN	DELVER		Fle	122
CHARLES	HIGDEN		Cur	121
JOHN	TAINE		Car	117
HENRY	WHITE		Fis	116
WILLIAM	KERL		Cur	105
	Tagg			71

Source: *Morning Chronicle*, 23 December 1802.

Table 8.3.15.10
Poll for common councilmen of Cripplegate Within, 8 January 1810

Forename	Surname	Precinct	Livery	Votes received
WILLIAM	HEYGATE		Met	161
WILLIAM	KERL		Cur	147
JONATHAN	DELVER		Fle	141
WILLIAM	HARDY		Gol	139
HENRY	WHITE		Fis	124
JAMES	BIRT		Uph	123
STEPHEN	HABBERTON		Whe	120
THOMAS	VALLANCE		Sta	116
William	Waterhouse		Inn	115
Charles	Higden		Cur	107
Thomas	Nightingale			91
John	Docksey			82
Thomas	Palmer			74

Note: Return of Habberton was declared void as he was not a freeman.
Source: LMA CLC/W/HH/001/Ms. 01561/001.

Table 8.3.15.11
Poll for common councilman of Cripplegate Within, 16 February 1810

Forename	Surname	Precinct	Livery	Votes received
FELTON	MATHEW		Cop	89
Stephen	Habberton		Whe	72

Source: LMA CLC/W/HH/001/Ms. 01561/001.

Table 8.3.15.12
Poll for common councilmen of Cripplegate Within, 7 January 1811

Forename	Surname	Precinct	Livery	Votes received
WILLIAM	HEYGATE		Met	106
JONATHAN	DELVER		Fle	96
THOMAS	VALLANCE		Sta	95
WILLIAM	KERL		Cur	95
WILLIAM	HARDY		Gol	90
STEPHEN	HABBERTON		Whe	82
WILLIAM	WATERHOUSE		Inn	74
JAMES	BIRT		Uph	69
Felton	Mathew		Cop	47

Source: LMA CLC/W/HH/001/Ms. 01561/001.

Table 8.3.15.13
Poll for common councilmen of Cripplegate Within, 6 January 1812

Forename	Surname	Precinct	Livery	Votes received
WILLIAM	WATERHOUSE		Inn	168
WILLIAM	KERL		Cur	158
WILLIAM	HEYGATE		Met	157
WILLIAM	HARDY		Gol	156
THOMAS	VALLANCE		Sta	155
STEPHEN	HABBERTON		Whe	152
JAMES	BIRT		Uph	149
JONATHAN	DELVER		Fle	142
Felton	Mathew		Cop	101
Edward	Heath		Sta	52

Source: LMA CLC/W/HH/001/Ms. 01561/001.

Table 8.3.15.14
Poll for common councilman of Cripplegate Within, 22 May 1812

Forename	Surname	Precinct	Livery	Votes received
FELTON	MATHEW		Cop	77
Edward	Heath		Sta	33

Source: LMA CLC/W/HH/001/Ms. 01561/001.

Table 8.3.15.15
Poll for common councilmen of Cripplegate Within, 11 January 1813

Forename	Surname	Precinct	Livery	Votes received
WILLIAM	WATERHOUSE		Inn	31
STEPHEN	HABBERTON		Whe	31
JONATHAN	DELVER		Fle	29
WILLIAM	KERL		Cur	28
THOMAS	VALLANCE		Sta	27
JAMES	BIRT		Uph	26
FELTON	MATHEW		Cop	24
WILLIAM	HARDY		Gol	23
Edward	Heath		Sta	9

Source: LMA CLC/W/HH/001/Ms. 01561/001.

Table 8.3.15.16
Poll for common councilmen of Cripplegate Within, 8 January 1816

Forename	Surname	Precinct	Livery	Votes received
WILLIAM	KERL		Cur	152
STEPHEN	HABBERTON		Whe	144
THOMAS	VALLANCE		Sta	143
WILLIAM	WATERHOUSE		Inn	143
FRANCIS	TOWERS		Wea	135
ARCHIBALD	HERRON		Wea	135
JAMES	BIRT		Uph	111
THOMAS	KIDDER		Bar	100
Felton	Mathew		Cop	82
Jonathan	Delver		Fle	61

Source: LMA CLC/W/HH/001/Ms. 01561/001.

Table 8.3.15.17
Poll for common councilmen of Cripplegate Within, 12 January 1818

Forename	Surname	Precinct	Livery	Votes received
THOMAS	VALLANCE		Sta	143
FRANCIS	TOWERS		Wea	144
WILLIAM	WATERHOUSE		Inn	139
THOMAS	KIDDER		Bar	134
WILLIAM	KERL		Cur	132
JONATHAN	DELVER		Fle	130
STEPHEN	HABBERTON		Whe	122
EDWARD	HEATH		Sta	105
Charles	Eicke		Gir	58
James	Birt		Uph	57

Source: LMA CLC/W/HH/001/Ms. 01561/001; *Morning Chronicle*, 25 December 1817.

Table 8.3.15.18
Poll for common councilman of Cripplegate Within, 9 September 1818

Forename	Surname	Precinct	Livery	Votes received
CHARLES	EICKE		Gir	65
Francis	Field		Gol	60

Source: LMA CLC/W/HH/001/Ms. 01561/001.

Table 8.3.15.19
Poll for beadle of Cripplegate Within, 19 April 1820

Forename	Surname	Votes received
JAMES	HEATHER	220
John	Glynn	141

Source: LMA CLC/W/HH/001/Ms. 01561/001.

Table 8.3.15.20
Poll for common councilmen of Cripplegate Within, 8 January 1821

Forename	Surname	Precinct	Livery	Votes received
THOMAS	VALLANCE		Sta	120
WILLIAM	WATERHOUSE		Inn	119
FRANCIS	FIELD		Gol	114
WILLIAM	KERL		Cur	112
FRANCIS	TOWERS		Wea	111
EDWARD	HEATH		Sta	105
CHARLES	EICKE		Gir	95
WILLIAM	CAPEL		Bow	87
Thomas	Kidder		Bar	42
Joseph	Alcock			41

Source: LMA CLC/W/HH/001/Ms. 01561/001.

Table 8.3.15.21
Poll for common councilmen of Cripplegate Within, 12 January 1824

Forename	Surname	Precinct	Livery	Votes received
WILLIAM	KERL		Cur	129
WILLIAM	WATERHOUSE		Inn	113
FRANCIS	FIELD		Gol	113
LEONARD	WILLSHIRE		Spe	111
JAMES C.	FORSYTH		Wea	107
THOMAS	GATES		Gol	98
HUGH	HERRON		Wea	97
BENJAMIN	SMITH		Bak	83
William	Capel		Bow	75
Frederick	Thorowgood			46

Source: LMA CLC/W/HH/001/Ms. 01561/001.

Table 8.3.15.22
Poll for common councilmen of Cripplegate Within, 8 January 1827

Forename	Surname	Precinct	Livery	Votes received
WILLIAM	KERL		Cur	125
BENJAMIN	SMITH		Bak	113
JAMES	PALMER		Pla	110
LEONARD	WILLSHIRE		Spe	100
WILLIAM	WATERHOUSE		Inn	97
SAMUEL	BEETON		Pat	97
FRANCIS	FIELD		Gol	76
JOHN OBADIAH	JAQUES		Nee	74
William	Brass		Whe	67
James	Richardson		Inn	50
Thomas	Gates		Gol	17

Source: LMA CLC/W/HH/001/Ms. 01561/001.

Table 8.3.15.23
Poll for common councilmen of Cripplegate Within, 7 January 1828

Forename	Surname	Precinct	Livery	Votes received
WILLIAM	KERL		Cur	150
BENJAMIN	SMITH		Bak	126
JOHN OBADIAH	JAQUES		Nee	126
LEONARD	WILLSHIRE		Spe	121
SAMUEL	BEETON		Pat	119
JAMES	PALMER		Pla	114
WILLIAM	WATERHOUSE		Inn	104
JAMES	RICHARDSON		Inn	98
Francis	Field		Gol	89
William	Brass		Whe	79
	Allcock			0

Source: LMA CLC/W/HH/001/Ms. 01561/001.

Table 8.3.15.24
Poll for common councilmen of Cripplegate Within, 12 January 1829

Forename	Surname	Precinct	Livery	Votes received
SAMUEL	BEETON		Pat	144
WILLIAM	KERL		Cur	143
JAMES	PALMER		Pla	142
JOHN OBADIAH	JAQUES		Nee	137
WILLIAM	WATERHOUSE		Inn	135
BENJAMIN	SMITH		Bak	134
LEONARD	WILLSHIRE		Spe	131
WILLIAM	BRASS		Whe	96
William	Ireland		Cur	80
James	Richardson		Inn	76

Source: LMA CLC/W/HH/001/Ms. 01561/001.

Table 8.3.15.25
Poll for common councilmen of Cripplegate Within, 11 January 1830

Forename	Surname	Precinct	Livery	Votes received
WILLIAM	KERL		Cur	150
SAMUEL	BEETON		Pat	143
JAMES	PALMER		Pla	140
JOHN OBADIAH	JAQUES		Nee	137
THOMAS	ORCHART		Bak	136
LEONARD	WILLSHIRE		Spe	122
WILLIAM	IRELAND		Cur	119
JAMES	RICHARDSON		Inn	106
William	Brass		Whe	102

Source: LMA CLC/W/HH/001/Ms. 01561/001.

Table 8.3.15.26
Poll for common councilmen of Cripplegate Within, 10 January 1831

Forename	Surname	Precinct	Livery	Votes received
JAMES	PALMER		Pla	130
SAMUEL	BEETON		Pat	129
THOMAS	ORCHART		Bak	127
WILLIAM	KERL		Cur	122
JAMES	RICHARDSON		Inn	120
JOHN OBADIAH	JAQUES		Nee	117
LEONARD	WILLSHIRE		Spe	112
WILLIAM	BRASS		Whe	99
William	Ireland		Cur	76

Source: LMA CLC/W/HH/001/Ms. 01561/001.

8.3.16 Cripplegate Without, 1720-1831: 20 polls

(4 common councilmen until 1825 and 8 from 1826; 434 freeman householders in 1831)

Table 8.3.16.1
Poll for common councilmen of Cripplegate Without, 11 January 1720

Forename	Surname	Precinct	Livery	Votes received
FELIX	FEAST			
EDMUND	JOYNER			
THOMAS	CATMUR			
RICHARD	FARRINGTON			

Source: *Weekly Journal*, 2 January 1720.

Table 8.3.16.2
Poll for common councilmen of Cripplegate Without, 8 January 1722

Forename	Surname	Precinct	Livery	Votes received	
				Poll	Scrutiny
JOHN	STYLES				260
JOHN	HARRIS				260
NATHANIEL	PHILIPS				260
					260
Thomas	Catmur			316	212
Richard	Farrington			316	212
Samuel	Cox			316	212
Henry	Southouse			316	212

Source: LMA COL/CC/13/01/025.

Table 8.3.16.3
Poll for common councilmen of Cripplegate Without, 7 January 1723

Forename	Surname	Precinct	Livery	Votes received	
				Poll	Scrutiny
THOMAS	CATMUR				
RICHARD	FARRINGTON				
HENRY	SOUTHOUSE				
SAMUEL	COX				
Nathaniel	Phillips				
John	Harris				
Samuel	Acton				
William	Tayleur				

Source: LMA COL/CC/13/01/012.

Table 8.3.16.4
Poll for common councilmen of Cripplegate Without, 10 January 1726

Forename	Surname	Precinct	Livery	Votes received	
				Poll	Scrutiny
RICHARD	FARRINGTON			201	
HENRY	SOUTHOUSE			183	
RICHARD	BARNWELL			184	
THOMAS	PIDDINGTON			195	
Nathaniel	Phillips			148	
Richard	Fowler			102	
John	Delafield			110	
David	Jones			113	

Source: *Parker's Penny Post*, 24 December 1725.

Table 8.3.16.5
Poll for common councilmen of Cripplegate Without, 10 January 1732

Forename	Surname	Precinct	Livery	Votes received
RICHARD	FARRINGTON			212
WILLIAM	COOPER			209
JOHN	DEERON			194
WILLIAM	MEREDITH			194
Thomas	Tew			194

Source: *Daily Courant*, 25 December 1731.

Table 8.3.16.6
Poll for common councilmen of Cripplegate Without, 7 January 1745

Forename	Surname	Precinct	Livery	Votes received	
				Poll	Scrutiny
Thomas	Bourne				
JOHN	DELL				

Note: Bourne died between the poll and the declaration of the scrutiny.
Source: *Daily Advertiser*, 3 January 1745.

Table 8.3.16.7
Poll for common councilman of Cripplegate Without, 2 March 1745

Forename	Surname	Precinct	Livery	Votes received
	COOPER			148
	Dell			129

Source: *Universal Spectator*, 2 March 1745.

Table 8.3.16.8
Poll for common councilman of Cripplegate Without, 12 August 1771

Forename	Surname	Precinct	Livery	Votes received
HENRY	BANNER		Joi	155
	Barnes			120

Source: *General Evening Post*, 13 August 1771.

Table 8.3.16.9
Poll for common councilmen of Cripplegate Without, 8 January 1776

Forename	Surname	Precinct	Livery	Votes received
JOHN	JONES		Fou	213
JOHN	BANNER		Plu	187
HENRY	BANNER		Joi	185
ROBERT	FRENCH		Tal	184
Mark	Jefferson			116

Source: *London Evening Post*, 23 December 1775.

Table 8.3.16.10
Poll for common councilmen of Cripplegate Without, 10 January 1780

Forename	Surname	Precinct	Livery	Votes received
JOHN	BANNER		Plu	290
HENRY	BANNER		Joi	289
ROBERT	FRENCH		Tal	284
JOHN	HALE		Bre	280
John	Jones		Fou	209

Source: *Public Ledger*, 24 December 1779.

Table 8.3.16.11
Poll for common councilmen of Cripplegate Without, 12 January 1795

Forename	Surname	Precinct	Livery	Votes received	
				Poll	Scrutiny
ROBERT	CLARK		Inn	299	272
NICHOLAS	BROWNING		Bak	300	265
THOMAS	SIMMONDS		Bre	262	245
JOHN	KNIGHT		Gol	217	215
Thomas	Dalby		But	226	125
John	Banner		Plu	165	99

Source: *London Packet*, 24 December 1794; 21 January 1795.

Table 8.3.16.12
Poll for common councilmen of Cripplegate Without, 11 January 1796

Forename	Surname	Precinct	Livery	Votes received
THOMAS	SIMMONDS		Bre	270
THOMAS	DALBY		But	226
ROBERT	CLARK		Inn	219
NICHOLAS	BROWNING		Bak	201
John	Knight		Gol	141

Source: *Morning Post*, 24 December 1795.

Table 8.3.16.13
Poll for common councilmen of Cripplegate Without, 10 January 1803

Forename	Surname	Precinct	Livery	Votes received
MATTHEW	WOOD		Fis	260
THOMAS	SIMMONDS		Bre	251
SAMUEL	LAKE		Bre	241
T.	DOLLY		Clm	233
	Browne			117
Robert	Clark		Inn	59

Source: *Morning Chronicle*, 24 December 1802.

Table 8.3.16.14
Poll for common councilmen of Cripplegate Without, 11 January 1808

Forename	Surname	Precinct	Livery	Votes received
RICHARD	DIXON		Inn	307
T.	DOLLY		Clm	280
JAMES	DACRE		Clw	273
GODFREY	BROWN			255
W.R.H.	Brown			235
	Gwyer			14

Source: *Morning Chronicle*, 24 December 1807.

Table 8.3.16.15
Poll for common councilmen of Cripplegate Without, 8 January 1810

Forename	Surname	Precinct	Livery	Votes received
RICHARD	DIXON		Inn	289
JOHN	CROUCH		Nee	258
JOHN	PULLEN		Joi	200
JAMES	DACRE		Clw	193
T.	Dolly		Clm	143

Source: *Morning Chronicle*, 25 December 1809.

Table 8.3.16.16
Poll for common councilmen of Cripplegate Without, 7 January 1811

Forename	Surname	Precinct	Livery	Votes received
RICHARD	DIXON		Inn	61
JAMES	DACRE		Clw	54
JOHN	PULLEN		Joi	53
JOHN	CROUCH		Nee	52
	Brown			17

Source: *Morning Chronicle*, 22 December 1810.

Table 8.3.16.17
Poll for common councilmen of Cripplegate Without, 8 January 1816

Forename	Surname	Precinct	Livery	Votes received
JOHN	BROGDEN		Gol	323
JAMES	DACRE		Clw	294
JOHN	PULLEN		Joi	245
JAMES	YELLOWLY		Car	245
Richard	Dixon		Inn	212

Source: *St James's Chronicle*, 23-26 December 1815.

Table 8.3.16.18
Poll for common councilmen of Cripplegate Without, 10 January 1820

Forename	Surname	Precinct	Livery	Votes received
JOHN	BROGDEN		Gol	312
JOHN	PULLEN		Joi	309
RICHARD L.	JONES		Bre	280
	CHALLIS			254
James	Yellowly		Car	251
	Banner			174

Source: *Morning Chronicle*, 24 December 1819.

Table 8.3.16.19
Poll for common councilmen of Cripplegate Without, 8 January 1827

Forename	Surname	Precinct	Livery	Votes received
JAMES	YELLOWLY		Car	349
RICHARD L.	JONES		Bre	331
JOHN	PULLEN		Joi	326
EDWIN	ALDERMAN		Clm	279
EDWARD	HALSE		Gir	278
EBENEZER	TAYLOR		Pew	259
JOHN	ATKINSON		Dra	258
H. ERCHARD B.	HAINES		Fis	224
	Stevens			189
	Gregory			108

Source: *Morning Chronicle*, 25 December 1826.

Table 8.3.16.20
Poll for common councilmen of Cripplegate Without, 10 January 1831

Forename	Surname	Precinct	Livery	Votes received
H. ERCHARD B.	HAINES		Fis	271
RICHARD L.	JONES		Bre	261
EDWARD	HALSE		Gir	261
EDWIN	ALDERMAN		Clm	256
JOHN	PULLEN		Joi	242
STEPHEN	CURTIS		Cur	230
JOHN	ATKINSON		Dra	218
JOSEPH	NEWELL		Uph	211
	Case			171

Source: *Morning Chronicle*, 24 December 1830.

8.3.17 Dowgate, 1769-1829: nine polls

(8 common councilmen; 139 freeman householders in 1833)

Table 8.3.17.1
Poll for common councilmen of Dowgate, 9 January 1769

Forename	Surname	Precinct	Livery	Votes received	
				Poll	Scrutiny
ROBERT	HOLDER		Mus		N
William	Gates				(N-7)

Source: *St James's Chronicle*, 5 January 1769.

Table 8.3.17.2
Poll for common councilmen of Dowgate, 6 January 1772

Forename	Surname	Precinct	Livery	Votes received
EDWARD	REYNOLDS		Vin	49
William	Gates			25

Source: *Middlesex Journal*, 21 December 1771.

Table 8.3.17.3
Poll for alderman of Dowgate, 5 January 1773

Forename	Surname	Livery	Votes received
WALTER	RAWLINSON	Gro	63
Robert	Macky	Joi	4

Source: Beaven, i, p. 142.

Table 8.3.17.4
Poll for common councilman of Dowgate, 7 May 1773

Forename	Surname	Precinct	Livery	Votes received
JOHN	PACKMAN		Tal	24
John	Salter			23

Source: *Morning Chronicle*, 8 May 1773.

Table 8.3.17.5
Poll for common councilmen of Dowgate, 10 January 1774

Forename	Surname	Precinct	Livery	Votes received
JOHN	GREENWOOD		Iro	
FRANCIS	HILTON		Dye	
JOHN	HART		Ski	
JOSEPH	STEVENSON		Coo	
ROBERT	HOLDER		Mus	
WILLIAM	GATES		Mas	57
JOHN	PACKMAN		Tal	56
HENRY	JANSON		Fis	55
Edward	Reynolds			36
John	Salter		Plu	34

Source: *London Evening Post*, 23 December 1773.

Table 8.3.17.6
Poll for common councilman of Dowgate, 28 June 1776

Forename	Surname	Precinct	Livery	Votes received
JOHN	SALTER		Plu	42
Edward	Simons			33

Source: *Daily Advertiser*, 29 June 1776.

Table 8.3.17.7
Poll for common councilman of Dowgate, 12 January 1795

Forename	Surname	Precinct	Livery	Votes received
JOHN	RAINE		Bla	40
James	Vandercom		Hab	31

Source: *Morning Post*, 26 December 1794.

Table 8.3.17.8
Poll for common councilmen of Dowgate, 7 January 1822

Forename	Surname	Precinct	Livery	Votes received
JAMES	SAUNDERS		Fis	63
JAMES EBENEZER	SAUNDERS		Fis	59
DAVID	PRICE		Hab	52
EDWARD J.	IANSON		Pat	51
JAMES SAMUEL	BENNETT		Pat	51
HUGH HAMILTON	MORTIMER		Pat	50
ALEXANDER	NESBITT		Pat	49
JOHN	FORSTER		Bre	46
Henry James	Combe			45
William	Wright			42
James F.	Vandercom		Hab	34
William Charles	Wright			16

Source: LMA CLC/W/IA/001/Ms. 01276/001.

Table 8.3.17.9
Poll for common councilmen of Dowgate, 12 January 1829

Forename	Surname	Precinct	Livery	Votes received
DAVID	PRICE		Hab	57
HUGH HAMILTON	MORTIMER		Pat	51
THOMAS	BRITTEN		Met	50
JOHN	FORSTER		Bre	50
WILLIAM	HEPWORTH		Bak	49
JAMES SAMUEL	BENNETT		Pat	46
MOSES	KIPLING		Bla	45
ALEXANDER	NESBITT		Pat	44
Henry James	Combe			35

Source: LMA CLC/W/IA/001/Ms. 01276/001.

8.3.18 Farringdon Within, 1715-1830: 34 polls

(15 common councilmen; 17 after 1736; from 1806, a double ward with two deputies; 570 freeman householders in 1833)

Table 8.3.18.a
Precincts in Farringdon Within

Code	Precinct
Anne	St Anne
August	St Augustine
Ch Ch 1	Christ Church 1
Ch Ch 2	Christ Church 2
Ewins	St Ewins
FaithP	St Faith St Pauls
Goldrow	Goldsmith's Row
Martin	St Martin
Matthew	St Matthew
Michael	St Michael
Monkw	Monkwell
Peter	St Peter
Patern	St Faith Paternoster
Sadler	Sadler's Hall
Sepul	St Sepulchre

Note: All electors in the ward were entitled to choose from among all the candidates but, in the larger wards, those elected as common councilmen were then taken to represent specific precincts or ward electoral sub-divisions (whose boundaries, confusingly, did not automatically match the parish's ecclesiastical boundaries).

Table 8.3.18.1

Poll for common councilmen of Farringdon Within, 10 January 1715

Forename	Surname	Precinct	Livery	Votes received	
				Poll	Scrutiny
WILLIAM	UNETT			386	
WILLIAM	CLINCH			374	
NEEDLER	WEBB			373	
JOHN	WHEATLY			364	
CHARLES	WOOD			361	
Humphry	Thayer			241	
John	Baskett			234	
Thomas	Simpson			220	
Anthony	Kingsley			220	
John	Hattley			208	

Source: *Post Boy*, 21 December 1714.

Table 8.3.18.2

Poll for common councilman of Farringdon Within, 7 May 1736

Forename	Surname	Precinct	Livery	Votes received	
				Poll	Scrutiny
JOHN	HUMPHRYS		Dra	357	
Richard	Sclater		Ski	251	

Source: *London Daily Post*, 8 May 1736; *Daily Gazetteer*, 8 June 1736.

Table 8.3.18.3

Poll for alderman of Farringdon Within, 10 November 1737

Forename	Surname	Livery	Votes received
HENRY	MARSHALL		383
William	Selwin		327

Source: Beaven, i, p. 151.

Table 8.3.18.4
Poll for common councilman of Farringdon Within, 12 January 1747

Forename	Surname	Precinct	Livery	Votes received
THOMAS	PARR			Unopposed
ROBERT	STRINGER			Unopposed
JAMES	PRICE			Unopposed
MICHAEL	MARTINDALE			Unopposed
JENNER	SWAINE			Unopposed
THOMAS	HODGES			Unopposed
JOSEPH	BAXTER			Unopposed
HENRY	SISSON			Unopposed
RICHARD	HOLLAND			Unopposed
GEORGE	HARRISON			Unopposed
RICHARD	SCLATER			Unopposed
SAMUEL	SEAWELL			Unopposed
JOHN	BLACKALL			Unopposed
ROBERT	WILLIS			Unopposed
RICHARD	GRANGER			Unopposed
EDWARD	NEWMAN			Unopposed
GILES	MILLS			226
John	Walker			156

Source: LMA CLC/W/JA/001/Ms. 00077.

Table 8.3.18.5
Poll for common councilman of Farringdon Within, 14 February 1747

Forename	Surname	Precinct	Livery	Votes received	
				Poll	Scrutiny
JOHN	BROWN			244	203
John	Walker			225	188

Source: LMA CLC/W/JA/001/Ms. 00077.

Table 8.3.18.6
Poll for common councilmen of Farringdon Within, 11 January 1748

Forename	Surname	Precinct	Livery	Votes received
JOHN	PATTERSON			340
THOMAS	REDBORD			324
ROBERT	STRINGER			319
THOMAS	SMITH			315
RICHARD	SCLATER			308
SAMUEL	SEAWELL			296
JOSEPH	BAXTER			295
MAURICE	GRIFFITH			294
JAMES	PRICE			291
MICHAEL	MARTINDALE			291
THOMAS	PARR			290
THOMAS	HODGES			289
HENRY	SISSON			289
GEORGE	HARRISON			288
JOSEPH	BROWN			286
EDWARD	NEWMAN			285
JENNER	SWAINE			245
John	Walker			233

Source: LMA CLC/W/JA/001/Ms. 00077.

Table 8.3.18.7
Poll for beadle of Farringdon Within, 28 June 1748

Forename	Surname	Votes received
JOHN	SAUNDERS	291
Robert	Stringer	246

Source: *General Evening Post*, 28 June 1748.

Table 8.3.18.8
Poll for common councilmen of Farringdon Within, 6 January 1755

Forename	Surname	Precinct	Livery	Votes received
THOMAS	PARR	Peter		Unopposed
ROBERT	MOHUN	Matthew		Unopposed
JOHN	FASHION	Goldrow		Unopposed
EDWARD	NEWMAN	August		Unopposed
RICHARD	STEVENS	Michael		Unopposed
JOHN	WALKER	Michael		Unopposed
DAVID	RICE	Patern		Unopposed
JOHN	RIVINGTON	FaithP		Unopposed
EDWARD	SAY	Martin		Unopposed
MAURICE	GRIFFITHS	Ch Ch 1		Unopposed
RANDLE	WICKSTED	Ch Ch 2		Unopposed
JOSEPH	SCLATER	Ewins		Unopposed
SAMUEL	SEAWELL	Sepul		Unopposed
JOHN	PATERSON	Monkw		Unopposed
THOMAS	SMITH	Anne		Unopposed
RICHARD	HARWOOD	Anne		Unopposed
MICHAEL	MARTINDALE	Sadler		168
Jenner	Swaine			78

Source: LMA CLC/W/JA/001/Ms. 00077.

Table 8.3.18.9
Poll for beadle of Farringdon Within, 20 January 1762

Forename	Surname	Votes received
PETER	LIME	280
Samuel	Spencer	232

Source: LMA CLC/W/JA/001/Ms. 00077.

Table 8.3.18.10
Poll for common councilmen of Farringdon Within, 8 January 1770

Forename	Surname	Precinct	Livery	Votes received	
				Poll	Scrutiny
JOHN	PATERSON	Monkw	Bar	351	
CHARLES	CLAVEY	Ch Ch 2	Mas	342	
WILLIAM	JONES	Peter	Glo	308	
DANIEL	PINDER	Anne	Dye	301	
DAVID	BUFFAR	Goldrow	Sal	295	
ARTHUR	HEMMING	Ewins	Gro	294	
RICHARD	HOLLYER	Matthew	Glz	290	
JOHN	CLEMENTS	Michael	Pew	289	
CHARLES G.	SAY	Martin	Sta	283	
RICHARD	FAWSON	FaithP	Car	280	
THOMAS	CASLON	Sadler	Sta	280	
JOHN	CUMBERLEGE	Sepul	Gol	277	
GEDELIAH	GATFIELD	Michael	Mus	273	
BENJAMIN	HAMNETT	Anne	Bas	273	
JARVIS	ADAMS	Patern	Wea	257	
JOHN	LOKES	Ch Ch 1	Wax	247	
CHARLES	MAYNARD	August	Uph	241	
John	Rivington			223	
John	Newcombe			218	
Edward	Bridgen			200	
Thomas	Woodroffe			196	

Source: LMA CLC/W/JA/001/Ms. 00077; *Whitehall Evening Post*, 23 December 1769; *Gazetteer and New Daily Advertiser*, 3 January 1770.

Table 8.3.18.11
Poll for common councilmen of Farringdon Within, 11 January 1773

Forename	Surname	Precinct	Livery	Votes received
CHARLES	CLAVEY	Ch Ch 2	Mas	273
THOMAS	HYDE	Sadler	Fis	264
EDWARD	UPTON	Monkw	Glo	263
CHARLES	MAYNARD	August	Uph	258
DANIEL	PINDAR	Anne	Dye	254
JOHN	LOKES	Ch Ch 1	Wax	250
WILLIAM	CARTER	Ewins	Met	250
STANLEY	CROWDER	Goldrow	Sta	243
JOHN	CLEMENTS	Michael	Pew	242
JOHN	RING	FaithP	Ski	242
BENJAMIN	HAMNETT	Anne	Bas	242
GEDELIAH	GATFIELD	Michael	Mus	241
SYLVANUS	HALL	Patern	Cur	239
GEORGE	CUMMINGS	Martin	Mus	233
THOMAS	VANHAGEN	Peter	Joi	223
JOHN	DOD	Sepul	Mus	218
JOHN	SMITH	Matthew		173
John	Miller			154
John	Cook			112

Source: LMA CLC/W/JA/001/Ms. 00077.

Table 8.3.18.12
Poll for assistant beadle of Farringdon Within, 14 January 1774

Forename	Surname	Votes received
JOHN	PROCKTER	319
John	Tringham	203

Source: LMA CLC/W/JA/001/Ms. 00077.

Table 8.3.18.13
Poll for beadle of Farringdon Within, 18 August 1774

Forename	Surname	Votes received
ROBERT	BEST	326
John	Prockter	275

Source: LMA CLC/W/JA/001/Ms.00077.

Table 8.3.18.14
Poll for alderman of Farringdon Within, 23 October 1779

Forename	Surname	Livery	Votes received
HENRY	KITCHIN	Cur	208
William	Axford	Mus	102

Source: LMA CLC/W/JA/001/Ms.00077; Beaven, i, p. 152.

Table 8.3.18.15
Poll for common councilmen of Farringdon Within, 8 January 1781

Forename	Surname	Precinct	Livery	Votes received
GEORGE	FLEMING	Sepul	Gol	362
DANIEL	PINDAR	Anne	Dye	347
JOHN	PEARKES	Ch Ch 2	Fis	346
WILLIAM	POWELL	Monkw	Pai	345
JOHN	COOKE	FaithP	Mus	340
THOMAS	VANHAGEN	Peter	Joi	335
SYLVANUS	HALL	Patern	Cur	332
JOHN	CLEMENTS	Michael	Pew	322
THOMAS	PATRICK	Ch Ch 1	Tin	322
GEDELIAH	GATFIELD	Michael	Mus	316
BENJAMIN	HAMNETT	Anne	Bas	311
THOMAS	LEDDIARD	Sadler	Clm	309
WILLIAM	CARTER	Ewins	Met	303
EDWARD	PARISH	Martin	Whe	302
STANLEY	CROWDER	Goldrow	Sta	295
CHARLES	MAYNARD	August	Uph	257
THOMAS	CASLON	Matthew	Sta	245
Thomas	Hyde			239
Samuel	Goodman			213

Source: LMA CLC/W/JA/001/Ms. 00077.

Table 8.3.18.16
Poll for assistant beadle of Farringdon Within, 4 January 1782

Forename	Surname	Livery	Votes received	
			Poll	Scrutiny
THOMAS	WARREN	Joi	355	291
Samuel	Shipley	Bar	318	286

Source: LMA CLC/W/JA/001/Ms. 00077.

Table 8.3.18.17
Poll for common councilman of Farringdon Within, 13 February 1790

Forename	Surname	Precinct	Livery	Votes received
JOHN	ASHBY		Hab	218
James	Slann			153

Source: LMA CLC/W/JA/001/Ms. 00077.

Table 8.3.18.18
Poll for schoolmaster of Farringdon Within, 16 November 1791

Forename	Surname	Votes received
JAMES	BUSHBY	121
John	Wills	48
Cornelius	Brown	36
Francis	Ventris	38

Source: *Public Advertiser*, 18 November 1791.

Table 8.3.18.19
Poll for common councilmen of Farringdon Within, 7 January 1793

Forename	Surname	Precinct	Livery	Votes received
DANIEL	PINDAR	Anne	Dye	408
RICHARD	WINSTANLEY	Matthew	Apo	407
WILLIAM	POWELL	Monkw	Pai	393
HENRY	GODFREY	Ch Ch 1	Gro	390
THOMAS	VANHAGEN	Peter	Joi	354
GEDELIAH	GATFIELD	Michael	Mus	352
JAMES	LEDDIARD	FaithP	Clm	351
EDWARD	PARISH	Martin	Whe	346
CHARLES	TURNER	Goldrow	Lea	345
JOHN	MOFFATT	Michael	Tur	333
JOHN	PEARKES	Ch Ch 2	Fis	330
JOHN	ASHBY	Sepul	Hab	321
WILLIAM	TILSLEY	Ewins	Sal	309
JOHN	STOKES	Sadler	Bar	308
THOMAS	SMITH	Anne	Lea	299
JOSEPH	POPE	August	Pla	295
WILLIAM	SLOMAN	Patern	Mus	267
William	Huson		Mus	259
William	Tremaine			240
Jonathan	Scott			231

Source: LMA CLC/W/JA/001/Ms. 00077; *Diary*, 26 December 1792.

Table 8.3.18.20
Poll for common councilman of Farringdon Within, 29 January 1796

Forename	Surname	Precinct	Livery	Votes received
JOHN	HAWKINS		Iro	225
Benjamin	Cooper			143

Source: *St James's Chronicle*, 30 January 1796.

Table 8.3.18.21

Poll for common councilmen of Farringdon Within, 11 January 1802

Forename	Surname	Precinct	Livery	Votes received
DANIEL	PINDAR	Anne	Dye	Unopposed
WILLIAM	POWELL	Monkw	Pai	314
WILLIAM	CADWELL	Michael	Cur	313
RICHARD	WINSTANLEY	Matthew	Apo	304
JOHN	STOKES	Sadler	Bar	285
JOHN	CROWDER	Ch Ch 1	Pcm	281
WILLIAM	HUSON	Sepul	Mus	272
THOMAS	ASHBY	August	Mus	271
THOMAS	SMITH		Hab	271
JOHN	HAYDON	Patern	Clm	270
JAMES	SMITH	Michael	Mus	259
JOHN	SMITH	Ewins	Hab	244
WILLIAM	HORTON	Ch Ch 2	Bla	243
THOMAS	SMITH		Lea	240
JOHN	WILKINSON	Martin	Spe	236
THOMAS	BREACH	FaithP	Sal	233
LEWIS	LEWIS	Peter	Vin	216
William	Roberts		Pla	206
George M.	Metcalfe		Clm	131

Source: LMA CLC/W/JA/001/Ms. 00077.

Table 8.3.18.22
Poll for common councilmen of Farringdon Within, 10 January 1803

Forename	Surname	Precinct	Livery	Votes received
DANIEL	PINDAR	Anne	Dye	Unopposed
JOHN	LEIGH	Anne	Met	340
WILLIAM	POWELL	Monkw	Pai	335
WILLIAM	CADWELL	Michael	Cur	330
RICHARD	WINSTANLEY	Matthew	Apo	325
WILLIAM	HUSON	FaithP	Mus	322
JOHN	CROWDER	Ch Ch 1	Pcm	317
JOHN	STOKES	Sadler	Bar	310
WILLIAM	ROBERTS	Peter	Pla	299
THOMAS	SMITH	Goldrow	Hab	291
THOMAS	ASHBY	August	Mus	291
JAMES	SMITH	Michael		278
JOHN	SMITH	Ewins	Hab	270
WILLIAM	HORTON	Ch Ch 2	Bla	269
JOHN	HAYDON	Patern	Clm	269
JOHN	WILKINSON	Martin	Spe	268
GEORGE M.	METCALFE	Sepul	Clm	223
Thomas	Breach			216

Source: LMA CLC/W/JA/001/Ms. 00077.

Table 8.3.18.23

Poll for common councilmen of Farringdon Within, 10 January 1804

Forename	Surname	Precinct	Livery	Votes received
DANIEL	PINDAR	Anne	Dye	Unopposed
WILLIAM	POWELL	Monkw	Pai	105
WILLIAM	CADWELL	Michael	Cur	103
RICHARD	WINSTANLEY	Matthew	Apo	101
GEORGE M.	METCALFE	Sepul	Clm	100
JOHN	LEIGH	Anne	Met	94
WILLIAM	HUSON	FaithP	Mus	93
JOHN	CROWDER	Ch Ch 1	Pcm	93
THOMAS	SMITH	Goldrow	Hab	93
JOHN	STOKES	Sadler	Bar	92
JOHN	SMITH	Ewins	Hab	91
JOHN	WILKINSON	Martin	Spe	91
WILLIAM	ROBERTS	Peter	Pla	88
JOHN	HAYDON	Patern	Clm	87
JAMES	SMITH	Michael		87
WILLIAM	HORTON	Ch Ch 2		77
LEWIS	LEWIS	August	Vin	77
George	Priest		Plu	44
Charles	Cook		Sta	39

Source: LMA CLC/W/JA/001/Ms. 00077.

Table 8.3.18.24
Poll for common councilmen of Farringdon Within, 6 January 1806

Forename	Surname	Precinct	Livery	Votes received
DANIEL	PINDAR	Anne	Dye	Unopposed
JOHN	LEIGH	Anne	Met	168
WILLIAM	CADWELL	Michael	Cur	160
WILLIAM	PRITCHARD	Monkw	Inn	153
JOHN	CROWDER	Ch Ch 1	Pcm	149
WILLIAM	ROBERTS	Peter	Pla	146
JOHN	STOKES	Sadler	Bar	145
JOHN	SMITH	Ewins	Hab	143
THOMAS	SMITH	Goldrow	Hab	143
GEORGE M.	METCALFE	Sepul	Clm	142
JAMES	SMITH	Michael	Mus	136
LEWIS	LEWIS	August	Vin	134
JOHN	WHEBLE	Ch Ch 2	Sta	134
CHARLES	COOK	Matthew	Sta	133
JOHN	WALKER	Patern	Mus	133
WILLIAM	WILLS	FaithP	Vin	129
JAMES	SCATCHERD	Martin	Sta	113
George	Winter		Bak	87
George	Priest		Plu	44

Source: LMA CLC/W/JA/001/Ms. 00077.

Table 8.3.18.25
Poll for common councilman of Farringdon Within, 31 October 1808

Forename	Surname	Precinct	Livery	Votes received
JOSEPH	DAW		Pai	187
George	Winter		Bak	131

Source: LMA CLC/W/JA/002/Ms. 03039.

Table 8.3.18.26
Poll for common councilmen of Farringdon Within, 9 January 1809

Forename	Surname	Precinct	Livery	Votes received
DANIEL	PINDAR	Ann	Dye	Unopposed
JOSEPH	DAW	FaithP	Pai	328
JAMES	SCATCHERD	Martin	Sta	308
CHARLES	COOKE	Matthew	Sta	295
WILLIAM	CADWELL	Michael	Cur	293
WILLIAM	PRITCHARD	Monkw	Inn	284
JOHN	CROWDER	Ch Ch 1	Pcm	281
JOHN	WHEBLE	Ch Ch 2	Sta	275
JOHN	LEIGH	Ann	Met	273
JOHN	STOKES	Sadler	Bar	270
THOMAS	SMITH	Goldrow	Hab	262
JOHN	WALKER	Ewins	Mus	260
LEWIS	LEWIS	August	Vin	256
GEORGE M.	METCALFE	Patern	Clm	255
WILLIAM	ROBERTS	Peter	Pla	249
JAMES	SMITH	Michael	Mus	243
GEORGE	WINTER	Sepul	Bak	233
John	Smith		Hab	225

Source: LMA CLC/W/JA/002/Ms. 03039.

Table 8.3.18.27

Poll for common councilmen of Farringdon Within, 11 January 1813

Forename	Surname	Precinct	Livery	Votes received
DANIEL	PINDAR		Dye	302
CHARLES	COOKE		Sta	288
MALCOLM	DUNNETT		Bar	287
GEORGE	WINTER		Bak	286
JOSEPH	DAW		Pai	284
WILLIAM	CADWELL		Cur	278
WILLIAM	PRITCHARD		Inn	276
LEWIS	LEWIS		Vin	275
JOHN	CROWDER		Pcm	273
JOHN	WHEBLE		Sta	273
WILLIAM	ROBERTS		Pla	267
JAMES	PEARSALL		Dye	267
JAMES	SCATCHERD		Sta	264
JOHN	WALKER		Mus	263
JOHN	STOKES		Bar	243
JOHN	LEIGH		Met	231
THOMAS	BLACKETT		Gls	175
Samuel	Case			152
Adam	Oldham		Wax	111

Source: LMA CLC/W/JA/002/Ms. 03039.

Table 8.3.18.28
Poll for common councilmen of Farringdon Within, 6 January 1817

Forename	Surname	Precinct	Livery	Votes received
DANIEL	PINDAR		Dye	352
THOMAS	BLACKETT		Gls	347
ROBERT	WESTWOOD		Iro	347
JAMES	HOWELL		Iro	343
JOHN	CROWDER		Pcm	339
JOHN	WALKER		Mus	339
WILLIAM	CADWELL		Cur	338
JOSEPH	DAW		Pai	338
ADAM	OLDHAM		Wax	334
WILLIAM	PRITCHARD		Inn	333
GEORGE	WINTER		Bak	332
JOHN	LEIGH		Met	328
JAMES	SCATCHERD		Sta	325
LEWIS	LEWIS		Vin	323
JOHN	WHEBLE		Sta	320
JAMES	PEARSALL		Dye	305
JOHN	MURCOTT		Dis	216
Malcolm	Dunnett		Bar	184

Source: LMA CLC/W/JA/002/Ms. 03039.

Table 8.3.18.29
Poll for common councilmen of Farringdon Within, 8 March 1817

Forename	Surname	Precinct	Livery	Votes received
MALCOLM	DUNNETT		Bar	303
JOHN PEARSON	HAYWARD		Gol	229
James	Hartley		Nee	168
John Jabez	Berrie			12

Source: LMA CLC/W/JA/002/Ms. 03039.

Table 8.3.18.30
Poll for common councilman of Farringdon Within, 21 October 1820

Forename	Surname	Precinct	Livery	Votes received
JAMES	PLUMMER		Pat	175
Charles	Woodward		Hab	103

Source: LMA CLC/W/JA/002/Ms. 03039.

Table 8.3.18.31
Poll for common councilmen of Farringdon Within, 7 January 1822

Forename	Surname	Precinct	Livery	Votes received
JOHN	CROWDER		Pcm	285
JAMES	PLUMMER		Pat	262
MALCOLM	DUNNETT		Bar	277
HENRY	PRITCHARD		Iro	276
JOSEPH	DAW		Pai	275
GEORGE	WINTER		Bak	274
ROBERT	WESTWOOD		Iro	274
ROBERT	HOGARD		Hab	272
JAMES	HOWELL		Iro	271
JOHN	MURCOTT		Dis	271
ADAM	OLDHAM		Wax	271
WILLIAM	PRITCHARD		Inn	271
JOHN PEARSON	HAYWARD		Gol	267
JAMES	HARTLEY		Nee	267
HENRY	GILBERTSON		Dra	262
JAMES	SCATCHERD		Sta	261
EDWARD	EAGLETON		Hab	167
Charles	Woodward		Hab	139

Source: LMA CLC/W/JA/002/Ms. 03039.

Table 8.3.18.32
Poll for common councilmen of Farringdon Within, 7 January 1828

Forename	Surname	Precinct	Livery	Votes received
JOSEPH	DAW		Pai	256
ADAM	OLDHAM		Wax	250
MALCOLM	DUNNETT		Bar	248
THOMAS	KELLY		Pla	247
WILLIAM	PRITCHARD		Inn	243
ROBERT	WESTWOOD		Iro	241
EDWARD	DUNSBY		Bar	240
MILES	FILBY		Met	238
JOHN	WILLIAMS		Pla	238
JOHN PEARSON	HAYWARD		Gol	236
JOHN	MURCOTT		Dis	235
SAMUEL	RIDLEY		Wea	234
WALTER	JACKSON		Gol	233
HENRY	PRITCHARD		Iro	220
JAMES WEBB	SOUTHGATE		Bar	192
JAMES	BEVERIDGE		Lor	167
JAMES	THOMPSON		Pai	157
Henry	Fisher		Gir	145
James	Hartley		Nee	46

Source: LMA CLC/W/JA/002/Ms. 03039.

Table 8.3.18.33
Poll for common councilmen of Farringdon Within, 11 January 1830

Forename	Surname	Precinct	Livery	Votes received
JOHN	ROBERTS		Hab	227
HENRY	FISHER		Gir	220
JOSEPH	DAW		Pai	219
EDWARD	DUNSBY		Bar	218
THOMAS	KELLY		Pla	217
ROBERT	WESTWOOD		Iro	216
JOHN PEARSON	HAYWARD		Gol	215
WILLIAM	PRITCHARD		Inn	213
JOHN	WILLIAMS		Pla	210
ADAM	OLDHAM		Wax	209
JOHN	MURCOTT		Dis	209
MALCOLM	DUNNETT		Bar	209
MILES	FILBY		Met	208
SAMUEL	RIDLEY		Wea	207
JAMES WEBB	SOUTHGATE		Bar	199
JAMES	THOMPSON		Pai	198
HENRY	PRITCHARD		Iro	158
James	Hartley		Nee	71

Source: LMA CLC/W/JA/002/Ms. 03039.

Table 8.3.18.34
Poll for under beadle of Farringdon Within, 24 December 1830

Forename	Surname	Votes received
HENRY	BURRELL	326
William Henry	Main	271

Source: LMA CLC/W/JA/002/Ms. 03039.

8.3.19 Farringdon Without, 1724-1829: 64 polls

(16 common councilmen; 835 inhabited houses in 1833)

Table 8.3.19.a
Precincts in Farringdon Without

Code	Precinct
Andrew	St Andrew
Bride	St Bride
Dunstan	St Dunstan
Martin	St Martin Ludgate
Sepul	St Sepulchre
Smith	Smithfield

Note: All electors in the ward were entitled to choose from among all the candidates but, in the larger wards, those elected as common councilmen were then taken to represent specific precincts or ward electoral sub-divisions (whose boundaries, confusingly, did not automatically match the parish's ecclesiastical boundaries).

Table 8.3.19.1
Poll for common councilmen of Farringdon Without, 6 January 1724

Forename	Surname	Votes received
HENRY	HOLLOWAY	1057
ROBERT	VINCENT	991
JOHN	ARNOLD	989
WALTER	PRYSE	975
JOHN	CHILD	956
John	Nash	851
George	Moody	851
John	Mead	827
George	Woodrove	814
Charles	Egerton	720

Source: Anon., *The art of managing popular elections* (1724), p. 63.

Table 8.3.19.2
Poll for common councilman of Farringdon Without, 27 January 1733

Forename	Surname	Precinct	Livery	Votes received	
				Poll	Scrutiny
PHILIP	ROBINSON	Bride		630	
	Fawconer			629	

Source: *London Evening Post*, 27 January 1733.

Table 8.3.19.3
Poll for beadle of Farringdon Without, 22 December 1735

Forename	Surname	Precinct	Livery	Votes received
ISAAC	WHITCHURCH			738
	Curtis			473

Source: *Read's Weekly Journal*, 27 December 1735.

Table 8.3.19.4
Poll for common councilmen of Farringdon Without, 7 January 1740

Forename	Surname	Precinct	Livery	Votes received
GEORGE	BURTON	Martin		744
	MASTER	Smith		665
	Tomkins			427
	DeWilde			223

Source: *London Evening Post*, 22 December 1739

Table 8.3.19.5
Poll for common councilman of Farringdon Without, 12 January 1741

Forename	Surname	Precinct	Livery	Votes received
JOHN	CHILD	Dunstan		469
William	Hart			305

Source: *London Evening Post*, 23 December 1740.

Table 8.3.19.6
Poll for common councilmen of Farringdon Without, 11 January 1742

Forename	Surname	Precinct	Livery	Votes received
GEORGE	GRAINGER	Bride		620
WILLIAM	SAVAGE	Smith		556
Charles	Gardner			447
Robert	Gammon			362

Source: *Champion*, 26 December 1741.

Table 8.3.19.7
Poll for beadle of Farringdon Without, 4 November 1742

Forename	Surname	Votes received
	BENN	754
	Atwood	713

Source: *London Evening Post*, 4 November 1742.

Table 8.3.19.8
Poll for common councilmen of Farringdon Without, 10 January 1743

Forename	Surname	Precinct	Livery	Votes received
JOHN	KING			62
CHRISTOPHER	MYNGS			59
ROBERT	GAMMON			580
CADWALLADER	COKER			544
William	Savage			472
	Astley			432

Note: Opposition to King and Myngs ended after a few hours. The four remaining candidates continued the poll.
Source: *London Evening Post*, 23 December 1742.

Table 8.3.19.9
Poll for common councilmen of Farringdon Without, 9 January 1744

Forename	Surname	Precinct	Livery	Votes received
JOHN	KING			190
CHRISTOPHER	MYNGS			186
ROBERT	GAMMON			192
CADWALLADER	COKER			187
CHARLES TAYLOR	BALLARD			164
EDWARD	WALMESLEY			185
CHARLES	GARDNER			541
James	Welch			324
William	Savage			*49*

Source: *Daily Post*, 26 December 1743.

Table 8.3.19.10
Poll for common councilmen of Farringdon Without, 12 January 1747

Forename	Surname	Precinct	Livery	Votes received
JOHN	HUGHES			422
Thomas	Nowell			275

Source: *London Evening Post*, 23 December 1746.

Table 8.3.19.11
Poll for beadle of Farringdon Without, 5 July 1748

Forename	Surname	Votes received
JOHN	CARPENDER	434
William	Bird	234

Source: *General Evening Post*, 7 July 1748.

Table 8.3.19.12
Poll for common councilmen of Farringdon Without, 9 January 1749

Forename	Surname	Precinct	Livery	Votes received
WILLIAM	HUTTON		Pou	513
THOMAS	TIBBS			430
Cadwallader	Coker			347

Source: *General Advertiser*, 24 December 1748; *London Evening Post*, 22-4 December 1748.

Table 8.3.19.13
Poll for beadle of Farringdon Without, 12 May 1749

Forename	Surname	Votes received
THOMAS	NICHOLLS	293
	Luff	115

Source: *General Advertiser*, 12 May 1749.

Table 8.3.19.14
Poll for common councilman of Farringdon Without, 8 January 1750

Forename	Surname	Precinct	Livery	Votes received
WILLIAM	HUTTON			328
Thomas	Tibbs			191

Source: *Whitehall Evening Post*, 21 December 1749.

Table 8.3.19.15
Poll for common councilmen of Farringdon Without, 6 January 1752

Forename	Surname	Precinct	Livery	Votes received
THOMAS	NOWELL	Old B		292
James	Steere			92

Source: *London Evening Post*, 21 December 1751.

Table 8.3.19.16
Poll for common councilman of Farringdon Without, 22 May 1762

Forename	Surname	Precinct	Livery	Votes received
	PLATT			250
John	Sibthorpe			75

Source: *Public Advertiser*, 22 May 1762.

Table 8.3.19.17
Poll for beadle of Farringdon Without, 21 April 1763

Forename	Surname	Votes received
RICHARD	STREETIN	791
John	Napper	570

Source: *London Evening Post*, 21 April 1763.

Table 8.3.19.18
Poll for collector of tithes of St Sepulchre, 19 October 1763

Forename	Surname	Votes received
	SELBY	68
	Towers	54

Source: *Lloyd's Evening Post*, 19 October 1763.

Table 8.3.19.20
Poll for alderman of Farringdon Without, 2 January 1769

Forename	Surname	Livery	Votes received
JOHN	WILKES	Joi	255
Thomas	Bromwich	Pai	69

Note: Election declared void. Wilkes elected unopposed, 27 January 1769.
Source: Beaven, i, p. 164.

Table 8.3.19.21
Poll for common councilmen of Farringdon Without, 8 January 1770

Forename	Surname	Precinct	Livery	Votes received
WILLIAM	RICHARDSON	Bride	Sta	585
THOMAS	SALTER	Sepul	Tur	483
THOMAS	SAINSBURY	Martin		464
WILLIAM	WATSON	Sepul	Bla	446
JOHN	HITCHCOCK	Andrew	Hab	438
ROBERT	GAMMON	Sepul	Apo	421
GEORGE	WYATT	Dunstan	Dra	419
JOHN	BROME	Dunstan	Met	412
THOMAS	TIBBS	Andrew		411
BENJAMIN	STEPHENSON	Bride	Gol	395
WILLIAM	CHAMBERLAYNE	Dunstan	Spe	388
JOHN	ADAMS	Bride	Fel	387
JOHN	MANSFIELD	Sepul	Joi	383
SAMUEL	SHARPE	Sepul	Bar	366
WILLIAM	AXFORD	Martin	Mus	361
JOHN	FOX	Sepul	Gro	348
Edward	Howse			336
Dryden	Leach			324
	Price			311
	Jones			306
Ralph	Young			283
William	Beetson			275
	Burnell			78
	Hutton			8

Source: *Whitehall Evening Post*, 23 December 1769.

Table 8.3.19.22
Poll for beadle of Farringdon Without, 18 January 1771

Forename	Surname	Votes received
WILLIAM	PEACHEY	485
	Hurst	227

Source: *Middlesex Journal*, 17 January 1771.

Table 8.3.19.23

Poll for common councilmen of Farringdon Without, 10 January 1774

Forename	Surname	Precinct	Livery	Votes received
EDWARD	HOWES		Tin	555
THOMAS	SAINSBURY			541
WILLIAM	RICHARDSON		Sta	529
JOHN	HITCHCOCK		Hab	516
RICHARD	BREWER		Joi	514
ROWLAND	ATKINSON		Whe	512
JOHN	ADAMS		Fel	493
GEORGE	WYATT		Dra	474
THOMAS	THORPE		Vin	472
BENJAMIN	STEPHENSON		Gol	467
WILLIAM	AXFORD		Mus	461
JOHN	MANSFIELD		Joi	461
JOHN	REYNOLDS		Fra	447
RICHARD	HEARNE		Uph	446
JOHN	FOX		Gro	436
EDWARD	YORKE		Pew	374
David	Williams			369
Hugh	James			184
Edward	Stone			141

Source: *London Chronicle*, 23 December 1773; *Daily Advertiser*, 24 December 1773; *Craftsman*, 25 December 1773; *Lloyd's Evening Post*, 22-24 December 1773.

Table 8.3.19.24
Poll for common councilmen of Farringdon Without, 9 January 1775

Forename	Surname	Precinct	Livery	Votes received
THOMAS	SAINSBURY			532
GEORGE	WYATT		Dra	516
JOHN	LOMAX			500
RICHARD	BREWER		Joi	496
RICHARD	OAKES		Lea	490
ROWLAND	ATKINSON		Whe	483
JOHN	CROCKETT		Met	468
RICHARD	HEARNE		Uph	462
WILLIAM	AXFORD		Mus	462
THOMAS	THORPE		Vin	454
JOHN	ADAMS		Fel	450
WILLIAM	RICHARDSON		Sta	449
BENJAMIN	STEPHENSON		Gol	432
WILLIAM	WRIGHT		Inn	432
JOHN	FOX		Gro	420
EDWARD	HOWSE		Tin	360
John	Burnell			347
Edward	Stone			294
John	Champion		Car	289
William	Howse			178

Source: *London Chronicle*, 22 December 1774.

Table 8.3.19.25
Poll for common councilmen of Farringdon Without, 6 January 1777

Forename	Surname	Precinct	Livery	Votes received
THOMAS	SAINSBURY			Unopposed
GEORGE	WYATT		Dra	546
RICHARD	BREWER		Joi	538
RICHARD	OAKES		Lea	521
JOHN	LOMAX			519
ROWLAND	ATKINSON		Whe	513
JOHN	CROCKETT		Met	497
RICHARD	HEARNE		Uph	497
WILLIAM	RICHARDSON		Sta	483
JOHN	ADAMS		Fel	460
THOMAS	THORPE		Vin	456
WILLIAM	AXFORD		Mus	453
BENJAMIN	STEPHENSON		Glo	450
WILLIAM	WRIGHT		Inn	435
WILLIAM	STYLES		Cok	429
JOHN	BURNELL		Car	416
John	Thorne			406

Source: *London Evening Post*, 24-26 December 1776.

Table 8.3.19.26
Poll for common councilmen of Farringdon Without, 11 January 1779

Forename	Surname	Precinct	Livery	Votes received
ROWLAND	ATKINSON			Unopposed
RICHARD	BREWER		Joi	517
RICHARD	OAKES		Lea	499
WILLIAM	SHARPE		Wea	484
JOHN	LOMAX			472
GEORGE	WYATT		Dra	452
EZEKIEL	DELIGHT		Vin	444
THOMAS	HARDER		Pai	441
THOMAS	THORPE		Vin	422
JOHN	MARSH			420
THOMAS	BURNELL		Mas	414
JOHN	CHAMPION		Car	402
WILLIAM	WRIGHT		Inn	401
THOMAS	GOODWYN		Pai	386
WILLIAM	AXFORD		Mus	371
WILLIAM	STILES		Cok	339
John	Chambers			288
Edward	Johnson			232
Thomas	Durke			216

Source: *London Evening Post*, 22-24 December 1778.

Table 8.3.19.27
Poll for common councilmen of Farringdon Without, 10 January 1780

Forename	Surname	Precinct	Livery	Votes received
ROWLAND	ATKINSON			Unopposed
RICHARD	BREWER		Joi	474
WILLIAM	SHARPE		Wea	445
JOHN	CHAMPION		Car	406
JOHN	MARSH		Dye	404
WILLIAM	NEWMAN		Cur	400
THOMAS	BURNELL		Mas	385
WILLIAM	WRIGHT		Inn	382
THOMAS	THORPE		Vin	378
GEORGE	WYATT		Dra	370
JOHN	LUCAS		But	365
THOMAS	GOODWYN		Pai	363
WILLIAM	AXFORD		Mus	346
EZEKIEL	DELIGHT		Vin	334
WILLIAM	STYLES		Cok	333
JAMES	BRANSCOMB		Dye	306
William	Miller		Gol	302
Edward	Johnson			127
Thomas	Hunter			126
	Merrick			41

Source: *Public Ledger*, 24 December 1779.

Table 8.3.19.28
Poll for common councilmen of Farringdon Without, 8 January 1781

Forename	Surname	Precinct	Livery	Votes received
THOMAS	THORPE		Vin	Unopposed
ROWLAND	ATKINSON			442
WILLIAM	SHARPE		Wea	430
JAMES	BRANSCOMB		Dye	425
WILLIAM	MILLER		Gol	389
RICHARD	BREWER		Joi	380
WILLIAM	NEWMAN		Cur	357
THOMAS	BURNELL		Mas	346
WILLIAM	WRIGHT		Inn	343
THOMAS	GOODWYN		Pai	342
EZEKIEL	DELIGHT		Vin	340
JOHN	CHAMPION		Car	337
JOHN	LUCAS		But	319
GEORGE	WYATT		Dra	306
GUY	WARWICK		Met	296
WILLIAM	STYLES		Cok	273
John	Squires		Wea	160

Source: *Morning Chronicle*, 25 December 1780.

Table 8.3.19.29
Poll for beadle of Farringdon Without, 20 February 1781

Forename	Surname	Votes received
	BIGGS	498
	Delegal	280

Source: *Whitehall Evening Post*, 20 February 1781.

Table 8.3.19.30
Poll for beadle of Farringdon Without, 13 May 1783

Forename	Surname	Votes received
	EDWARDS	397
	Thompson	119

Source: *London Chronicle*, 13 May 1783.

Table 8.3.19.31
Poll for common councilman of Farringdon Without, 17 May 1784

Forename	Surname	Precinct	Livery	Votes received
WILLIAM	SHARP		Wea	212
	Hooper			128

Source: *London Chronicle*, 15 May 1784.

Table 8.3.19.32
Poll for common councilmen of Farringdon Without, 10 January 1785

Forename	Surname	Precinct	Livery	Votes received
ROWLAND	ATKINSON			Unopposed
THOMAS	THORP		Vin	Unopposed
JOHN	NICHOLS		Sta	665
RICHARD	BREWER		Joi	599
WILLIAM	SHARP		Wea	594
CHARLES	SHARP		Spe	590
JAMES	BREWER		Joi	573
WILLIAM	WRIGHT		Inn	558
JAMES	BRANSCOMB		Dye	558
ROBERT	BERESFORD		Lor	498
WILLIAM	MILLER		Gol	487
WILLIAM	NEWMAN		Cur	485
GUY	WARWICK		Met	470
JOHN	SQUIRE		Wea	462
THOMAS	GOODWIN		Pai	444
EDWARD	JOHNSON		Gls	417
George	Wyatt		Dra	367
John	Butts			359
Robert	Threlfall			284
William	Stiles		Cok	72

Source: *Morning Chronicle*, 24 December 1784.

Table 8.3.19.33
Poll for common councilmen of Farringdon Without, 9 January 1786

Forename	Surname	Precinct	Livery	Votes received
ROWLAND	ATKINSON			608
JOHN	NICHOLS		Sta	550
RICHARD	BREWER		Joi	546
JAMES	BREWER		Joi	534
WILLIAM	SHARPE		Wea	534
WILLIAM	MILLER		Gol	533
JAMES	BRANSCOMB		Lor	530
CHARLES	SHARP		Spe	517
THOMAS	THORP		Vin	503
THOMAS	BURNELL		Mas	485
THOMAS	BERESFORD		Lor	483
WILLIAM	WRIGHT		Inn	483
JOHN	ALMON		Glo	467
WILLIAM	NEWMAN		Cur	462
THOMAS	GOODWYN		Pai	406
GUY	WARWICK		Met	404
Andrew	Abbott		Car	354
Edward	Johnson		Gls	281
John	Lambe		Gol	184

Source: *Whitehall Evening Post*, 24-27 December 1785.

Table 8.3.19.34
Poll for common councilman of Farringdon without, 17 October 1786

Forename	Surname	Precinct	Livery	Votes received	
				Poll	Scrutiny
EDWARD	WORLEY		Joi	392	
Andrew	Abbott		Car	383	

Source: *Daily Universal Register*, 19 October 1786.

Table 8.3.19.35
Poll for common councilmen of Farringdon Without, 8 January 1787

Forename	Surname	Precinct	Livery	Votes received
THOMAS	THORPE	Bride	Vin	611
JAMES	BRANSCOMB	Andrew	Lor	585
THOMAS	BURNELL	Dunstan	Mas	562
WILLIAM	SHARPE	Andrew	Wea	542
ROBERT	HERRING	Andrew	Uph	530
CHARLES	SHARP	Andrew	Spe	499
ANDREW	ABBOTT	Andrew	Car	494
RICHARD	BREWER	Sepul	Joi	494
JAMES	BREWER	Sepul	Joi	487
EDWARD	WORSLEY	Sepul	Joi	485
GUY	WARWICK	Sepul	Met	472
JOHN	LAMBE	Dunstan	Gol	470
WILLIAM	WRIGHT		Inn	450
WILLIAM	CROCKETT	Sepul	Met	443
JOHN	ALMON	Dunstan	Glo	439
WILLIAM	MILLER	Martin	Gol	417
Thomas	Beresford		Lor	415
Thomas	Goodwyn		Pai	409
John	Nichols		Sta	408
S.	Roberts			300
Simeon	Pope			300

Source: *Morning Chronicle*, 25 December 1786.

Table 8.3.19.36
Poll for common councilmen of Farringdon Without, 12 January 1789

Forename	Surname	Precinct	Livery	Votes received
JOHN	NICHOLS		Sta	Unopposed
RICHARD	BREWER		Joi	Unopposed
ROBERT	HERRING		Uph	642
CHARLES	SHARPE		Spe	628
JAMES	BRANSCOMB		Lor	620
THOMAS	BERESFORD		Lor	612
WILLIAM	SHARPE		Wea	606
WILLIAM	WRIGHT		Inn	599
JAMES	BREWER		Joi	597
THOMAS	GURNEY		Pav	564
JOHN	LAMBE		Gol	559
WILLIAM	CROCKETT		Met	513
EDWARD	WORSLEY		Joi	491
WILLIAM E.	ROGERS		Bak	459
WILLIAM	MILLER		Gol	448
THOMAS	BURNELL		Mas	426
Jacob	Meane		Tin	423
S.	Roberts			314

Source: *Whitehall Evening Post*, 23 December 1788.

Table 8.3.19.37
Poll for beadle of Farringdon Without, 17 February 1790

Forename	Surname	Votes received
WILLIAM	MARCH	932
	Stacey	829

Source: *St James's Chronicle*, 18 February 1790.

Table 8.3.19.38

Poll for common councilmen of Farringdon Without, 7 January 1793

Forename	Surname	Precinct	Livery	Votes received
JOHN	NICHOLS		Sta	Unopposed
RICHARD	BREWER		Joi	Unopposed
ROBERT	HERRING		Uph	578
JAMES	BREWER		Joi	573
JOSEPH	BOUCOCK		Gol	569
WILLIAM	SHARPE		Wea	557
WILLIAM	MARRIOTT		Vin	531
WILLIAM	WRIGHT		Inn	525
WILLIAM	CROCKETT		Met	514
JOHN	LAMBE		Gol	513
JAMES	BRANSCOMB		Dye	510
WILLIAM E.	ROGERS		Bak	497
THOMAS	BERESFORD		Lor	490
JACOB	MEANE		Tin	471
THOMAS	GURNEY		Pav	468
RICHARD	TOWNSHEND		Clw	450
John	Warner		Fou	344

Source: *St James's Chronicle*, 22 December 1792.

Table 8.3.19.39
Poll for common councilmen of Farringdon Without, 12 January 1795

Forename	Surname	Precinct	Livery	Votes received
RICHARD	BREWER		Joi	Unopposed
JOHN	NICHOLS		Sta	Unopposed
ROBERT	HERRING		Uph	560
JAMES	BREWER		Joi	550
JOHN	LAMBE		Gol	545
JOSEPH	BOUCOCK		Gol	541
WILLIAM	WRIGHT		Inn	533
WILLIAM	SHARPE		Wea	514
JOHN	WARNER		Fou	498
JAMES	BRANSCOMB		Dye	487
WILLIAM E.	ROGERS		Bak	483
THOMAS	BERESFORD		Lor	477
WILLIAM	CROCKETT		Met	457
JACOB	MEANE		Tin	420
RICHARD	TOWNSEND		Clw	402
JONATHAN	PERKINS		Gol	325
Joseph	Bracebridge			312
Thomas	Gurney		Pav	294

Source: *Morning Chronicle*, 26 December 1794.

Table 8.3.19.40
Poll for common councilmen of Farringdon Without, 11 January 1796

Forename	Surname	Precinct	Livery	Votes received
RICHARD	BREWER		Joi	675
ROBERT	HERRING		Uph	656
WILLIAM	WRIGHT		Inn	655
JOHN	LAMBE		Gol	616
JAMES	BRANSCOMB		Dye	609
WILLIAM	SHARP		Wea	609
JOSEPH	BOUCOCK		Gol	568
JOHN	NICHOLS		Sta	529
JAMES	BREWER		Joi	521
WILLIAM E.	ROGERS		Bak	498
CHARLES WERY	CLARK		Tyl	484
JONATHAN	PERKINS		Gol	479
ROBERT	WAITHMAN		Fra	463
THOMAS	BERESFORD		Lor	455
WILLIAM	CROCKETT		Met	444
LUKE	HODGSON		Whe	412
John	Wheeler		Gol	403
Thomas	Reeve		Iro	377
William	Evans			366
Richard	Townsend		Clw	359
John	Terry			343
John	Warner		Fou	316

Source: *Morning Post*, 24 December 1795; *Morning Chronicle*, 24 December 1795.

Table 8.3.19.41
Poll for common councilmen of Farringdon Without, 9 January 1797

Forename	Surname	Precinct	Livery	Votes received
ROBERT	HERRING		Uph	558
WILLIAM	WRIGHT		Inn	553
WILLIAM	SHARPE		Wea	550
RICHARD	BREWER		Joi	543
JAMES	BRANSCOMB		Dye	538
JOHN	NICHOLS		Sta	507
JOHN	LAMBE		Gol	502
JAMES	BREWER		Joi	492
ROBERT	WAITHMAN		Fra	483
LUKE	HODGSON		Whe	472
JOSEPH	BOUCOCK		Gol	450
THOMAS	REEVE		Iro	442
JONATHAN	PERKINS		Gol	433
CHARLES WERY	CLARK		Tyl	418
JOHN	WHEELER		Gol	377
WILLIAM E.	ROGERS		Bak	364
C. W.	Collins			338
Thomas	Burnell		Mas	334
John	Terry			256
John	Warner		Fou	249

Source: *Oracle and Public Advertiser*, 24 December 1796.

Table 8.3.19.42
Poll for alderman of Farringdon Without, 1 January 1798

Forename	Surname	Livery	Votes received
CHARLES	PRICE	Iro	606
Samuel Ferrand	Waddington	Joi	399

Source: Beaven, i, p. 165.

Table 8.3.19.43
Poll for common councilmen of Farringdon Without, 7 January 1799

Forename	Surname	Precinct	Livery	Votes received
ROBERT	HERRING		Uph	571
JAMES	SHEARS		Arm	521
WILLIAM	WRIGHT		Inn	493
JAMES	BRANSCOMB		Dye	490
RICHARD	BREWER		Joi	484
JOSEPH	BOUCOCK		Gol	459
ROBERT	WAITHMAN		Fra	452
JOHN	LAMBE		Gol	443
JAMES	BREWER		Joi	431
CHARLES WERY	CLARKE		Tyl	425
WILLIAM	SHARPE		Wea	409
LUKE	HODGSON		Whe	400
WILLIAM E.	ROGERS		Bak	396
JOHN	NICHOLS		Sta	386
JONATHAN	PERKINS		Gol	365
THOMAS	HARPER		Tur	352
Thomas	Burnell		Mas	345
Thomas	Reeve		Iro	331
John	Wheeler		Gol	326
John	Axford		Mus	182

Source: *Observer*, 30 December 1798.

Table 8.3.19.44
Poll for common councilmen of Farringdon Without, 6 January 1800

Forename	Surname	Precinct	Livery	Votes received
ROBERT	HERRING		Uph	507
JAMES	SHEARS		Arm	500
JAMES	BRANSCOMB		Dye	491
WILLIAM	WRIGHT		Inn	455
JOSEPH	BOUCOCK		Gol	453
JOHN	NICHOLS		Sta	440
JAMES	BREWER		Joi	430
JONATHAN	PERKINS		Gol	425
RICHARD	BREWER		Joi	418
CHARLES W.	CLARKE		Tyl	399
LUKE	HODGSON		Whe	397
ROBERT	WAITHMAN		Fra	395
THOMAS	HARPER		Tur	377
THOMAS	REEVE		Iro	365
SAMUEL	CLANFIELD		Tur	350
THOMAS	BURNELL		Mas	338
William	Robins		Clm	304

Source: *Oracle and Daily Advertiser*, 25 December 1799.

Table 8.3.19.45
Poll for common councilmen of Farringdon Without, 9 January 1804

Forename	Surname	Precinct	Livery	Votes received
ROBERT	HERRING		Uph	609
JAMES	SHEARS		Arm	591
THOMAS M.	BARDIN		Lor	591
JAMES	BRANSCOMB		Dye	558
JOSEPH	BOUCOCK		Gol	540
WILLIAM	WRIGHT		Inn	522
RICHARD	BREWER		Joi	520
ROBERT	WAITHMAN		Fra	512
JOHN	DAWSON		Pla	493
ABRAHAM	YOUNG		Tur	491
JOHN	NICHOLS		Sta	489
JAMES	BREWER		Joi	486
THOMAS	HARPER		Tur	468
THOMAS	REEVE		Iro	418
JOHN	NEWMAN		Cur	394
William	Robins		Clm	366
	Burkit			143

Source: *Morning Chronicle*, 24 December 1803.

Table 8.3.19.46
Poll for common councilmen of Farringdon Without, 12 January 1807

Forename	Surname	Precinct	Livery	Votes received
ROBERT	WAITHMAN		Fra	578
EDWARD	QUIN		Clm	574
THOMAS M.	BARDIN		Lor	549
JAMES	BRANSCOMB		Dye	530
ROBERT	HERRING		Uph	499
JOHN	DAWSON		Pla	495
WILLIAM	WRIGHT		Inn	492
WILLIAM JOHN	REEVES		Bla	484
RICHARD	BREWER		Joi	483
JAMES	BREWER		Joi	482
ABRAHAM	YOUNG		Tur	467
THOMAS	HARPER		Tur	466
WILLIAM	GRIFFITH		Sta	454
THOMAS	REEVE		Iro	451
JOHN	NEWMAN		Cur	450
JOHN	NICHOLS		Sta	446
John	Axford		Mus	168

Source: *Morning Chronicle*, 25 December 1806.

Table 8.3.19.47
Poll for common councilmen of Farringdon Without, 11 January 1808

Forename	Surname	Precinct	Livery	Votes received
EDWARD	QUIN		Clm	667
THOMAS M.	BARDIN		Lor	649
ROBERT	HERRING		Uph	621
ROBERT	WAITHMAN		Fra	615
JAMES	BRANSCOMB		Dye	613
JOHN	NICHOLS		Sta	596
WILLIAM JOHN	REEVES		Bla	576
WILLIAM	WRIGHT		Inn	550
JOHN	DAWSON		Pla	544
ABRAHAM	YOUNG		Tur	541
RICHARD	BREWER		Joi	523
JAMES	BREWER		Joi	515
WILLIAM	GRIFFITH		Sta	512
THOMAS	HARPER		Tur	505
JOHN	NEWMAN		Cur	482
THOMAS	REEVE		Iro	455
James	Crook		Cor	394

Source: *Morning Chronicle*, 24 December 1807.

Table 8.3.19.48
Poll for common councilman of Farringdon Without, 22 October 1808

Forename	Surname	Precinct	Livery	Votes received
WILLIAM	MURRELL		Bar	401
James	Crook		Cor	343
Samuel	Miller		Cor	36

Source: *Morning Chronicle*, 22 October 1808.

Table 8.3.19.49
Poll for common councilmen of Farringdon Without, 24 December 1808

Forename	Surname	Precinct	Livery	Votes received
ROBERT	WAITHMAN		Fra	729
JAMES	CROOK		Cor	712
WILLIAM	MURRELL		Bar	664
ROBERT	HERRING		Uph	659
THOMAS M.	BARDIN		Lor	642
WILLIAM JOHN	REEVES		Bla	640
THOMAS	REEVE		Iro	616
JAMES	BRANSCOMB		Dye	616
JOHN	NICHOLS		Sta	580
SAMUEL	MILLER		Cor	570
WILLIAM	WRIGHT		Inn	560
THOMAS	HARPER		Tur	558
JOHN	DAWSON		Pla	545
ABRAHAM	YOUNG		Tur	521
WILLIAM	GRIFFITH		Sta	480
RICHARD	BREWER		Joi	476
James	Brewer		Joi	430

Source: *Morning Chronicle*, 24 December 1808.

Table 8.3.19.50
Poll for common councilmen of Farringdon Without, 8 January 1810

Forename	Surname	Precinct	Livery	Votes received
ROBERT	WAITHMAN		Fra	713
WILLIAM	PONTIFEX		Arm	658
ROBERT	HERRING		Uph	628
EDWARD	QUIN		Clm	625
JAMES	CROOK		Cor	615
THOMAS M.	BARDIN		Lor	601
WILLIAM JOHN	REEVES		Bla	584
SAMUEL	MILLER		Cor	584
ABRAHAM	YOUNG		Tur	532
JOHN	DAWSON		Pla	531
JOHN	NICHOLLS		Sta	515
WILLIAM	GRIFFITH		Sta	512
THOMAS	REEVE		Iro	509
WILLIAM	WRIGHT		Inn	502
WILLIAM	MURRELL		Bar	501
RICHARD	BREWER		Joi	483
Thomas	Harper		Tur	448

Source: *Morning Chronicle*, 25 December 1809.

Table 8.3.19.51
Poll for unknown office of Farringdon Without, 19 July 1810

Forename	Surname	Precinct	Livery	Votes received
JOHN	HICKIN			57
	Farlow			39
	Edmonds			21

Source: John Hickin, *To the worthy inhabitants of the parish of St Dunstan in the west* (1810).

Table 8.3.19.52
Poll for common councilmen of Farringdon Without, 7 January 1811

Forename	Surname	Precinct	Livery	Votes received
EDWARD	QUIN		Clm	662
ROBERT	WAITHMAN		Fra	617
ROBERT	HERRING		Uph	547
WILLIAM JOHN	REEVES		Bla	507
JOHN	NICHOLS		Sta	505
JAMES	CROOK		Cor	485
WILLIAM	WRIGHT		Inn	467
THOMAS	REEVE		Iro	464
SAMUEL	MILLER		Cor	458
JOHN	DAWSON		Pla	451
ABRAHAM	YOUNG		Tur	446
RICHARD	BREWER		Joi	442
WILLIAM	GRIFFITH		Sta	439
WILLIAM	MURRELL		Bar	438
THOMAS	HARPER		Tur	436
WILLIAM	PONTIFEX		Arm	435
John	Blackett		Gls	305
Bezer	Blundell		Car	304

Source: *Morning Chronicle*, 25 December 1825.

Table 8.3.19.53
Poll for common councilmen of Farringdon Without, 6 January 1812

Forename	Surname	Precinct	Livery	Votes received
ROBERT	WAITHMAN		Fra	628
EDWARD	QUIN		Clm	628
WILLIAM JOHN	REEVES		Bla	581
ROBERT	HERRING		Uph	553
JAMES	CROOK		Cor	547
THOMAS M.	BARDIN		Lor	527
JOHN	DAWSON		Pla	512
ABRAHAM	YOUNG		Tur	482
TTHOMAS	REEVE		Iro	481
WILLIAM	PONTIFEX		Arm	471
ROBERT	HEDGES		Cop	471
WILLIAM	MURRELL		Bar	466
WILLIAM	GRIFFITH		Sta	445
THOMAS	HARPER		Tur	443
RICHARD	BREWER		Joi	420
BEZER	BLUNDELL		Car	407
	Robins			360
	Hoare			306

Source: *Morning Chronicle*, 25 December 1811.

Table 8.3.19.54
Poll for common councilmen of Farringdon Without, 11 January 1813

Forename	Surname	Precinct	Livery	Votes received
ROBERT	WAITHMAN		Fra	575
EDWARD	QUIN		Clm	542
ROBERT	HERRING		Uph	528
WILLIAM JOHN	REEVES		Bla	515
JAMES	CROOK		Cor	500
THOMAS M.	BARDIN		Lor	471
ABRAHAM	YOUNG		Tur	449
THOMAS	REEVE		Iro	444
WILLIAM	MURRELL		Bar	440
JOHN	DAWSON		Pla	440
WILLIAM	GRIFFITH		Sta	435
ROBERT	HEDGES		Cop	422
WILLIAM	PONTIFEX		Arm	418
THOMAS	HARPER		Tur	407
JOHN	BLACKETT		Gls	380
HENRY	MARRIOTT		Arm	356
	Robins			324
Richard	Brewer		Joi	313
Richard	Rosser			192

Source: *Morning Chronicle*, 24 December 1812.

Table 8.3.19.55
Poll for common councilmen of Farringdon Without, 9 January 1815

Forename	Surname	Precinct	Livery	Votes received
ROBERT	WAITHMAN		Fra	656
WILLIAM	VALE		Bar	559
ROBERT	HERRING		Uph	536
WILLIAM JOHN	REEVES		Bla	512
JAMES	CROOK		Cor	495
WILLIAM	GRIFFITH		Sta	467
ABRAHAM	YOUNG		Tur	460
THOMAS	REEVE		Iro	453
THOMAS OAK	SMITH		Glz	445
JOHN	BLACKETT		Gls	442
WILLIAM	MURRELL		Bar	439
WILLIAM	PONTIFEX		Arm	423
THOMAS	HARPER		Tur	421
CHARLES A.	SAVAGE		Inn	408
WILLIAM	PATTEN		Gol	396
ROBERT	HEDGES		Cop	393
Samuel	Miller		Cor	302

Source: *Morning Chronicle*, 24 December 1814.

Table 8.3.19.56
Poll for common councilmen of Farringdon Without, 12 January 1818

Forename	Surname	Precinct	Livery	Votes received
ROBERT	WAITHMAN		Fra	560
ROBERT	HERRING		Uph	528
WILLIAM JOHN	REEVES		Bla	515
WILLIAM	VALE		Bar	507
JAMES	CROOK		Cor	506
JAMES	WILLIAMS		Gol	490
JOHN	BLACKETT		Gls	463
WILLIAM	GRIFFITH		Sta	461
ABRAHAM	YOUNG		Tur	454
WILLIAM A.	BECKWITH		Gun	445
WILLIAM	PONTIFEX		Arm	421
CHARLES A.	SAVAGE		Inn	418
THOMAS	REEVE		Iro	411
THOMAS OAK	SMITH		Glz	379
WILLIAM	PATTEN		Gol	368
THOMAS	HARPER		Tur	309
William	Murrell			236
	Sparrow			137

Source: *Morning Chronicle*, 25 December 1817.

Table 8.3.19.57
Poll for common councilmen of Farringdon Without, 10 January 1820

Forename	Surname	Precinct	Livery	Votes received
ROBERT	HERRING		Uph	507
WILLIAM JOHN	REEVES		Bla	497
JAMES	CROOK		Cor	451
WILLIAM	VALE		Bar	448
WILLIAM	GRIFFITH		Sta	429
JAMES	WILLIAMS		Gol	428
ABRAHAM	YOUNG		Tur	426
JOHN	BLACKETT		Gls	422
CHARLES A.	SAVAGE		Inn	414
WILLIAM A.	BECKWITH		Gun	413
WILLIAM	PONTIFEX		Arm	402
RICHARD	TAYLOR		Sta	394
THOMAS OAK	SMITH		Glz	389
WILLIAM	PATTEN		Gol	378
JAMES WEBB	SOUTHGATE		Bar	369
SAMUEL	ROBERTS		Pai	329
Thomas	Harper		Tur	297

Source: *Morning Chronicle*, 25 December 1819.

Table 8.3.19.58
Poll for common councilmen of Farringdon Without, 8 January 1821

Forename	Surname	Precinct	Livery	Votes received
WILLIAM JOHN	REEVES		Bla	521
JAMES	WILLIAMS		Gol	517
JAMES	CROOK		Cor	488
WILLIAM	VALE		Bar	485
WILLIAM	GRIFFITHS		Sta	484
JOHN	BLACKETT		Gls	484
CHARLES A.	SAVAGE		Inn	479
RICHARD	TAYLOR		Sta	474
WILLIAM A.	BECKWITH		Gun	469
VINCENT	FIGGINS		Sta	467
SAMUEL	ROBERTS		Pai	456
JAMES WEBB	SOUTHGATE		Bar	441
GEORGE	TURNER		Far	438
WILLIAM	PATTEN		Gol	429
THOMAS CURSON	HANSARD		Sta	420
ALEXANDER	GALLOWAY		Lea	404
Thomas	Harper		Tur	171

Source: *Morning Chronicle*, 25 December 1820.

Table 8.3.19.59

Poll for common councilmen of Farringdon Without, 12 January 1824

Forename	Surname	Precinct	Livery	Votes received
WILLIAM JOHN	REEVES		Bla	515
WILLIAM	VALE		Bar	496
JOHN	BLACKETT		Gls	481
JAMES	CROOK		Cor	477
CHARLES A.	SAVAGE		Inn	477
WILLIAM	GRIFFITHS		Sta	475
WILLIAM A.	BECKWITH		Gun	461
ABRAHAM	YOUNG		Tur	460
SAMUEL	ROBERTS		Pai	459
JAMES WEBB	SOUTHGATE		Bar	458
RICHARD	TAYLOR		Sta	458
VINCENT	FIGGINS		Sta	444
THOMAS C.	HANSARD		Sta	430
GEORGE	TURNER		Far	423
WILLIAM	PATTEN		Gol	411
HENRY	BUTTERWORTH		Sta	382
Alexander	Galloway		Lea	378

Source: *St James's Chronicle*, 23-25 December 1823.

Table 8.3.19.60
Poll for common councilmen of Farringdon Without, 10 January 1825

Forename	Surname	Precinct	Livery	Votes received
HENRY	BUTTERWORTH		Sta	531
EDWARD	TICKNER		Lea	523
WILLIAM JOHN	REEVES		Bla	470
JOHN	BLACKETT		Gls	448
JAMES	CROOK		Cor	426
WILLIAM	VALE		Bar	412
RICHARD	TAYLOR		Sta	404
JAMES WEBB	SOUTHGATE		Bar	380
ALEXANDER	GALLOWAY		Lea	377
WILLIAM	GRIFFITH		Sta	374
CHARLES A.	SAVAGE		Inn	362
WILLIAM	PATTEN		Gol	360
WILLIAM A.	BECKWITH		Gun	351
SAMUEL	ROBERTS		Pai	350
VINCENT	FIGGINS		Sta	345
ABRAHAM	YOUNG		Tur	330
George	Turner		Far	326
Thomas C.	Hansard		Sta	302
James	Ramshaw		Sta	227

Source: *St James's Chronicle*, 23-25 December 1824.

Table 8.3.19.61
Poll for common councilmen of Farringdon Without, 9 January 1826

Forename	Surname	Precinct	Livery	Votes received
WILLIAM JOHN	REEVES		Bla	541
WILLIAM	VALE		Bar	497
JAMES	CROOK		Cor	483
EDWARD	TICKNER		Lea	470
WILLIAM	GRIFFITH		Sta	466
HENRY	BUTTERWORTH		Sta	453
JOHN	BLACKETT		Gls	447
VINCENT	FIGGINS		Sta	446
RICHARD	TAYLOR		Sta	433
JAMES WEBB	SOUTHGATE		Bar	426
SAMUEL	ROBERTS		Pai	423
CHARLES A.	SAVAGE		Inn	420
WILLIAM A.	BECKWITH		Gun	415
JAMES	RAMSHAW		Sta	405
JAMES	HARMER		Spe	404
ALEXANDER	GALLOWAY		Lea	404
Robert	Obbard		Pai	386
William Cheek	Bousfield		Arm	363
	Jones			213
	Charles			162

Source: *St James's Chronicle*, 22-24 December 1825.

Table 8.3.19.62
Poll for common councilmen of Farringdon Without, 8 January 1827

Forename	Surname	Precinct	Livery	Votes received
WILLIAM JOHN	REEVES		Bla	Unopposed
WILLIAM	VALE		Bar	Unopposed
EDWARD	TICKNER		Lea	350
SAMUEL	ROBERTS		Pai	331
JAMES	CROOK		Cor	328
VINCENT	FIGGINS		Sta	324
RICHARD	TAYLOR		Sta	324
CHARLES A.	SAVAGE		Inn	322
HENRY	BUTTERWORTH		Sta	318
ROBERT	OBBARD		Pai	316
WILLIAM	GRIFFITH		Sta	314
JAMES	HARMER		Spe	308
WILLIAM A.	BECKWITH		Gun	306
JOHN	BLACKETT		Gls	300
JAMES	RAMSHAW		Sta	296
ALEXANDER	GALLOWAY		Lea	253
	Barrett			176

Source: *Morning Chronicle*, 25 December 1826.

Table 8.3.19.63
Poll for common councilmen of Farringdon Without, 7 January 1828

Forename	Surname	Precinct	Livery	Votes received
JAMES	RAMSHAW		Sta	536
WILLIAM CHEEK	BOUSFIELD		Arm	535
EDWARD	TICKNER		Lea	534
JAMES	HARMER		Spe	521
WILLIAM	VALE		Bar	496
JOSEPH THOMAS	BEDFORD		Joi	495
RICHARD	TAYLOR		Sta	485
VINCENT	FIGGINS		Sta	472
JOHN	BLACKETT		Gls	461
HENRY	BUTTERWORTH		Sta	461
WILLIAM A.	BECKWITH		Gun	451
GEORGE F.	HARMS		Inn	443
SAMUEL	ROBERTS		Pai	433
UNDERWOOD	PRICE		Tin	404
ROBERT	OBBARD		Pai	391
ALEXANDER	GALLOWAY		Lea	390
Charles A.	Savage		Inn	385
Henry	Hunt			348

Source: Anon., *A collection of particulars* (1829).

Table 8.3.19.64
Poll for common councilmen of Farringdon Without, 12 January 1829

Forename	Surname	Precinct	Livery	Votes received
WILLIAM CHEEK	BOUSFIELD		Arm	526
CHARLES A.	SAVAGE		Inn	513
EDWARD	TICKNER		Lea	484
RICHARD	TAYLOR		Sta	481
GEORGE F.	HARMS		Inn	481
HENRY	BUTTERWORTH		Sta	471
JAMES	HARMER		Spe	469
SAMUEL	ROBERTS		Pai	457
JOHN	BLACKETT		Gls	453
JAMES	RAMSHAW		Sta	448
ROBERT	OBBARD		Pai	445
JOSHUA THOMAS	BEDFORD		Joi	443
WILLIAM A.	BECKWITH		Gun	423
VINCENT	FIGGINS		Sta	416
ALEXANDER	GALLOWAY		Lea	411
UNDERWOOD	PRICE		Tin	390
Henry	Hunt			298

Source: Anon., *A collection of the particulars* (1829).

8.3.20 Langbourn, 1712-1831: 24 polls

(10 common councilmen; 305 freeman householders in 1833)

Table 8.3.20.1
Poll for aldermanic candidates of Langbourn, 9 July 1712

Forename	Surname	Livery	Votes received	
			Poll	Scrutiny
PETER	DELMÉ	Fis	219	156
Robert	Beachcroft		218	169
William	Askey		247	169
Samuel	Clark		247	156

Source: Beaven, i, p. 123.

Table 8.3.20.2
Poll for common councilmen of Langbourn, 6 January 1729

Forename	Surname	Precinct	Livery	Votes received	
				Poll	Scrutiny
GABRIEL	SMYTH				
JAMES	MARTIN				
GEORGE	CHAMPION				
GEORGE	CASWALL				
JOHN	COLT				
THOMAS	RAVENSCROFT				
JOSEPH	HANKEY				
THOMAS	HOARE				
WILLIAM	HAWYS				
THOMAS	OYLES				

Source: LMA COL/CC/13/01/012.

Table 8.3.20.3
Poll for alderman of Langbourn, 4 September 1728

Forename	Surname	Livery	Votes received
HENRY	HANKEY	Hab	146
Edward	Bridgen	Cut	90

Source: Beaven, i, p. 171.

Table 8.3.20.4
Poll for common councilmen of Langbourn, 9 January 1738

Forename	Surname	Precinct	Livery	Votes received	
				Poll	**Scrutiny**
GABRIEL	SMYTH				Unopposed
JOHN	CASWALL			224	204
THOMAS	THOMPSON			204	183
JAMES	CREED			192	178
JOHN	TOWNSEND			195	175
THOMAS	OYLES			173	164
EDWARD	IRONSIDES			183	163
JOHN	BARKER			180	160
JOSHUA	BAKER			163	155
SAMUEL	SYDEBOTHAM			174	153
George	Caswall			158	150
George	Scullard			156	
Samuel	Herring			152	
William	Knight			149	
William	Pepys			144	
James	Hebert			133	

Source: *London Evening Post*, 22 December 1737; 19 January 1738.

Table 8.3.20.5
Poll for common councilmen of Langbourn, 9 January 1739

Forename	Surname	Precinct	Livery	Votes received	
				Poll	Scrutiny
THOMAS	OYLES			192	184
JAMES	CREED			189	183
SAMUEL	HERRING			187	181
WILLIAM	KNIGHT			174	167
JOHN	CASWALL			180	165
WILLIAM	PEPYS			172	163
HENRY	LAWTON			166	161
EDWARD	NEAL			160	154
JOHN	TOWNSEND			175	154
JAMES	HEBERT			157	150
Edward	Ironsides			165	149
John	Barker			161	146
George	Caswall			155	142
Thomas	Thompson			141	128
Samuel	Sydebotham			136	121
John	Hawkins			124	119
John	Cheslyn			130	116
James	Littlebury			74	106
George	Scullard			115	102
James	Wicks			104	100

Source: *London Evening Post*, 21-23 December 1738; *Read's Weekly Journal*, 27 January 1739.

Table 8.3.20.6
Poll for common councilmen of Langbourn, 7 January 1740

Forename	Surname	Precinct	Livery	Votes received
THOMAS	OYLES			
JOHN	CASWALL			
JAMES	CREED			
EDWARD	NEAL			
WILLIAM	PEPYS			
WILLIAM	KNIGHT			
SAMUEL	HERRING			
HENRY	LAWTON			
EDWARD	IRONSIDES			
JAMES	HAWKINS			

Source: *London Evening Post*, 22-25 December 1739.

Table 8.3.20.7
Poll for common councilmen of Langbourn, 9 January 1744

Forename	Surname	Precinct	Livery	Votes received
JOHN	BARKER			185
EDWARD	IRONSIDES			182
HENRY	LAWTON			180
JOHN	TOWNSEND			174
THOMAS	RAWLINSON			173
ROBERT	WILSON			170
THOMAS	MINORS			168
JOHN	SPRINGETT			164
WILLIAM	BIRTON			154
JAMES	ANDERTON			142
William	Hunter			104

Source: *Daily Advertiser*, 24 December 1743.

Table 8.3.20.8
Poll for common councilmen of Langbourn, 7 January 1771

Forename	Surname	Precinct	Livery	Votes received	
				Poll	**Scrutiny**
INGHAM	FOSTER		Iro	193	170
WILLIAM	LEM		Sal	184	161
JAMES	THOMPSON		Dra	186	161
WILLIAM	CHESSON		Hab	181	158
GEORGE	MAYNARD		Vin	178	156
CHRISTOPHER	CORRALL		Gol	174	151
MATTHIAS	PALLING		Joi	171	149
THOMAS	WITHERBY		Cop	159	137
JOHN	REYNOLDS			142	131
ROBERT	WILSON		Met	146	125
	Burrow			145	121

Source: *General Evening Post*, 22-25 December 1770; *Middlesex Journal*, 15-17 January 1771; *Public Advertiser*, 16 January 1771.

Table 8.3.20.9
Poll for common councilmen of Langbourn, 6 January 1783

Forename	Surname	Precinct	Livery	Votes received
THOMAS	WITHERBY		Cop	129
GEORGE	BODLEY		Fis	125
JOHN	NEWMAN		Joi	125
EDWARD	TUTET		Clm	124
CHRISTOPHER	CORRALL		Gol	120
PETER	POPE		Hab	119
JOHN	PHILLIPS		Uph	119
THOMAS	HUDSON		Car	119
CHARLES EDWARD	WILSON		Sta	119
ROBERT	GOSLING		Sal	115
Francis	Pyner			46

Source: *Morning Chronicle*, 24 December 1782.

Table 8.3.20.10
Poll for common councilmen of Langbourn, 9 January 1792

Forename	Surname	Precinct	Livery	Votes received
JOHN	PHILLIPS		Uph	152
THOMAS	DERMER		Car	149
HENRY	MITTON		Gol	147
GEORGE	BODLEY		Fis	144
THOMAS	WITHERBY		Cop	143
JOHN	DOD		Gro	143
PETER	POPE		Hab	137
HILTON	WRAY		Apo	136
RICHARD	RANKIN		Bar	114
THOMAS	AYRES		Gol	109
James	Davis, jnr			79

Source: *Lloyd's Evening Post,* 23-26 December 1791.

Table 8.3.20.11
Poll for alderman of Langbourn, 26 February 1795

Forename	Surname	Livery	Votes received
JOHN	EAMER	Sal	123
Matthew	Bloxham	Sta	94

Source: Beaven, i, p. 172.

Table 8.3.20.12
Poll for common councilmen of Langbourn, 11 January 1796

Forename	Surname	Precinct	Livery	Votes received
THOMAS	AYRES		Gol	181
THOMAS	WITHERBY		Cop	179
GEORGE	BODLEY		Fis	178
PETER	POPE		Hab	177
THOMAS	DERMER		Car	177
HENRY	MITTON		Gol	172
HILTON	WRAY		Apo	168
JOHN	PHILLIPS		Uph	144
RICHARD	RANKIN		Bar	136
WILLIAM	PINCHBACK		Cor	119
Richard	Dixon		Fis	116

Source: *Morning Post*, 24 December 1795.

Table 8.3.20.13
Poll for common councilmen of Langbourn, 9 January 1797

Forename	Surname	Precinct	Livery	Votes received
JOHN	PHILLIPS		Uph	45
THOMAS	DERMER		Car	45
THOMAS	AYRES		Gol	44
THOMAS	WITHERBY		Cop	43
PETER	POPE		Hab	43
RICHARD	RANKIN		Bar	43
HILTON	WRAY		Apo	42
GEORGE	BODLEY		Fis	41
WILLIAM	PINCHBACK		Cor	41
RICHARD	DIXON		Fis	39
Henry	Goldfinch			11

Source: *Daily Advertiser*, 23 December 1796.

Table 8.3.20.14
Poll for common councilmen of Langbourn, 8 January 1810

Forename	Surname	Precinct	Livery	Votes received
JOHN	PHILLIPS		Uph	195
RICHARD	RANKIN		Bar	180
THOMAS	AYRES		Gol	175
GEORGE	BODLEY		Fis	168
THOMAS	WILTSHIRE		Clw	160
RICHARD	DIXON		Fis	159
JOHN	TAYLOR		Iro	147
MILES	MASKEW		Arm	135
WILLIAM	WITHERBY		Sta	121
ROBERT	ELLIOTT		Gls	115
Benjamin	Stubbing		But	105
William	Pinchback		Cor	86
Andrew	Anderson		Bak	73

Source: LMA CLC/W/KA/001/Ms. 05678.

Table 8.3.20.15
Poll for common councilmen of Langbourn, 7 January 1811

Forename	Surname	Precinct	Livery	Votes received
JOHN	PHILLIPS		Uph	178
THOMAS	WILTSHIRE		Clw	170
RICHARD	RANKIN		Bar	167
THOMAS	AYRES		Gol	167
GEORGE	BODLEY		Fis	163
BENJAMIN	STUBBING		But	162
WILLIAM	WITHERBY		Sta	152
ROBERT	ELLIOTT		Gls	150
RICHARD	DIXON		Fis	142
THOMAS	THOMPSON		Fel	105
Andrew	Anderson		Bak	92

Source: LMA CLC/W/KA/001/Ms. 05678.

Table 8.3.20.16
Poll for common councilmen of Langbourn, 6 January 1812

Forename	Surname	Precinct	Livery	Votes received
JOHN	PHILLIPS		Uph	111
THOMAS	AYRES		Gol	109
THOMAS	WILTSHIRE		Clw	108
BENJAMIN	STUBBING		But	105
RICHARD	DIXON		Fis	104
RICHARD	RANKIN		Bar	102
ROBERT	ELLIOTT		Gls	100
WILLIAM	WITHERBY		Sta	97
GEORGE	BODLEY		Fis	88
THOMAS	THOMPSON		Fel	84
Andrew	Anderson		Bak	43

Source: LMA CLC/W/KA/001/Ms. 05678.

Table 8.3.20.17
Poll for common councilmen of Langbourn, 11 January 1813

Forename	Surname	Precinct	Livery	Votes received
JOHN	PHILLIPS		Uph	209
THOMAS	AYRES		Gol	206
THOMAS	WILTSHIRE		Clw	205
ROBERT	ELLIOTT		Gls	204
BENJAMIN	STUBBING		But	197
RICHARD	RANKIN		Bar	196
WILLIAM	WITHERBY		Sta	194
RICHARD	DIXON		Fis	190
JAMES	CARTER		Wea	146
EDWARD	POYNDER		Plu	134
Andrew	Anderson		Bak	101

Source: LMA CLC/W/KA/001/Ms. 05678.

Table 8.3.20.18
Poll for common councilman of Langbourn, 20 October 1813

Forename	Surname	Precinct	Livery	Votes received
SAMUEL	JOYCE		Clm	17
Andrew	Anderson		Bak	5
John Holmes	Gibson		Scr	3

Source: LMA CLC/W/KA/001/Ms. 05678.

Table 8.3.20.19
Poll for common councilmen of Langbourn, 8 January 1821

Forename	Surname	Precinct	Livery	Votes received
THOMAS	AYRES		Gol	189
THOMAS	WILTSHIRE		Clw	177
BENJAMIN	STUBBING		But	174
JAMES	CARTER		Wea	165
RICHARD	DIXON		Fis	163
JOHN HOLMES	GIBSON		Scr	163
WILLIAM	WITHERBY		Sta	159
ROBERT	ELLIOTT		Gls	153
SAMUEL	JOYCE		Clm	151
THOMAS	MILROY		Sad	108
William	Rice		Bak	96
William	Beddom			92

Source: *Morning Chronicle*, 25 December 1820.

Table 8.3.20.20
Poll for common councilmen of Langbourn, 7 January 1822

Forename	Surname	Precinct	Livery	Votes received
ROBERT	ELLIOTT		Gls	174
JOHN HOLMES	GIBSON		Scr	174
THOMAS	MILROY		Sad	173
JAMES	CARTER		Wea	170
RICHARD	DIXON		Fis	166
THOMAS	WILTSHIRE		Clw	164
BENJAMIN	STUBBING		But	162
THOMAS	AYRES		Gol	160
SAMUEL	JOYCE		Clm	134
WILLIAM	RICE		Bak	122
Robert	Haswell		Pai	101
	Wright			87
William	Beddom			26

Source: *St James's Chronicle*, 22-25 December 1821.

Table 8.3.20.21
Poll for common councilman of Langbourn, 4 February 1822

Forename	Surname	Precinct	Livery	Votes received
THOMAS	WILTSHIRE		Clw	139
Robert	Haswell		Pai	74

Source: *The Times*, 7 February 1822.

Table 8.3.20.22
Poll for alderman of Langbourn, 10 April 1823

Forename	Surname	Livery	Votes received
JOHN	KEY	Sta	135
Francis	Desanges	Dye	89

Source: Beaven, i, p. 172.

Table 8.3.20.23
Poll for common councilmen of Langbourn, 7 January 1828

Forename	Surname	Precinct	Livery	Votes received
THOMAS	AYRES		Gol	86
ROBERT	HASWELL		Pai	85
WILLIAM	BARBER		Sal	85
ROBERT	ELLIOTT		Gls	84
JAMES	CARTER		Wea	83
JOHN	DIXON		Met	83
BENJAMIN	STUBBING		But	81
WILLIAM	NICHOLLS		Scr	80
JAMES	LAYTON		Gro	78
SAMUEL	UNWIN		Fel	74
	Stewart			14
	Creed			12

Source: *Morning Chronicle*, 24 December 1827.

Table 8.3.20.24
Poll for common councilmen of Langbourn, 10 January 1831

Forename	Surname	Precinct	Livery	Votes received
JAMES	CARTER		Wea	160
BENJAMIN	STUBBING		But	158
THOMAS	AYRES		Gol	157
SAMUEL	UNWIN		Fel	151
ROBERT	HASWELL		Pai	150
JOHN	DIXON		Met	150
ROBERT	ELLIOTT		Gls	147
WILLIAM	NICHOLLS		Scr	141
WILLIAM	MARCHANT		Sta	135
WILLIAM	MORRISON		Fel	96
William	Stewart		Met	86
	Killick			76
	Hunt			17

Source: *Morning Chronicle*, 24 December 1830.

8.3.21 Lime Street, 1724-1825: 14 polls

(4 common councilmen; number of freeman householders in 1833 unrecorded, but *c.* 100)

Table 8.3.21.1
Poll for alderman of Lime Street, 31 January 1724

Forename	Surname	Livery	Votes received	
			Poll	Scrutiny
RICHARD	HOPKINS	Cut	88	66
Edward	Bridgen	Cut	72	48

Source: Beaven, i, p. 177.

Table 8.3.21.2
Poll for common councilmen of Lime Street, 8 January 1728

Forename	Surname	Precinct	Livery	Votes received	
				Poll	Scrutiny
HENRY	TOMBS				
JOHN	HARDMAN				
JAMES	SMITH				
JAMES	PHILLIPS				
William	Pomeroy				
Thomas	Johnson				

Source: LMA COL/CC/13/01/012.

Table 8.3.21.3
Poll for alderman of Lime Street, 5 January 1736

Forename	Surname	Livery	Votes received	
			Poll	Scrutiny
ROBERT	WILLIMOTT	Coo	62	56
Robert	Pomeroy	Met	61	47

Source: Beaven, i, p. 177.

Table 8.3.21.4
Poll for beadle of Lime Street, 13 September 1739

Forename	Surname	Votes received
BENJAMIN	HUGHES	60
Edward	Harvey	24

Source: LMA CLC/W/KB/001/Ms. 01169/001.

Table 8.3.21.5
Poll for alderman of Lime Street, 23 December 1746

Forename	Surname	Livery	Votes received	
			Poll	Scrutiny
WILLIAM	WHITAKER	Clo	58	48
John	Tuff	Scr	52	43

Source: Beaven, i, p. 177.

Table 8.3.21.6
Poll for alderman of Lime Street, 6 August 1752

Forename	Surname	Livery	Votes received
JOHN	PORTER	Sal	68
William	Alexander	Tal	34

Source: Beaven, i, p. 177.

Table 8.3.21.7
Poll for common councilmen of Lime Street, 6 January 1755

Forename	Surname	Precinct	Livery	Votes received
SAMUEL	SOUTHOUSE			68
GEORGE	MASON			61
WILLIAM	BURGIS			54
LANCELOT	SHADWELL			53
Samuel	Freeman			29

Source: LMA CLC/W/KB/001/Ms. 01169/001.

Table 8.3.21.8
Poll for common councilmen of Lime Street, 8 January 1770

Forename	Surname	Precinct	Livery	Votes received
SAMUEL	FREEMAN		Gol	101
JAMES	SHARP		Dra	101
JOHN	HARDY		Mus	78
HUMPHRY	JONES		Glo	65
	Moody			54

Source: LMA CLC/W/KB/001/Ms. 01169/001.

Table 8.3.21.9
Poll for alderman of Lime Street, 26 September 1772

Forename	Surname	Livery	Votes received
WATKIN	LEWES	Joi	59
Benjamin	Hammett	Hab	34

Source: Beaven, i, p. 177; but for variant, see *London Evening Post*, 23 December 1772.

Table 8.3.21.10
Poll for beadle of Lime Street, 30 May 1780

Forename	Surname	Votes received
WILLIAM	HUMMERSTON	62
John	Letts	15

Source: LMA CLC/W/KB/001/Ms. 01169/002.

Table 8.3.21.11
Poll for common councilman of Lime Street, 6 January 1800

Forename	Surname	Precinct	Livery	Votes received
SAMUEL	BROWN			
JOHN	ADCOCK		Sal	
JACOB	BOAK			
THOMAS	PRICE		Met	45
John	Wilt			40

Source: *Morning Post*, 25 December 1799.

Table 8.3.21.12
Poll for common councilmen of Lime Street, 8 January 1821

Forename	Surname	Precinct	Livery	Votes received
THOMAS	PRICE		Met	57
JOHN	DYSTER		Met	54
JOHN	ADCOCK		Sal	52
WILLIAM	SHEARMAN		Fel	47
John	Prince		Met	21

Source: LMA CLC/W/KB/001/Ms. 01169/002.

Table 8.3.21.13
Poll for common councilmen of Lime Street, 7 January 1822

Forename	Surname	Precinct	Livery	Votes received
THOMAS	PRICE		Met	52
JOHN	PRINCE		Met	46
JOHN	DYSTER		Met	45
WILLIAM	SHEARMAN		Fel	40
Peter	Jones			30

Source: LMA CLC/W/KB/001/Ms. 01169/002.

Table 8.3.21.14
Poll for common councilmen of Lime Street, 10 January 1825

Forename	Surname	Precinct	Livery	Votes received
THOMAS	PRICE		Met	61
THOMAS	MITCHELL		Dra	61
JOHN	DYSTER		Met	59
WILLIAM	SHEARMAN		Fel	51
John	Prince		Met	31

Source: LMA CLC/W/KB/001/Ms. 01169/001.

8.3.22 Portsoken, 1708-1831: 22 polls

(5 common councilmen; 123 freeman householders in 1833)

Table 8.3.22.1
Poll for common councilmen of Portsoken, 12 January 1708

Forename	Surname	Precinct	Livery	Votes received
JOHN	CRADDOCK			
John	Dodson			

Source: LMA COL/CC/13/01/012.

Table 8.3.22.2
Poll for alderman of Portsoken, 8 July 1718

Forename	Surname	Livery	Votes received
JOHN	GREEN	Dis	329
Robert	Dennet		186

Source: LMA COL/WD/04/040. Poll not recorded in Beaven.

Table 8.3.22.3
Poll for common councilmen of Portsoken, 8 January 1728

Forename	Surname	Precinct	Livery	Votes received	
				Poll	Scrutiny
THOMAS	HARDWELL				
DANIEL	COLLART				
JOHN	BOSWELL				
VALENTINE	BREWIS				
ROBERT	HALL				
James	Rochester				
Richard	Bridgman				
Robert	Pycroft				
Peter	Spitser				

Source: LMA COL/CC/13/01/012.

Table 8.3.22.4
Poll for common councilmen of Portsoken, 12 January 1736

Forename	Surname	Precinct	Livery	Votes received
ROBERT	PYCROFT			232
VALENTINE	BREWIS			214
DANIEL	COLLCUTT			181
JAMES	ROCHESTER			168
RICHARD	BRIDGMAN			136
Thomas	Hardwell			128

Source: *London Evening Post*, 20 December 1735.

Table 8.3.22.5
Poll for common councilman of Portsoken, 10 January 1737

Forename	Surname	Precinct	Livery	Votes received
JAMES	ROCHESTER			197
	Warner			161

Source: *London Evening Post*, 23 December 1736.

Table 8.3.22.6
Poll for common councilmen of Portsoken, 11 January 1748

Forename	Surname	Precinct	Livery	Votes received
RICHARD	WILSON			238
ROBERT	PYCROFT			201
RICHARD	BRIDGMAN			194
PHILIP	GRAFTON			190
LOWE	MANSFIELD			187
Jeremiah	Bentham			79

Source: *London Evening Post*, 22 December 1747.

Table 8.3.22.7
Poll for common councilmen of Portsoken, 9 January 1749

Forename	Surname	Precinct	Livery	Votes received
RICHARD	BRIDGMAN			217
ROBERT	PYCROFT			210
RICHARD	WILSON			200
LOWE	MANSFIELD			198
PHILIP	GRAFTON			195
Richard	Sharp			135

Source: *London Evening Post*, 22-24 December 1748.

Table 8.3.22.8
Poll for common councilmen of Portsoken, 6 January 1772

Forename	Surname	Precinct	Livery	Votes received	
				Poll	Scrutiny
ROBERT	HARDING		Sal	278	
WILLIAM	ROGERS		Dis	267	
ABRAHAM	BRECKNOCK		Inn	254	
WILLIAM	WILSON		Gun	213	200
PHILIP	GRAFTON		Tur	205	200
George	Holgate			194	180
John Cottewell	Hatcher			175	

Source: *London Evening Post*, 24 December 1771; *Middlesex Journal*, 16 January 1772.

Table 8.3.22.9
Poll for common councilman of Portsoken, 13 January 1774

Forename	Surname	Precinct	Livery	Votes received
JAMES	WISE			147
George	Holgate			81

Source: *London Chronicle*, 13 January 1774.

Table 8.3.22.10
Poll for alderman of Portsoken, 3 June 1785

Forename	Surname	Livery	Votes received
BENJAMIN	HAMNETT	Hab	168
Josiah	Dornford	Coo	127

Source: Beaven, i, p. 186.

Table 8.3.22.11
Poll for common councilmen of Portsoken, 9 January 1786

Forename	Surname	Precinct	Livery	Votes received
JOHN	TAYLOR		Gol	64
BENJAMIN	CURTIS		Dra	64
THOMAS	TUCKER		Joi	63
BENJAMIN	BUNN		Lor	63
ROBERT	HARDING		Sal	61
Thomas	Evans			4

Source: *Whitehall Evening Post*, 22-24 December 1785.

Table 8.3.22.12
Poll for alderman of Portsoken, 19 September 1798

Forename	Surname	Livery	Votes received
JAMES	SHAW	Scr	117
Charles	Flower	Fra	78

Source: Beaven, i, p. 186.

Table 8.3.22.13
Poll for common councilmen of Portsoken, 8 January 1810

Forename	Surname	Precinct	Livery	Votes received
EDWARD	COLEBATCH		Hab	268
ROBERT	ATKINSON		Whe	260
JAMES	HOPPE		Cor	258
ROBERT	CARTER		Cop	217
JOHN	REA		Fou	170
John	Briscoe		Glz	168
William	Hewson		Gls	96

Source: *Morning Chronicle*, 25 December 1809.

Table 8.3.22.14
Poll for common councilmen of Portsoken, 7 January 1811

Forename	Surname	Precinct	Livery	Votes received
ROBERT	ATKINSON		Whe	120
EDWARD	COLEBATCH		Hab	116
ROBERT	CARTER		Cop	114
JOHN	HOPPE		Cor	110
JOHN	BRISCOE		Glz	73
John	Rea		Fou	16

Source: *Morning Chronicle*, 24 December 1810.

Table 8.3.22.15
Poll for common councilmen of Portsoken, 7 January 1822

Forename	Surname	Precinct	Livery	Votes received
EDWARD	COLEBATCH		Hab	211
ROBERT	CARTER		Cop	200
PETER	PERRY		Clm	190
JOHN	SMITH		Bow	187
THOMAS	PARKER		Whe	178
	Cundell			91

Source: *The Times*, 25 December 1821.

Table 8.3.22.16
Poll for common councilmen of Portsoken, 7 January 1828

Forename	Surname	Precinct	Livery	Votes received
EDWARD	COLEBATCH		Hab	190
PETER	PERRY		Clm	177
ROBERT	CARTER		Cop	172
JOHN	SMITH		Bow	169
JOHN	PRESTED		Whe	164
Michael	Scales		But	92

Source: *Morning Chronicle*, 25 December 1827.

Table 8.3.22.17
Poll for common councilmen of Portsoken, 12 January 1829

Forename	Surname	Precinct	Livery	Votes received
EDWARD	COLEBATCH		Hab	168
PETER	PERRY		Clm	157
ROBERT	CARTER		Cop	153
JOHN	PRESTED		Whe	151
JOHN	SMITH		Bow	149
Michael	Scales		But	66

Source: *Morning Chronicle*, 25 December 1828.

Table 8.3.22.18
Poll for common councilmen of Portsoken, 11 January 1830

Forename	Surname	Precinct	Livery	Votes received
EDWARD	COLEBATCH		Hab	207
ROBERT	CARTER		Cop	199
JOHN	SMITH		Bow	186
JOHN	PRESTED		Whe	159
MICHAEL	SCALES		But	151
Peter	Perry		Clm	133
Nathaniel	Negus		Bak	129

Source: *Morning Chronicle*, 24 December 1829.

Table 8.3.22.19
Poll for common councilmen of Portsoken, 10 January 1831

Forename	Surname	Precinct	Livery	Votes received
EDWARD	COLEBATCH		Hab	203
ROBERT	CARTER		Cop	187
JOHN	SMITH		Bow	174
JOHN	PRESTED		Whe	172
PETER	PERRY		Clm	154
Michael	Scales		But	150
	Manning			20

Source: *Morning Chronicle*, 24 December 1830.

Table 8.3.22.20
Poll for alderman of Portsoken, 10 February 1831

Forename	Surname	Livery	Votes received
Michael	Scales	But	155
Daniel Whittle	Harvey	Gir	127

Source: Beaven, i, p. 188.

Table 8.3.22.21
Poll for alderman of Portsoken, 7 December 1831

Forename	Surname	Livery	Votes received
Michael	Scales	But	169
William Hughes	Hughes	Cor	74

Source: Beaven, i, p.188.

Table 8.3.22.22
Poll for common councilmen of Portsoken, 9 January 1832

Forename	Surname	Precinct	Livery	Votes received	
				Poll	Scrutiny
JOHN	PARKER		Whe	204	
JOHN	CLARK		Pat	192	
NATHAN	NEGUS		Bak	174	
THOMAS E.	DEATH		Mus	169	
EDWARD	COLEBATCH		Hab	149	
	Saul			160	
Robert	Carter			126	
Peter	Perry			116	

Source: *St James's Chronicle*, 22-24 December 1831.

8.3.23 Queenhithe, 1710-1827: nine polls

(6 common councilmen; 123 freeman householders in 1833)

Table 8.3.23.1
Poll for common councilman of Queenhithe, 8 February 1710

Forename	Surname	Precinct	Livery	Votes received	
				Poll	Scrutiny
JOHN	TOOLY			86	
John	Barber			85	

Source: LMA COL/CC/13/01/028; COL/CC/13/01/012; COL/WD/04/040;

Table 8.3.23.2
Poll for common councilmen of Queenhithe, 6 January 1766

Forename	Surname	Precinct	Livery	Votes received
ABRAHAM	GREEN			71
WILLIAM	HUMPHREYS			70
Richard	Clarke			45
John	Mills			43

Source: *Public Advertiser*, 24 December 1765.

Table 8.3.23.3
Poll for beadle of Queenhithe, 3 November 1767

Forename	Surname	Votes received
HENRY	BALDWIN	105
John	March	66

Source: *London Evening Post*, 3 November 1767.

Table 8.3.23.4
Poll for alderman of Queenhithe, 29 June 1772

Forename	Surname	Livery	Votes received Poll	Scrutiny
FREDERICK	BULL	Sal	83	53
Walter	Rawlinson	Gro	73	47

Source: Beaven, i, p. 195.

Table 8.3.23.5
Poll for alderman of Queenhithe, 15 January 1784

Forename	Surname	Precinct	Livery	Votes received
JOHN	BATES		Vin	87
George	Macauley		Bow	49
Mackenzie				

Source: Beaven, i, p. 195.

Table 8.3.23.6
Poll for common councilmen of Queenhithe, 7 January 1788

Forename	Surname	Precinct	Livery	Votes received
Charles	Iliff		Car	

Source: *World*, 24 December 1787; *Morning Chronicle*, 24 December 1787.

Table 8.3.23.7
Poll for common councilmen of Queenhithe, 12 January 1795

Forename	Surname	Precinct	Livery	Votes received
BENJAMIN	WINKWORTH		Dra	77
BENJAMIN	SHAW		Cop	74
WILLIAM	BESWICK		Cop	74
CHARLES	ILIFF		Car	70
MATTHEW	BRICKWOOD		Fis	69
WILLIAM	CHAMPION		Car	65
William	Humphreys		Cop	45

Source: *London Packet*, 24 December 1794.

Table 8.3.23.8
Poll for alderman of Queenhithe, 21 May 1821

Forename	Surname	Precinct	Livery	Votes received	
				Poll	Scrutiny
WILLIAM	VENABLES		Sta	59	50
John	Capel		Bro	45	31

Source: T. Hathway, *A report of the decisions* (London, 1821).

Table 8.3.23.9
Poll for common councilmen of Queenhithe, 8 January 1827

Forename	Surname	Precinct	Livery	Votes received
WILLIAM	ROUTH		Fru	71
ROBERT PHILIP	JONES		Mus	71
EDWARD	HUGHES		Gro	70
THOMAS	DUTTON		Inn	69
JOHN	HOWELL		Fru	62
THOMAS	HATHWAY		Inn	44
	Fellowes			39

Source: *Morning Chronicle*, 25 December 1826.

8.3.24 Tower, 1714-1827: 24 polls

(10 common councilmen; 381 freeman householders in 1833)

Table 8.3.24.1
Poll for common councilmen of Tower, 11 January 1714

Forename	Surname	Precinct	Livery	Votes received	
				Poll	Scrutiny
PETER	BOULTON				
JOHN	ELDERTON				
ROBERT	EVANS				
PETER	EATON				
JAMES	BARDOE				
NICHOLAS	BATCHELOR				
GOSTWICK	COX				
NICHOLAS	HANBURY				
SAMUEL	CLARKE				
Richard	Lechmere				

Source: LMA COL/CC/13/01/012.

Table 8.3.24.2
Poll for common councilmen of Tower, 10 January 1715

Forename	Surname	Precinct	Livery	Votes received
PETER	EATON			235
RICHARD	LECHMERE			227
SAMUEL	BEACHCROFT			222
JOHN	BRITTON			217
HARCOURT	MASTERS			215
James	Bordoe			214
THOMAS	CLARKE			212
RICHARD	HARRIS			212
STEPHEN	KING			209
P.	GODFREY			206
Peter	Boulton			206
Samuel	Clarke			206
Gostwick	Cox			202
Nicholas	Hanbury			202
Robert	Evans			199
John	Elderton			197
	Bolthole			192
	Shirley			185

Source: LMA COL/WD/03/040.

Table 8.3.24.3
Poll for common councilmen of Tower, 9 January 1716

Forename	Surname	Precinct	Livery	Votes received
PETER	EATON			298
HARCOURT	MASTERS			297
JOHN	BRITTAIN			295
FRANCIS	PORTEEN			287
SAMUEL	BEACHCROFT			286
RICHARD	LECHMERE			284
RICHARD	HARRIS			281
THOMAS	CLARK			281
ROBERT	JEFFS			269
Thomas	Loveday			204
Samuel	Clark			195
Gostwick	Cox			193
John	Elderton			190
Nicholas	Batcheldore			189
Peter	Boulton			189
Edward	Bridgen			181
James	Bardoe			180
Robert	Evans			178

Source: *Flying Post*, 22 December 1715.

Table 8.3.24.4
Poll for common councilmen of Tower, 7 January 1717

Forename	Surname	Precinct	Livery	Votes received
RICHARD	HARRIS			
THOMAS	CLARKE			
ROBERT	JEFFS			
THOMAS	LOVEDAY			
JOHN	BRITTAN			
PETER	EATON			
HARCOURT	MASTERS			
NICHOLAS	BATCHELOR			
THOMAS	HEATON			
NICHOLAS	HANBURY			
John	Langton			
Joseph	Taylor			

Source: LMA COL/CC/13/01/012.

Table 8.3.24.5
Poll for common councilmen of Tower, 6 January 1718

Forename	Surname	Precinct	Livery	Votes received	
				Poll	Scrutiny
JAMES	BERDOE			200	158
JOHN	ELDERTON			189	148
EDWARD	BRIDGEN			184	143
Robert	Jeffs			204	140
Thomas	Loveday			199	136
Richard	Harris			193	130

Source: LMA COL/CC/13/01/012.

Table 8.3.24.6
Poll for common councilman of Tower, 10 January 1737

Forename	Surname	Precinct	Livery	Votes received
JAMES	PHILLIPS			155
	Hatley			75

Source: *London Evening Post*, 21 December 1736.

Table 8.3.24.7
Poll for alderman of Tower, 2 February 1737

Forename	Surname	Livery	Votes received
DANIEL	LAMBERT	Cop	196
Peter	Burrell	Hab	98

Source: Beaven, i, p. 203.

Table 8.3.24.8
Poll for common councilman of Tower, 8 January 1750

Forename	Surname	Precinct	Livery	Votes received
WALTER	JONES			134
Edward	Floyd			104

Source: *London Evening Post*, 23 December 1749.

Table 8.3.24.9
Poll for alderman of Tower, 16 May 1750

Forename	Surname	Livery	Votes received
THOMAS	CHITTY	Sal	20
James	Creed	Hab	0

Source: Beaven, i, p. 203.

Table 8.3.24.10
Poll for common councilman of Tower, 9 January 1758

Forename	Surname	Precinct	Livery	Votes received
BRASS	CROSBY			149
	Field			75

Source: *London Evening Post*, 22 December 1757.

Table 8.3.24.11
Poll for common councilmen of Tower, 8 January 1770

Forename	Surname	Precinct	Livery	Votes received	
				Poll	Scrutiny
CHARLES	WILKINS		Sal	182	
SAMUEL	FREEMAN		Wax	171	
RICHARD	ROMAN		Dye	170	
HAMNETT	TOWNLEY		Fis	156	
JAMES	ANSELL		Cop	153	
WILLIAM	CHIVERS		Mus	150	
JOSEPH	SPECK		Cop	147	
JOHN	STAINBANK		Glo	144	
RICHARD	NEAVE		Dra	144	
HENRY	BULLOCK			139	
SAMUEL	PLUMMER		Clw	131	
William	Prowting			124	112
Isaac	Elliott			124	112
Edward	Alexander			108	
Richard	Brooke			98	
William	Mills			96	
William	Worsfold			89	
Eustace	Kentish			74	

Note: No return was made between Prowting and Elliott.
Source: *Independent Chronicle*, 25 December 1769; LMA COL/AD/04/048.

Table 8.3.24.12
Poll for alderman of Tower, 12 October 1775

Forename	Surname	Livery	Votes received
HUGH	SMITH	Sal	141
Thomas	Wooldridge	Mus	88

Source: Beaven, i, p. 203.

Table 8.3.24.13
Poll for common councilmen of Tower, 7 January 1788

Forename	Surname	Precinct	Livery	Votes received
CHARLES	WILKINS		Sal	124
WILLIAM	SHONE		Gls	103
WILLIAM	SURMAN		Iro	103
JAMES	GASCOIGN		Sal	102
THOMAS	ROGERS		Spe	101
JAMES	ANSELL		Cop	100
WILLIAM	BROADHURST		Iro	99
SAMUEL	DIXON		Fis	99
WILLIAM	BAGSTER		Apo	97
SAMUEL	TOWNLEY		Fis	96
JOHN	HEWETSON		Pav	88
JOHN	CLOSE		Whe	87
	Alexander			49

Source: *Whitehall Evening Post*, 22 December 1787.

Table 8.3.24.14
Poll for common councilmen of Tower, 10 January 1791

Forename	Surname	Precinct	Livery	Votes received
CHARLES	WILKINS		Sal	224
SAMUEL	DIXON		Fis	195
JAMES	GASCOIGN		Sal	193
THOMAS	FOTHERGILL		Dra	190
THOMAS	ROGERS		Spe	172
JOSEPH	PHILLIPS		Cop	170
JAMES	ALLEN		Clw	169
JOHN	PRESTWICH		Joi	164
JOHN	CLOSE		Whe	163
JAMES	WOODBRIDGE		Cop	157
JOHN	HEWETSON		Pav	151
WILLIAM	BAGSTER		Apo	150
Samuel	Hutchinson		Met	109
	Aldous			62
	Bales			41

Source: *Whitehall Evening Post*, 23 December 1790.

Table 8.3.24.15
Poll for common councilmen of Tower, 11 January 1796

Forename	Surname	Precinct	Livery	Votes received
CHARLES	WILKINS		Sal	245
JAMES	DIXON		Met	240
SAMUEL	DIXON		Fis	221
JAMES	WOODBRIDGE		Cop	221
JAMES	WOODHOUSE		Cop	198
DANIEL	COXE		Whe	190
THOMAS	FOTHERGILL		Dra	188
SAMUEL	HUTCHINSON		Met	180
JOSEPH	PHILLIPS		Cop	178
THOMAS	ROGERS		Spe	178
JAMES	GASCOIGNE		Sal	169
SAMUEL	WRIGHT		Whe	167
William	Bagster		Apo	150
John	Prestwich		Joi	122
John	Hewetson		Pav	106

Source: *Lloyd's Evening Post*, 23 December 1795.

Table 8.3.24.16
Poll for common councilmen of Tower, 6 January 1800

Forename	Surname	Precinct	Livery	Votes received
SAMUEL	HUTCHINSON		Met	248
JAMES	DIXON		Met	241
SAMUEL	WRIGHT		Whe	241
SAMUEL	DIXON		Fis	239
MATTHEW	LUCAS		Vin	229
THOMAS	DAWSON		Iro	224
THOMAS	FOTHERGILL		Dra	222
SAMUEL	WALKER		Spe	217
CHARLES	STUART		Bak	212
DAVID	LAING		Tyl	188
LEWIS	GILSON		Fis	171
JAMES	GASCOIGNE		Sal	159
John	Hartshorne		Dra	141

Source: *Oracle and Daily Advertiser*, 25 December 1799.

Table 8.3.24.17
Poll for common councilmen of Tower, 7 January 1805

Forename	Surname	Precinct	Livery	Votes received
SAMUEL	HUTCHINSON		Met	104
SAMUEL	DIXON		Fis	104
JAMES	DIXON		Met	103
MATHEW	LUCAS		Vin	101
THOMAS	DAWSON		Iro	100
DAVID	LAING		Tyl	98
SAMUEL	WRIGHT		Whe	97
THOMAS	BRIDGES		Vin	95
THOMAS	FOTHERGILL		Dra	94
CHARLES	STUART		Bak	91
SAMUEL	WALKER		Spe	89
JOHN	HARTSHORNE		Dra	78
Lewis	Gilson		Fis	34

Source: *Morning Chronicle*, 25 December 1804.

Table 8.3.24.18
Poll for common councilmen of Tower, 6 January 1806

Forename	Surname	Precinct	Livery	Votes received
JAMES	DIXON		Met	250
SAMUEL	WRIGHT		Whe	250
SAMUEL	HUTCHINSON		Met	249
SAMUEL	DIXON		Fis	247
THOMAS	BRIDGES		Vin	231
MATTHEW	LUCAS		Vin	224
PETER	SKIPPER		Bar	223
CHARLES	STUART		Bak	212
WILLIAM	CAWTHORN		Spe	202
THOMAS	FOTHERGILL		Dra	196
DAVID	LAING		Tyl	195
GILPIN	GORST		Vin	183
Samuel	Walker		Spe	178
John	Hartshorne		Dra	157
Lewis	Gilson		Fis	86

Source: *Morning Chronicle*, 24 December 1805.

Table 8.3.24.19
Poll for common councilmen of Tower, 8 January 1810

Forename	Surname	Precinct	Livery	Votes received
SAMUEL	WRIGHT		Whe	186
JOHN	DRINKALD, JNR		Vin	177
SAMUEL	HUTCHINSON		Met	176
PETER	SKIPPER		Bar	173
THOMAS	BRIDGES		Vin	169
MATTHEW	LUCAS		Vin	166
SAMUEL	DIXON		Fis	164
CHARLES	STUART		Bak	160
DAVID	LAING		Tyl	157
WILLIAM	CAWTHORN		Spe	152
GILPIN	GORST		Vin	148
ROBERT	SMITH		Hab	141
John	Hartshorne		Dra	72

Source: *Morning Chronicle*, 25 December 1809.

Table 8.3.24.20
Poll for common councilmen of Tower, 6 January 1817

Forename	Surname	Precinct	Livery	Votes received
SAMUEL	WRIGHT		Whe	241
JOHN	DRINKALD		Vin	233
ROBERT	SMITH		Hab	228
PETER	SKIPPER		Bar	223
WILLIAM	CAWTHORNE		Spe	215
THOMAS	BRIDGES		Vin	209
SAMUEL	HUTCHINSON		Met	207
MATTHEW PRIME	LUCAS		Vin	206
CHARLES	STUART		Bak	206
SAMUEL	DIXON		Fis	200
DAVID	LAING		Tyl	183
GILPIN	GORST		Vin	183
Brian	Corcoran			140

Source: *Morning Chronicle*, 25 December 1816.

Table 8.3.24.21
Poll for common councilmen of Tower, 10 January 1820

Forename	Surname	Precinct	Livery	Votes received
SAMUEL	WRIGHT		Whe	239
JOHN	DRINKALD		Vin	237
MATTHIAS PRIME	LUCAS		Vin	233
PETER	SKIPPER		Bar	232
WILLIAM	CAWTHORNE		Spe	226
CHARLES	STUART		Bak	223
GILPIN	GORST		Vin	216
MATTHEW	CLARKE		Met	212
WILLIAM	RUSTON		Whe	207
ROBERT	SMITH		Hab	203
JAMES	HUNT		Met	200
SAMUEL	DIXON		Fis	176
David	Laing		Tyl	146

Source: *Morning Chronicle*, 24 December 1819.

Table 8.3.24.22
Poll for common councilmen of Tower, 9 January 1826

Forename	Surname	Precinct	Livery	Votes received
PETER	SKIPPER		Bar	62
SAMUEL	DIXON		Fis	62
SAMUEL	WRIGHT		Whe	62
WILLIAM	CAWTHORNE		Spe	62
CHARLES	STUART		Bak	61
ROBERT	SMITH		Hab	61
EDWARD H.	NOY		Gol	61
JAMES	HUNT		Met	60
JOHN	DRINKALD		Vin	60
GILPIN	GORST		Vin	59
WILLIAM	ROBINSON		Bar	59
THOMAS	HOWELL		Hab	59
John	Hartshorne		Dra	8

Source: *St James's Chronicle*, 20-22 December 1825.

Table 8.3.24.23
Poll for common councilmen of Tower, 8 January 1827

Forename	Surname	Precinct	Livery	Votes received
PETER	SKIPPER		Bar	200
SAMUEL	WRIGHT		Whe	195
JOHN	DRINKALD		Vin	193
EDWARD H.	NOY		Gol	181
CHARLES	STUART		Bak	177
ROBERT	SMITH		Hab	177
SAMUEL	DIXON		Fis	176
WILLIAM	ROBINSON		Bar	172
WILLIAM	CAWTHORNE		Spe	167
JAMES	HUNT		Met	164
WILLIAM JOHN	HALL		Clw	163
GILPIN	GORST		Vin	144
Thomas	Howell		Hab	143

Source: *Morning Chronicle*, 25 December 1826.

Table 8.3.24.24
Poll for common councilmen of Tower, 7 January 1828

Forename	Surname	Precinct	Livery	Votes received
PETER	SKIPPER		Bar	266
THOMAS	HOWELL		Hab	258
SAMUEL	WRIGHT		Whe	255
JOHN	DRINKALD		Vin	252
WILLIAM	ROBINSON		Bar	240
ROBERT	SMITH		Hab	233
GILPIN	GORST		Vin	231
CHARLES	STUART		Bak	229
EDWARD H.	NOY		Gol	222
WILLIAM	CAWTHORNE		Fis	209
JAMES	HUNT		Met	196
SAMUEL	DIXON		Fis	177
William John	Hall		Clw	158

Source: *Morning Chronicle*, 25 December 1827.

8.3.25 Vintry, 1717-1828: 19 polls

(9 common councilmen; freeman householders in 1833 unrecorded, but *c.* 100)

Table 8.3.25.1
Poll for common councilmen of Vintry, 7 January 1717

Forename	Surname	Precinct	Livery	Votes received	
				Poll	Scrutiny
WILLIAM	COOKE				
JOHN	SAMWAYS				
JOHN	COOPER				
HENRY	GREENWAY				
JOHN	YERBURY				
SAMUEL	PALMER				
GEORGE	VERNON				
SAMUEL	WESTALL				
Edmund	Trench				
Francis	Bullock				
John	Bailey				
Robert	Smith				
George	Vernon				
Isaac	Fryer				
Philip	Pintles				
Richard	Pitts				

Note: Trench and Bullock having an equal number of votes after the scrutiny, the election was referred to the Court of Aldermen which declared it to be void.
Source: LMA COL/CC/13/01/012.

Table 8.3.25.2
Poll for common councilmen of Vintry, 14 February 1717

Forename	Surname	Precinct	Livery	Votes received	
				Poll	Scrutiny
EDMUND	TRENCH				
Francis	Bullock				

Source: LMA COL/CC/13/01/012.

Table 8.3.25.3
Poll for common councilmen of Vintry, 8 January 1722

Forename	Surname	Precinct	Livery	Votes received	
				Poll	Scrutiny
EDMUND	TRENCH				
James	Kelham			89	
Samuel	Palmer			87	
George	Smith, snr			86	
John	Parker			85	
John	Bayley			85	
Richard	Lockwood			84	
Robert	Smith			84	
Joseph	Wrigglesworth			84	
JOHN	SAMWAYS			61	
JOHN	YERBURY			58	
SAMUEL	WESTALL			57	
JAMES	COOPER			57	
CHRISTOPHER	CHEESEBROUGH			57	
HENRY	GREENAWAY			57	
THOMAS	BARKER			56	
THOMAS	CORBETT			56	

Source: *Daily Post*, 23 December 1721; 16 January 1722.

Table 8.3.25.4
Poll for common councilmen of Vintry, 10 January 1726

Forename	Surname	Precinct	Livery	Votes received
ROBERT	SMITH			74
JEREMIAH	BRAITHWAIT			73
JOHN	PARKER			73
JOHN	BROOKE			73
RICHARD	LOCKWOOD			73
SAMUEL	PALMER			73
JAMES	KELHAM			72
JOHN	HOAR			72
JOHN	ENGLAND			71
William	Poyntz			63
Edmund	Trench			61
Christopher	Cheesebrough			60
Henry	Emmett			60
Stephen	Prew			60
Thomas	Corbett			60
William	Vere			59
Samuel	Westall			59
James	Pittson			58

Source: *Daily Journal*, 22 December 1725.

Table 8.3.25.5
Poll for common councilmen of Vintry, 8 January 1728

Forename	Surname	Precinct	Livery	Votes received	
				Poll	Scrutiny
DANIEL	TOWNE				
JEREMIAH	BRAITHWAITE				
THOMAS	CORBETT				
ROBERT	KIDD				
THOMAS	GREGG				
CHRISTOPHER	CHEESEBROUGH				
STEPHEN	PREW				
WILLIAM	ROUSE				
EDMUND	TRENCH				
James	Kelham				
John	Hoar				
John	Brookes				
John	Parker				
George	Smith, snr				
John	Yerbury				
Henry	Emmett				

Source: LMA COL/CC/13/01/012.

Table 8.3.25.6
Poll for common councilmen of Vintry, 28 January 1730

Forename	Surname	Precinct	Livery	Votes received	
				Poll	Scrutiny
EDMUND	TRENCH				
WILLIAM	ROUS				
ROBERT	KID				
CHRISTOPHER	CHEESEBROUGH				
THOMAS	GREGG				
JOHN	HARBIN				
SAMUEL	ALLEN				
STEPHEN	PREW				
DANIEL	THORNE				

Source: *Daily Journal*, 22 January 1730.

Table 8.3.25.7
Poll for common councilmen of Vintry, 11 January 1731

Forename	Surname	Precinct	Livery	Votes received	
				Poll	Scrutiny
WILLIAM	ROUS			95	
EDMUND	TRENCH			91	
ROBERT	KIDD			91	
THOMAS	GREGG			91	
JOHN	HARBIN			88	
STEPHEN	PREW			83	
SAMUEL	ALLEN			83	
CHRISTOPHER	CHEESEBROUGH			80	
WILLIAM	WHITAKER			78	
John	Brooks			63	
Daniel	Towne			63	
George	Smith, snr			57	
Peter	St Hill			54	
John	Parker			53	
Marshe	Dickenson			50	

Source: *British Journal*, 26 December 1730; LMA COL/CC/13/01/012.

Table 8.3.25.8
Poll for common councilmen of Vintry, 8 January 1739

Forename	Surname	Precinct	Livery	Votes received
DANIEL	TOWN			75
JAMES	KELHAM			74
EDMUND	TRENCH			71
THOMAS	ROUSE			71
THOMAS	GREGG			70
MARSHE	DICKENSON			70
STEPHEN	PREW			62
CHRISTOPHER	CHEESEBROUGH			62
NATHANIEL	HIGHMORE			61
Robert	Rampshire			58
	Hoggard			52

Source: *London Evening Post*, 21-23 December 1738.

Table 8.3.25.9
Poll for common councilmen of Vintry, 7 January 1740

Forename	Surname	Precinct	Livery	Votes received	
				Poll	Scrutiny
THOMAS	GREGG			92	
MARSH	DICKENSON			89	
THOMAS	ROWSE			79	
EDMUND	TRENCH			78	
WILLIAM	BEDELL			79	
DANIEL	TOWN			77	
NATHANIEL	HIGHMORE			61	
ROBERT	RAMPSHIRE			60	
THOMAS	ROBERTS			59	
Martin	Wardell			76	
William	Mills			76	
James	Kelham			73	
John	Tew			57	
Thomas	Delamot			56	

Source: *Daily Post*, 22 December 1739; *Daily Post*, 25 January 1740.

Table 8.3.25.10
Poll for common councilmen of Vintry, 8 January 1759

Forename	Surname	Precinct	Livery	Votes received
BENJAMIN	GASCOIGNE			64
THOMAS	GREGG			63
GODFREY	WILSON			62
STEPHEN	HUNT			62
MOSES	ALLNUT			62
JOHN	GOULD			61
HIGGINS	EDEN			60
JOHN	KENT			60
Daniel	De St Leu			55
Peter	Furnell			19

Source: *London Evening Post*, 21-23 December 1758.

Table 8.3.25.11
Poll for common councilmen of Vintry, 10 January 1774

Forename	Surname	Precinct	Livery	Votes received
THOMAS	WATKINSON		Bak	84
LAURENCE	HOLKER		Iro	83
PRIEST	SHRUBB		Plu	83
WILLIAM	WRIGHT		Glo	78
JOSEPH	DOWNES		Hab	77
THOMAS	FUNNELL		Gol	77
GODFREY	WILSON		Far	68
JOHN	ELMES		Tyl	62
ROBERT	BENSON		Nee	55
	Maskall			39
Robert	Evered			38
	Walford			29

Source: *General Evening Post*, 23 December 1773.

Table 8.3.25.12
Poll for alderman of Vintry, 5 November 1774

Forename	Surname	Livery	Votes received
NATHANIEL	NEWMAN, JNR	Mer	60
William	Lee	Hab	46

Source: Beaven, i, p. 214.

Table 8.3.25.13
Poll for common councilmen of Vintry, 7 January 1811

Forename	Surname	Precinct	Livery	Votes received
WILLIAM	PICKERING		Vin	57
THOMAS	WHITBY		Dra	57
JAMES	CADE		Dra	56
JAMES	GATTY		Pai	56
HERMAN	SHRODER		Vin	56
JOHN ERNEST	GROB		Met	55
HENRY	COOPER		Car	53
CHARLES	MARTIN		Vin	50
WILLIAM	SPEAR		Met	48
Thomas	Crook		Cor	10

Source: *Morning Chronicle*, 25 December 1810.

Table 8.3.25.14
Poll for common councilmen of Vintry, 6 January 1812

Forename	Surname	Precinct	Livery	Votes received
CHARLES	MARTIN		Vin	81
THOMAS	WHITBY, JNR		Dra	79
WILLIAM	PICKERING		Vin	76
JAMES	GATTY		Pai	72
THOMAS	CONWAY		Car	66
JAMES	CADE		Dra	62
WILLIAM	SPEAR		Met	60
JOHN	HARDIE		Gir	55
STEPHEN	GRIFFIN		Apo	53
Henry	Cooper			51
Thomas	Crook		Cor	32

Source: *The Times*, 25 December 1811. The *Morning Chronicle*, 25 December 1811 reports Whitby as receiving 97 votes, which would be on the high side and looks like a misprint.

Table 8.3.25.15
Poll for common councilmen of Vintry, 11 January 1813

Forename	Surname	Precinct	Livery	Votes received
THOMAS	WHITBY, JNR		Dra	71
WILLIAM	PICKERING		Vin	71
CHARLES	MARTIN		Vin	70
JAMES	GATTY		Pai	70
THOMAS	CONWAY		Car	68
JOHN	HARDIE		Gir	65
WILLIAM	SPEAR		Met	63
THOMAS	GARRETT		Bow	59
JOHN	COMBES		Pat	48
Thomas	Crook		Cor	45

Source: *Morning Chronicle*, 24 December 1812.

Table 8.3.25.16
Poll for common councilmen of Vintry, 10 January 1825

Forename	Surname	Precinct	Livery	Votes received
THOMAS	WHITBY, JNR		Dra	63
HENRY JOHN	ELMES		Gol	59
CHARLES	INGALL		Vin	57
JOHN	COMBES		Pat	57
THOMAS	CONWAY		Car	57
CHAPMAN	MARSHALL		Inn	56
THOMAS	GARRETT		Bow	52
THOMAS	MARSDEN		Tyl	50
FRANK	DICKENS		Cop	41
Thomas	Crook		Cor	34
Richard	Woodward		Sal	24

Source: *St James's Chronicle*, 23-25 December 1824.

Table 8.3.25.17
Poll for alderman of Vintry 4 November 1826

Forename	Surname	Livery	Votes received	
			Poll	Scrutiny
Henry	Winchester	Cut	30	26
Edward Archer	Wilde	Dye	27	23
Thomas	Cooke	Cor	3	3

Note: Election declared void.
Source: Beaven, i, pp. 214-15; *Morning Chronicle*, 30 December 1826.

Table 8.3.25.18
Poll for alderman of Vintry, 4 January 1827

Forename	Surname	Livery	Votes received	
			Poll	Scrutiny
HENRY	WINCHESTER	Cut	52	38
Edward Archer	Wilde	Dye	52	35

Source: Beaven, i, p. 215.

Table 8.3.25.19
Poll for common councilmen of Vintry, 7 January 1828

Forename	Surname	Precinct	Livery	Votes received
THOMAS	WHITBY, JNR		Dra	43
JOHN	COMBS		Pat	42
THOMAS	CONWAY		Cor	41
HARVEY JOHN	ELMES		Gol	40
THOMAS	MARSDEN		Tyl	38
CHARLES	INGALL		Vin	37
GEORGE	MARTIN		Inn	37
CHAPMAN	MARSHALL		Inn	37
JOHN	ION		Clm	34
Thomas	Crook		Cor	11

Source: *Morning Chronicle*, 25 December 1827.

8.3.26 Walbrook, 1702-1831: 26 polls

(8 common councilmen; 126 freeman householders in 1833)

Table 8.3.26.1
Poll for aldermanic candidates of Walbrook, 19 June 1702

Forename	Surname	Precinct	Livery	Votes received
GILBERT	HEATHCOTE		Vin	94
HENRY	FURNES			90
Robert	Beachcroft			80

Source: *Flying Post*, 20 June 1702.

Table 8.3.26.2
Poll for alderman of Walbrook, 18 March 1725

Forename	Surname	Livery	Votes received
JOHN	TASH	Vin	111
Roger	Hudson	Gol	63

Source: Beaven, i, p. 224.

Table 8.3.26.3
Poll for common councilmen of Walbrook, 8 January 1728

Forename	Surname	Precinct	Livery	Votes received	
				Poll	Scrutiny
JOHN	GRAINGE				
MICHAEL	HILLERSDON				

Source: LMA COL/CC/13/01/012.

Table 8.3.26.4
Poll for common councilmen of Walbrook, 12 January 1730

Forename	Surname	Precinct	Livery	Votes received	
				Poll	Scrutiny
THOMAS	KNAPP			90	
SAMUEL	KEYNTON			89	
WILLIAM	FARMER			89	
WILLIAM	ARNOLD			89	
EDWIN	SANDYS			88	
ROBERT	HENSHAW			87	
MICHAEL	HILLERSDON			83	
ROBERT	PIERCE			81	
John	Hill			81	
William	Jakeman			78	
Thomas	Simms			75	
James	D'Argent			75	
William	Stevens			72	
John	Stanley			66	
John	Shepherd			46	

Source: *Daily Journal*, 24 December 1729; 20 January 1730.

Table 8.3.26.5
Poll for common councilmen of Walbrook, 10 January 1732

Forename	Surname	Precinct	Livery	Votes received	
				Poll	Scrutiny
ROBERT	PIERCE			103	
SAMUEL	KEYNTON			95	
WILLIAM	WILKINS			91	
JOHN	HILL			89	
JOHN	SHORTHAZELL			88	
WILLIAM	FARMER			88	
THOMAS	SIMS			75	
Robert	Henshaw			75	
HEZEKIAH	WALKER			74	
Edward	Faulkner			66	
William	Arnold			64	
Michael	Hillersdon			59	
Thomas	D'Argent			58	
James	Armson			51	
Thomas	Browne			50	

Source: *London Evening Post*, 21 December 1731; 15 January 1732.

Table 8.3.26.6
Poll for common councilmen of Walbrook, 8 January 1733

Forename	Surname	Precinct	Livery	Votes received
William	Arnold			
Robert	Henshaw			

Source: *Read's Weekly Journal*, 23 December 1732.

Table 8.3.26.7
Poll for common councilmen of Walbrook, 8 January 1739

Forename	Surname	Precinct	Livery	Votes received
WILLIAM	WILKINS			117
RICHARD	MARTIN			115
WILLIAM	ARNOLD			113
HEZEKIAH	WALKER			106
ROBERT	PIERCE			102
WILLIAM	BELCHIER			100
WILLIAM	FARMER			98
JOHN	HILL			93
Samuel	Keynton			74

Source: *London Evening Post*, 21 December 1738.

Table 8.3.26.8
Poll for beadle of Walbrook, 24 December 1743

Forename	Surname	Votes received	
		Poll	Scrutiny
	PROUDMAN	106	
	Wootten	96	

Source: *Daily Advertiser*, 23 December 1743; *Penny Morning London Advertiser*, 20 January 1744.

Table 8.3.26.9
Poll for common councilmen of Walbrook, 8 January 1753

Forename	Surname	Precinct	Livery	Votes received	
				Poll	Scrutiny
JAMES	ENNIS			82	79
ROBERT	NORRIS			79	76
RICHARD	REYNELL			74	71
JOSEPH	BLANDFORD			71	68
NATHANIEL	THOMAS			68	65
WILLIAM	WALTERS			62	61
MATTHEW	PERCHARD			62	59
WILLIAM	WHIPHAM			58	56
Basil	Brown			53	51
Robert	Feverall			49	47

Source: *London Daily Advertiser*, 23 December 1752; 22 January 1753.

Table 8.3.26.10
Poll for alderman of Walbrook, 3 November 1758

Forename	Surname	Livery	Votes received
ALEXANDER	MASTER	Dra	43
Thomas	Crozier	Wax	9

Source: Beaven, i, p. 224.

Table 8.3.26.11
Poll for alderman of Walbrook, 6 June 1766

Forename	Surname	Livery	Votes received
WILLIAM	NASH	Sal	53
Brackley	Kennett	Vin	11

Source: Beaven, i, p. 224.

Table 8.3.26.12
Poll for common councilmen of Walbrook, 8 January 1770

Forename	Surname	Precinct	Livery	Votes received	
				Poll	Scrutiny
WILLIAM	WHIPHAM		Cop	105	
JOHN	SHORE		Shi	100	
NATHANIEL	THOMAS		Wax	99	
RICHARD	DIXON		Cop	97	
RICHARD	ALSAGER		Clw	96	
ARTHUR	BEARDMORE			79	
WILLIAM	ARNOLD			60	55
Charles	Summers			58	53
Clement	Bellamy			56	53
John	Raincock			55	52
Robert	Ellis			41	

Note: Neither Summers nor Bellamy was returned.
Source: *Lloyd's Evening Post*, 22 December 1769; 19 January 1770; LMA COL/AD/04/048.

Table 8.3.26.13
Poll for common councilman of Walbrook, 8 March 1770

Forename	Surname	Precinct	Livery	Votes received
JOHN	RAINCOCK			59
Charles	Summers			54

Source: *London Evening Post*, 8 March 1770.

Table 8.3.26.14
Poll for common councilmen of Walbrook, 12 January 1784

Forename	Surname	Precinct	Livery	Votes received
ROBERT	WYATT		Ski	86
SAMUEL	TOULMIN		Bar	86
RICHARD	DIXON		Cop	84
CHRISTOPHER	PARKER		Glo	83
NATHANIEL	SERGEANT		Clm	82
THOMAS	AXFORD		Mus	80
JONATHAN	TURNER		Lea	79
WILLIAM	GRICE		Glo	74
	Orton			36
John	Lewis		Clw	28

Source: *Morning Chronicle*, 25 December 1783.

Table 8.3.26.15
Poll for common councilmen of Walbrook, 9 January 1792

Forename	Surname	Precinct	Livery	Votes received
ROBERT	WYATT		Ski	98
NATHANIEL	SERGEANT		Clm	97
THOMAS	AXFORD		Mus	93
SAMUEL	TOULMIN		Bar	92
JOHN	WINTER		Ski	89
CHRISTOPHER	PORTER		Cor	89
WILLIAM	GRICE		Glo	75
THOMAS	SPEED		Gro	74
	Stapleton			53

Source: LMA CLC/W/PA/007/Ms. 00470.

Table 8.3.26.16
Poll for common councilmen of Walbrook, 11 January 1808

Forename	Surname	Precinct	Livery	Votes received
WILLIAM	PEARCE		Clm	99
THOMAS	WILLIAMS		Whe	94
THOMAS	BELL		Nee	89
THOMAS	WALL		Bar	84
SAMUEL	TOULMIN		Bar	81
THOMAS	MARGAREY		Sal	81
CHARLES	ALSAGER		Clw	78
ROBERT	ASHBY		Hab	71
John	Winter		Ski	44
P.	Sills			41

Source: LMA CLC/W/PA/007/Ms. 00470.

Table 8.3.26.17
Poll for common councilmen of Walbrook, 8 January 1810

Forename	Surname	Precinct	Livery	Votes received
ROBERT	ASHBY		Hab	84
THOMAS	WILLIAMS		Whe	83
WILLIAM	PEARCE		Clm	83
THOMAS	BELL		Nee	81
THOMAS	MARGAREY		Sal	77
WILLIAM	RYDE		Wax	73
WILLIAM	ROSS		Gro	71
EPHRAIM	HEYWOOD		Bar	68
	James			44

Source: LMA CLC/W/PA/007/Ms. 00470.

Table 8.3.26.18
Poll for common councilmen of Walbrook, 12 January 1818

Forename	Surname	Precinct	Livery	Votes received
THOMAS	WILLIAMS		Whe	99
EPHRAIM	HEYWOOD		Bar	96
THOMAS	BELL		Nee	92
WILLIAM	PEARCE		Clm	91
THOMAS	HALE		Hab	89
WILLIAM	ROSS		Gro	88
WILLIAM	RYDE			82
WILLIAM	WOODWARD		Joi	78
George Edward	Shuttleworth		Ski	37
Thomas Nathaniel	Williams		Nee	32

Source: LMA CLC/W/PA/007/Ms. 00470. Shuttleworth was later common councilman in Cheap, 1821-35.

Table 8.3.26.19
Poll for common councilman of Walbrook, 9 May 1818

Forename	Surname	Precinct	Livery	Votes received
MICHAEL	GIBBS		Fis	32
Thomas Nathaniel	Williams		Nee	28

Source: LMA CLC/W/PA/007/Ms. 00470.

Table 8.3.26.20
Poll for common councilmen of Walbrook, 27 January 1819

Forename	Surname	Precinct	Livery	Votes received
EPHRAIM	HEYWOOD		Bar	82
MICHAEL	GIBBS		Fis	79
WILLIAM	PEARCE		Clm	78
THOMAS	BELL		Nee	76
THOMAS	WILLIAMS		Whe	75
THOMAS	HALE		Hab	75
THOMAS N.	WILLIAMS		Nee	71
WILLIAM	WOODWARD		Joi	58
JACOB GEORGE	COPE		Fis	44
George Edward	Shuttleworth		Ski	31

Source: LMA CLC/W/PA/007/Ms. 00470.

Table 8.3.26.21
Poll for common councilmen of Walbrook, 8 January 1821

Forename	Surname	Precinct	Livery	Votes received
WILLIAM	PEARCE		Clm	78
THOMAS	WILLIAMS		Whe	77
THOMAS	HALE		Hab	74
WILLIAM	RICHARDSON		Joi	70
JACOB GEORGE	COPE		Fis	70
WILLIAM	WOODWARD		Joi	63
THOMAS N.	WILLIAMS		Nee	53
G.	CURTIS			23
Thomas Ford	Hale		Hab	9
Michael	Gibbs		Fis	8

Source: *St James's Chronicle*, 23-26 December 1820.

Table 8.3.26.22
Poll for common councilmen of Walbrook, 7 January 1822

Forename	Surname	Precinct	Livery	Votes received
THOMAS	WILLIAMS		Whe	72
WILLIAM	PEARCE		Clm	70
JACOB GEORGE	COPE		Fis	70
WILLIAM	RICHARDSON		Joi	70
MICHAEL	GIBBS		Fis	67
WILLIAM	WOODWARD		Joi	61
THOMAS FORD	HALE		Hab	58
THOMAS	WATKINS		Gir	49
Thomas N.	Williams		Nee	41

Source: *The Times*, 25 December 1821.

Table 8.3.26.23
Poll for common councilmen of Walbrook, 9 January 1826

Forename	Surname	Precinct	Livery	Votes received	
				Poll	Scrutiny
THOMAS	WILLIAMS		Whe	38	
MICHAEL	GIBBS		Fis	38	
THOMAS	WATKINS		Gir	38	
WILLIAM	RICHARDSON		Joi	37	
THOMAS FORD	HALE		Hab	36	
JACOB GEORGE	COPE		Fis	34	
WILLIAM	WOODWARD		Joi	34	
WILLIAM	RYDE		Wax	19	
J.	Deans			25	

Source: *St James's Chronicle*, 20-22 December 1825.

Table 8.3.26.24
Poll for common councilmen of Walbrook, 8 January 1827

Forename	Surname	Precinct	Livery	Votes received
THOMAS	WILLIAMS		Whe	50
MICHAEL	GIBBS		Fis	49
WILLIAM	RICHARDSON		Joi	48
THOMAS	WATKINS		Gir	46
WILLIAM	WOODWARD		Joi	44
THOMAS	HALE		Hab	43
THOMAS FORD	HALE		Hab	43
JACOB GEORGE	COPE		Fis	40
William	Ryde		Wax	21

Source: *Morning Chronicle*, 23 December 1826.

Table 8.3.26.25
Poll for common councilmen of Walbrook, 10 January 1831

Forename	Surname	Precinct	Livery	Votes received
THOMAS FORD	HALE		Hab	55
THOMAS	WATKINS		Gir	53
THOMAS	WILLIAMS		Whe	51
MICHAEL	GIBBS		Fis	51
WILLIAM	WOODWARD		Joi	50
WILLIAM	RICHARDSON		Joi	49
JACOB GEORGE	COPE		Fis	40
THOMAS	HALE		Hab	39
Thomas	Harrison			27

Source: LMA CLC/W/PA/007/Ms. 00470.

Table 8.3.26.26
Poll for common councilmen of Walbrook, 9 January 1832

Forename	Surname	Precinct	Livery	Votes received
WILLIAM	RICHARDSON		Joi	87
THOMAS	WATKINS		Gir	85
THOMAS	WILLIAMS		Whe	85
FORD	HALE		Hab	85
MICHAEL	GIBBS		Fis	77
JACOB GEORGE	COPE		Fis	67
JOSEPH	RICE		Bak	63
LEWIS	WILLIAMS		Sta	61
Thomas	Harrison			57

Source: *St James's Chronicle*, 22-24 December 1831.

8.4 MIDDLESEX CORONERS, 1733-1830: 11 polls

Note (1): The coroners of Middlesex were elected, like the county's MPs, by the Middlesex freeholders: for further details of Middlesex franchise, see Section 3.2.

Note (2): The names of successful candidates are given in SMALL CAPITALS and those of unsuccessful candidates in lower case.

Table 8.4.1
Poll for coroner of eastern division, 26 April 1733

Candidate	Votes received
JOHN KING	466
Francis Wherry	172
Zouch Troughton	107

Source: *London Evening Post*, 26 April 1733.

Table 8.4.2
Poll for coroner of western division, 29 May 1738

Candidate	Votes received
ROBERT WRIGHT	473
Thomas Haywood	409
Henry Laremore	283
Zouch Troughton	72
William Davids	53

Source: *London Evening Post*, 30 May 1738.

Table 8.4.3
Poll for coroner of western division, 10 January 1754

Candidate	Votes received
EDWARD UMFREVILLE	953
George Grew	482
William Davids	371

Source: *London Evening Post*, 10 January 1754.

Table 8.4.4
Poll for coroner of eastern division, 8 May 1755

Candidate	Votes received
GEORGE GREW	N
William Davids	(N-48)

Source: *London Evening Post*, 3 May 1755.

Table 8.4.5
Poll for coroner of eastern division, 27 February 1764

Candidate	Votes received
THOMAS PHILLIPS	817
Samuel Greer	467
William Davids	323
John Banyard	235

Source: *London Evening Post*, 28 February 1764.

Table 8.4.6
Poll for coroner of western division, 14 July 1786

Candidate	Votes received
WILLIAM WILSON	1,013
Peregrine Phillips	27

Source: *General Advertiser*, 15 July 1786.

Table 8.4.7
Poll for coroner of eastern division, 4 November 1786

Candidate	Votes received
EDWARD WALTER	1,192
Samuel Hill	336

Source: *General Advertiser*, 4 November 1786.

Table 8.4.8
Poll for coroner of western division, 7 December 1786

Candidate	Votes received
RICHARD COLLETT	1,199
Thomas Stirling	501
Samuel Hill	458

Source: *Morning Post and Daily Advertiser*, 8 December 1786.

Table 8.4.9
Poll for coroner of eastern division, 26 April 1804

Candidate	Votes received
JOHN WRIGHT UNWIN	962
J. Augustus Bonney	139

Source: *Morning Chronicle*, 27 April 1804.

Table 8.4.10
Poll for coroner of western division, 19 March 1816

Candidate	Votes received
THOMAS STIRLING	1,763
John S. Taylor	1,614
Richard Gude	1,596

Source: *Ipswich Journal*, 23 March 1816.

Table 8.4.11
Poll for coroner of eastern division, 20 September 1830

Candidate	Votes received
WILLIAM BAKER	3,670
Thomas Wakley	3,534

Source: *Ipswich Journal*, 25 September 1830.